STANDARD LOAN

UNLESS RECALLED BY ANOTHER READER
THIS ITEM MAY BE BORROWED FOR
FOUR WEEKS

To renew, telephone:
01243 816089 (Bishop Otter)
01243 816099 (Bognor Regis)

Writ

Writing in a Film Age

Essays by Contemporary Novelists

Keith Cohen, editor

University Press of Colorado

Copyright © 1991 by the University Press of Colorado
P.O. Box 849
Niwot, Colorado 80544

The University Press of Colorado is a cooperative publishing enterprise supported, in part, by Adams State College, Colorado State University, Fort Lewis College, Mesa State College, Metropolitan State College of Denver, University of Colorado, University of Northern Colorado, University of Southern Colorado, and Western State College.

Library of Congress Cataloging-in-Publication Data

Writing in a film age: essays by contemporary novelists / edited by Keith Cohen.
    p. cm.
    Includes bibliographical references and index.
    ISBN 0-87081-183-5 (alk. paper). — ISBN 0-87081-180-0 (pbk.: alk. paper).
    1. Motion pictures and literature. I. Cohen, Keith.
  PN1995.3.W75   1991
  809'.04—dc20   91-12271
                                                      CIP

10 9 8 7 6 5 4 3 2 1

for Paula, Alex, Marc, and Benjamin

Contents

Preface

I inherited this project from Frederick Ramey, who, as editor at Arden Press, first had the idea of gathering together original essays by writers whose works have crossed over into film. As Ramey worked with other editors in compiling the essays, he determined the scope of the selections and the cultural diversity of the authors. By the time I was brought onto the project, Ramey had generated five of the ten essays. He deserves credit for this initial compilation. I was charged with further expanding the international cast of writers, which I did by soliciting new essays. I also began the arduous task of editing the existing essays.

When the list of contributors was finalized, I was pleased by the intellectual diversity and broad cultural spectrum it represented. The authors include four North Americans, two Argentines, one Frenchman and one French woman, one German, and one Italian. For the most part, the essays were written recently, within the past decade. In the case of Borges and Pasolini, the writing dates from an earlier period; what prompted me to include their essays was the freshness and originality of their perceptions.

Four of the essays, those by Kluge, Sukenick, Borges, and Pasolini, have been published before, usually in a different form. The other six are appearing for the first time or else for the first time in English.

I have organized the essays into three main categories. In Part 1, "Up Against Cinema," the authors (Burroughs, Duras, Robbe-Grillet, Kluge, and Sukenick) outline their theories of how film challenges traditional modes of writing. They isolate similar structures in written language and film, pinpoint the limits of each art form, describe the cultural changes effected by innovations in communications technology and mass media, or focus on those aspects of writing that could be further expanded or renovated by cinematic expression.

In Part 2, "Writing Film Into a System," film is viewed as an alternate art form whose systematic differences from other art forms teach us about literature, or about art in general. Borges sees films as revealing, in their adaptations of well-known plays or novels, the shortcomings of the originals or the potentials of the story material. Pasolini maintains that film functions according to linguistic laws similar to those that govern literary language but that the material of film is so dissimilar from that of literature that an entirely new system of codification is needed.

Part 3, "Cinema: The Other Apprenticeship," includes the essays of those authors — Baumbach, Stoltzfus, and Puig — who have found in cinema a specific means of learning more about the literary craft. Emphasizing the powerful impact cinema made on their artistic development, they account for the specific ways they changed their writing after being apprenticed, literally or figuratively, to filmmakers.

The volume includes a Bibliography and Filmography intended to aid the reader in finding out more about the works of the contributors and in tracing some of the relationships between films and literary texts mentioned by the contributors. The Filmography, in particular, makes it possible to view films that the authors collaborated on or actually scripted. It can also be used to put together a group of films that would illustrate a major theme addressed by one or more of the authors or that would represent either a sampling or a comprehensive program of the titles with which a particular author has been associated.

One aim of this volume is to facilitate further research for literary and film scholars. To this end, I have included as much information as practical regarding dates of publication and release and availability of translations. If a novel has been translated or if a film has been released in the United States, then the current translated title is given for that work in parentheses following its first mention. If a novel has not been translated or if a film has not been released here, then a literal translation is given in parentheses.

KC

Writing in a Film Age

Introduction

I can no longer think what I want to think. My thoughts have been replaced by images.
                                   — Georges Duhamel, *Scènes de la vie future*

The powerful effect that cinema has exercised upon literature and the other arts, as well as upon nearly every aspect of daily life in the twentieth century, is well known. Filmmaking, an artistic practice that from its earliest days combined the artisanal "hands-on" qualities of crafts and the visual arts with the imaginative rigors of such temporal arts as novel writing and drama, can be seen as the first wholly *invented* art. Its development relied on scientific breakthroughs in optics and chemistry that occurred during the nineteenth century.[1] If you also consider the central importance to the cinematographic process of industrially produced machinery — from recording camera to projector — and the new art's appeal to a mass audience, you will begin to see why cinema has been heralded as the "most representative" art of the high-technology era.[2]

The new art was to work its effects upon artists and the general public at varying rates. Although the impact was immediate on certain writers, such as John Dos Passos and Gertrude Stein, who spoke of the new aesthetic potentials opened up by cinema and integrated cinematic techniques into their writing, the response by others was delayed.[3] It was as if the strikingly new ways of seeing and sequencing afforded by the movies had to have time to sink into the sensibilities of the wide-eyed spectators before they could react. It has been shown that cinema gradually displaced the novel as the primary form of popular entertainment during the first three decades of the twentieth century.

A keen film sensibility and cinematic frames of reference gradually became the norms for new generations in Europe and the United States, where most of the pioneering work in film took place. Other nations looked to these countries, particularly to the picture of American life presented by Hollywood, for a view of what was considered by many to be life as it was supposed to be lived in the modern world.

This book is a testimony to the permeation of film sensibility into the second and third generations of postcinema artists. Of the ten writers and filmmakers who have contributed to the volume, one was born at the turn of the twentieth century, two were born at the onset of World War I, three during the 1920s, and the other four in 1932 or 1933. Thus, their formative years cover the period between the two world wars, when movies were in their heyday of popularity and artistic inventiveness.

Jorge Luis Borges, whose life literally spans the history of cinema, grew up at a time when filmmakers were beginning to discover the possibilities of narration in their films. Although his prose remains, unlike that of others, untouched by the devices of cinema, his frame of reference, especially during the time that he wrote movie reviews on a regular basis, was frequently the cinema.

William Burroughs and **Marguerite Duras** consider, in their essays in this volume, the influence cinema had on their own artistic formation. They approach questions about cinema as both writers and filmmakers. Burroughs reveals some of the unexplored potentials of cinema and suggests how they might be exploited through screenwriting and literary experimentation. Duras, for whom writing and filmmaking are part of a single artistic continuum, reflects on those aspects of film practice that allow her to go beyond the literary word.

Alain Robbe-Grillet, whose name was for two decades more closely associated with the aesthetics of cinema than that of any other novelist, propounds in his essay a theory that writers can adopt cinematic techniques and develop new writing styles. A spin-off of his influential collection of theoretical essays, *Pour un nouveau roman* (1963; translated as *For a New Novel,* 1965), his essay joins Burroughs's in calling for greater exploitation of the inherent signifying potentials of cinema in order to forge new and radical forms of expression. **Ben Stoltzfus,** a major commentator on Robbe-Grillet's works in the United States, stresses in his essay the formative part film technique played in his own development as a fiction writer. Like Robbe-Grillet and Burroughs, he discovers in cinema a virtual gold mine of new ways of seeing and, consequently, new ways of writing.

Pier Paolo Pasolini, an Italian artist who is equally celebrated as a poet and filmmaker, relates in his essay that his critical sensibility was greatly influenced by the developing science of signs, semiotics. He forges a theory of cinema that sees in reality a vast but nevertheless catalogable series of signs. The views propounded in his essay throw an extraordinary light upon his films.

Each of the four writers born in the 1930s attests to the profound effect of the classic Hollywood style and its European counterpart on his artistic sensibilities. **Manuel Puig** explains his decision to study film in Italy by evoking the "parallel reality" that movies provided for him as a child growing up in the Argentine hinterlands. Although he discovered early on that filmmaking was, for him, a dead-end career, his experiences in Rome served as an almost unconscious apprenticeship in the means of depicting narrative space — not in film but in the novel. A work like *El Beso de la mujer araña* (1976; translated as *Kiss of the Spider Woman,* 1978) vividly reflects this apprenticeship.

Alexander Kluge's disillusionment with the Hollywood dream was both more immediate and more extensive than Puig's. Whereas Puig maintains the idols of the silver screen as integral parts of his image repertoire, the German novelist and filmmaker takes them on as aesthetic adversaries. His essay is a manifesto for developing the margins around the conventional means of signification in cinema; and his films attest to his genuine attempt to match theory with practice.

Jonathan Baumbach and **Ronald Sukenick** chronicle in their essays the experience of growing up in America during the 1930s and 1940s with the movies. Baumbach, like Puig, records the degree to which Saturday matinees saturated his fantasy life. The murky borderland between dream and reality first charted by the movies formed the founding point of reference for his writing. Sukenick went through the same rite of passage — consisting of weekly matinees — however, he draws more general conclusions than Baumbach from his early experiences. For him, growing up in the modern electronic world — which he calls the "electrosphere" — meant conditioning one's mind to integrating events in a very special manner. What once may have been called film sensibility becomes for Sukenick the very condition for making sense of modern everyday life. He contends that film today cannot be considered in an aesthetic vacuum because of its permeability with other arts (painting, music, video) and electronic languages.

Capacities of Cinema: Thoughts, Dreams, and Repetition

Critics have speculated at some length about the sources of cinema: industrial and technological innovations, carry-overs of literary techniques from theater and the novel, mass culture of the nineteenth century, and so on. Although on the surface cinema and writing have very different histories — cinema being a recent brainchild of industrial science and writing being a fundamental, "primitive" form of communication linked with the beginnings of civilization as we know it — many writers sense a kinship with the cinematic way of telling stories or the particular view of reality offered by the film medium. Postulating a close tie between cinema and literature requires careful scrutiny of the manner in which we apprehend "images," be they visual and therefore entirely outside ourselves or linguistically generated in our minds as we read. If the tie is there, it must have something to do with similarities in the book-reading and film-viewing processes. And so, what begins as a question about the relationship between two forms of art ends up as a question about the functioning of the mind. Thus, thinking about the history of cinema and its effects on other arts leads one to think about the thought process itself.

What constitutes the thoughts that stream through our minds? Is it the words of our language — or some fair semblance of words — those signifiers that account for so much in our waking state? Or is it some primordial, ill-defined images, which, as soon as they are cognated by our reflective minds, vanish like smoke? Plato maintained that cognition consists of remembering, that when we "learn" something we are actually bringing into consciousness images that we had previously formed in our heads. For example, when we learn about the sides of a square, we are really just comparing what we see in a diagram with an image, already in our minds, of an equilateral, equiangular parallelogram.[4] As the writers of the following essays grapple with the relationship between visual signs and verbal signs in the cinema and in literature, most often expressing themselves in terms of their own writing or film experiences, it is this (ultimately philosophical) issue of the content of consciousness that they address, directly or indirectly, over and over.

William Burroughs, probably best known for successfully putting into practice the cut-up method of literary composition, ponders the nature of consciousness as he attempts to explain the appeal of his method. The cut-up technique, developed in the late 1950s by Burroughs in collaboration with Brion Gysin, consists of randomly juxtaposing texts from a wide variety of sources. Burroughs would, for example, take pages from a newspaper, paste them up next to pages from a pulp novel, and then arbitrarily cut the mock-up horizontally or vertically. The result would be a text whose consistency and continuity were always in question, where the reader, vaguely aware that two unrelated, nonsimultaneous events were being presented at the same time, would be jarred by thematic dissonances and unexpected connections, the rewards of this aleatory method.[5] Comparing Burroughs's cut-ups to Antonin Artaud's work, Julia Kristeva distinguishes the cut-up composition from earlier modern experiments by its "asymbolicity," that is, the apparent short-circuiting of the function of language to communicate coherent, sequential ideas through symbols. This trait, which, according to Kristeva, is "peculiar to psychosis or the logical and phonetic drifting that pulverizes and multiplies meaning while pretending to play with it or flee from it," lends significance to the writing by "unfolding and suspending discursive logic and the speaking subject."[6]

Following a precedence established in the nineteenth century by the impressionist painters and carried on by many innovators in modern art and literature, from the naturalists to the surrealists, Burroughs claims that the cut-up method portrays what consciousness is really like, how life is actually experienced: "Consciousness is a cut-up, and life is a cut-up." Far from distorting the way things are, as it may seem when first reading a text composed of juxtaposed fragments of other texts, the cut-up method, according to Burroughs, shows us life as it happens to us, in bits and pieces, traversed by memories and fantasies and never cut from whole cloth.

Pasolini would agree. We are all constantly in the process, according to Pasolini, of making cinema. All of life in the entirety of its actions is a natural, living film; in this sense, it is the linguistic equivalent of oral language in its natural and biological aspect. Thus, life is one continuous Burroughs cut-up.

Whether consciously or not, Burroughs derived inspiration for the cut-up experiments from cinematic montage. The aesthetic values emphasized in the cut-up — juxtaposition, conflict, reader participation — are the same values Sergei Eisenstein claimed for montage in the early days of film theorizing. Established by the Soviets as the "nerve of cinema," montage is, in Eisenstein's view, opposed to the "dramatic" or "unrolling" methods of representation associated with the theater. Instead, it is "an idea that arises from the collision of independent shots."[7] The connection between montage and the cut-up method is clearest when we consider the tape-recording cut-up. In this influential variation of Burroughs's textual cut-up, pieces of tapes are randomly spliced together, or "edited" in the cinematic sense. The finished tape, which is sometimes transcribed, presents a collision of voice and sound — a kind of audio montage.

Ronald Sukenick espouses a method that is similar to the cut-up and has similar aims. Modern narrative, for him, is not merely a bag of tricks designed to titillate the reader. It is capable of expanding our consciousness through techniques such as collage, improvisation, and arbitrary form. According to this argument, discursive thought, associated with traditional rationality, establishes frames and boundaries beyond which the ordinary mind is not allowed to venture. The montage techniques of modern narrative break down such boundaries, setting up a dialogue "between the possible and the impossible" intended, according to Sukenick, "to reclaim the impossible." Going beyond the conventional processes of signification in language, these techniques use image, association, metaphor, and chance to jar the reader's mind outside of chronology and rational cause-and-effect.

Sukenick goes a step beyond Burroughs when he maintains in his essay that the modern electronic world in which we live requires us to process information in new ways. He contends that artistic innovation has developed as a means for coping with the new conditions of our lives. Cinema, which many have called the typical art of the twentieth century because of the way it deals with time, relative perspective, and discontinuity, seems to express best the experience of living in a post-industrial, electronic, mass-media world. For Sukenick, films, like radio and television, feed back to us, by means of narrative, the information we could not possibly deal with intelligently by traditional means. Thus, we "narrate ourselves"; our fantasies become amazingly similar to films because, Sukenick claims, "We have to imagine ourselves in terms of the way information comes in at us."

Yet, as critics have pointed out since cinema's first days, the capacity for film to deal with conceptual thought is severely limited. What impressed every class of viewer from the beginning of film was its capacity to imitate objects exactly (theorists call this "iconicity"). Because of the nature of the photographic process, by which the light rays reflecting off an object are actually *impressed* onto the celluloid by means of a chemical transformation involving silver bromide, the cinematic image of an object is very similar to the object that produced the image. In the case of a wooden table, the cinematic image, though very much like the actual table, is obviously not identical to it, since it is produced from strong light beams passing through the variously configurated celluloid and not from wood and nails and varnish. This iconicity led many film commentators throughout the first part of the twentieth century to emphasize film's potential for capturing objects and actions rather than moods and ideas. Cinema was the new instrument of popular journalism, recording for the masses important events that could be witnessed firsthand by only a few.

Consequently, theorists depreciated the medium's capacity for representing thought.[8] Literature, we know, has always explored the internal aspects of men and women as well as their external aspects, such as physiognomy, actions, and spoken words. Twentieth-century literature, in fact, has given high priority to discovering the linguistic means by which the psyche can be investigated, ways in which the reader can glimpse the rush of consciousness that we sense going on deep within ourselves. The novel has historically been the province for exploring consciousness, with the masterpieces of classic modernism — for example, *Ulysses* (1922), *Three Lives* (1909), *The Sound and the Fury* (1929), *To the Lighthouse* (1927), *Remembrance of Things Past* (1913–1927) — taking part in this enterprise. And cinema has excelled in the recording of action, developing during its classic period those genres that depend precisely upon carefully detailed and motivated actions: the western, the detective film, the adventure film.

Sergei Eisenstein looked beyond this distinction between literature/thought and cinema/action, claiming that the sound film was "capable of reconstructing all phases and all specifics of the course of thought."[9] Discussing the possibilities of representing Clyde Griffith's inner debate in his projected (though never realized) adaptation of Theodore Dreiser's *An American Tragedy* (1925), Eisenstein showed how the use of sound, rather than simply increasing the iconicity of cinema, could enhance the subjective presentation of the feverish race of thoughts through a troubled mind. The effect could be achieved through synchronized or nonsynchronized sounds and images, sounds alone, or images alone; the sounds and images could be representational or nonrepresentational.

It is interesting to think of which filmmakers have attempted to use the film medium in the way suggested by Eisenstein. The French so-called impressionist filmmakers of the 1920s, such as Germaine Dulac and Jean Epstein, as well as American independents, such as Maya Deren and Stan Brakhage, have expressed interior states and oneiric visions — if not the stream of consciousness — in their films. (Their works are discussed in greater detail below.) German expressionist filmmakers of the 1920s and 1930s used stylized sets and acting to create moods that reflected the protagonists' dominant states of mind. Psychological thrillers of the 1930s and 1940s, which comprise several Hollywood subgenres, including the detective film and the woman's film, used flashbacks to reveal the subjective attitudes of central characters toward events they recalled.

Later filmmakers continued to speculate about the relation between thought and cinema. Pasolini points out in his essay that because not all thought is verbal, it is logical to assume that the cinematic image chain could be at least suggestive of what goes through the human mind. Marguerite Duras, whose career has shuttled continually between filmmaking and novel writing, agrees with Eisenstein that the sound film is capable — indeed, destined — to present subjectivity. Her own films, *Nathalie Granger* (1972), *Détruire, dit-elle* (*Destroy, She Said,* 1969), and *India Song* (1975), delve deeply into women's states of mind. She notes, however, that few films have succeeded at approximating concepts or ideas. A rare exception, according to Duras, is Carl Dreyer's *Ordet* (1955), which deals directly with the idea of God. Borges points to the film *The Green Pastures* (1936) as an example of the more commonly observed gap between idea and actualization: When God appears in that film, walking around and speaking like an ordinary human being, the audience is amused, not filled with the awe reserved for the idea of true divinity.

Alexander Kluge, the German director and writer, discusses the difficulty of expressing a passage of highly figurative prose in film terms. Phrases like "fits of fury" and "down to his bones" are figures of speech that have no equivalent in filmic expression. In attempting, nevertheless, to match the prose, phrase for phrase, with film images, Kluge demonstrates how limited cinematic language is for dealing with the intangible. He maintains that film is not altogether incapable of handling abstractions; it is montage that confers upon cinema its "conceptual possibilities." As such, film "offers a form of expression which is as capable of a dialectical relationship between concept and perception as is verbal language without, however, stabilizing this relationship, as language is bound to do." Language is obliged to "stabilize" concepts in figures of speech that rapidly become clichés (e.g., "fits of fury"). Film, by means of montage, has the potential for creating figures without fixing them in clichés.

Kluge concludes that we might foresee a time when filmmakers have developed a battery of film metaphors that vie with those of literature. He discerns developments in this direction even today, citing as examples the way Louis Malle makes allusion to Charlie Chaplin's films and the existence of a whole vocabulary specific to the western.

Cinema has the means of developing, according to some theorists, a set lexicon for each genre or for major forms, such as the fiction film and the documentary. Christian Metz and other semioticians may disagree over the exact nature of these linguistic properties, but the basic claim is that cinema resembles language.[10] A related claim is that the film's unfolding corresponds to the thought process. Whereas cinema may directly articulate concepts only with difficulty, its signifying chain has been compared repeatedly to the images that pass through our minds. Retelling myths and fashioning figures of speech for the way consciousness works are, of course, as old as philosophy. It is curious that these figures and tales resemble so frequently the cinematic process or some aspect of it. Plato's myth for the relation between real and ideal (or conceptual) forms is set in the celebrated cave, where people are positioned with their backs to the source of light and their eyes are aimed toward shadows reflected on an inner wall, very much the way spectators are seated in the darkened cinema as they focus on the bright screen's "shadows." (Plato's point is that what we experience in reality — the cave — is no more than the reflections of ideal forms we never actually see.) In trying to describe how our thoughts proceed, John Locke offered an image of so many slides on a magic lantern; just as the slides revolve around the candle at the center of the lantern, so thoughts swirl around in our heads.[11] Indeed, it is the philosophers' use of images such as the cave and the magic lantern that makes it seem as if cinema, though so recently invented, has existed as metaphor and aspiration for centuries.[12]

In addition to being compared to the thought process, film has often been related to dreams. Both share a fundamental trait: a succession of discontinuous images that seemingly cannot be stopped.[13] Although literary fictions have dealt with the material of dreams since the earliest Greek poets, the mechanisms and effects of film have led writers again and again to detect in this medium a secret parallel with dream work. Jonathan Baumbach considers the relationship between film and dreams to be reciprocal. "Perhaps film interests me because of its relation to dreams," he writes; "and then, it may be the other way around, that dreams intrigue me because of their cinemalike ambience." Baumbach discovers in movie plots, which he would "rehearse" to himself as a child before going to sleep, the same "coded mysteriousness" that is characteristic of dreams. Like Molina in Manuel Puig's *Kiss of the Spider Woman,* Baumbach finds that simple movie plots have the capacity to release us from the world of rationality, from the real. Movie plots sparked his dreams as a child, and he says, without exaggeration, that his novels are based on the films he has seen — films that have led him into a dream world that furnished the ideas for his books.

For Burroughs, the similarity between dreaming and watching a movie — the darkened space, the seeming absence of others, the brightly lit screen — is so great that he hypothesizes a therapy whereby people who miss their REM (rapid eye movement) sleep could make it up by seeing a film. Inversely, recurrent dreams could be used as the basis for a filmscript. Following this line of reasoning, we might imagine a film director employed to shoot a person's most pleasurable dream; then, when the person wanted a lift, he or she would have only to see that film.

In the essays that follow, the dream analogy is also drawn to support claims of verisimilitude in film. Alain Robbe-Grillet, inveighing against the "realist" tendency of traditional fiction, charges that the very assumptions of representationalism are false. Far from leading lives carefully organized around clear-cut aims, where effects logically follow from causes in a neat motivational chain, we inhabit, in Robbe-Grillet's words, a "universe of dreams, sexual fantasies, and nocturnal anxieties." The "new cinema" must, accordingly, open itself up further to such unconscious promptings.

It is significant to note in this connection that Robbe-Grillet's prescription for the "new cinema" bears a striking resemblance to the "new novel" that he and other French writers began creating in the 1950s. In these works, narrative presence is constantly undercut or transformed by the pressure of dreams and anxieties. In *La Maison de rendez-vous* (1965), for example, Robbe-Grillet shifts perspective from person to person and shifts from one scene to another without any discursive markers. The result is a nightmarish description of a high-class brothel in Hong Kong where sequences of a narrator watching from the streets outside become inextricably mixed with actions on a stage inside the brothel and with other Hong Kong scenes whose details do not square with earlier views. The effect suggests fantasies on the part of the very unstable narrator. Despite the difficulties such writing creates for reading such a novel, the effect is of a hallucinatory eyewitness report in which the viewer unwittingly becomes part of the drama.

If cinema were to follow Robbe-Grillet's suggestions and open itself further to the realm of the unconscious, a controversy would arise over precisely how cinema can overcome its limitation in presenting the stuff of thought, be it dream or waking consciousness. Burroughs, speaking mainly about conventional scriptwriting, warns against even attempting to show dreams, thoughts, or fantasies on the screen. He feels that the heavy-handed means by which such excursuses are introduced are aggravating to the audience, which nullifies their potential as narrative devices. Manuel Puig, whose novels mix film accounts, dreams, thoughts, and memories, disagrees, claiming that film does indeed have the potential for presenting dreams. Even though in one sense film synthesizes the real and the fantastic, it is nevertheless, according to Puig, the "ideal vehicle" for dreams. Puig illuminates this unusual contention by avowing what some might consider a cultural bias. The Argentine writer describes the Hollywood movies of the 1930s and 1940s not as idealized representations of interpersonal relations and situations but as dreams in the form of images. Thus, he arrives at a creative method similar to Baumbach's: By allowing the films he has seen to intermingle with his dreams, he generates a new kind of novelistic material that is partway between a dream and a film. In *La Traición de Rita Hayworth* (1968; translated as *Betrayed by Rita Hayworth*, 1971), for example, films are the primary oneiric medium by which Toto expresses for himself the contradictions he sees all around him. In *Kiss of the Spider Woman*, film narratives, recounted by Molina, are the sole means by which the two prisoners can escape the confines of their cell.

The dream analogy can be further explored by considering the prevalence of repetition in both films and dreams. The film process is, of course, based on a particular kind of repetition: The flickering of similar, or slightly varying images at the rate of twenty-four frames per second gives the viewer the impression of continuous action due to the phenomenon known as persistence of vision. But another important kind of repetition in film is in the insistent return of the camera to significant objects, scenes, or other configurations of the narrative development in order to emphasize either those objects and scenes themselves or a particular character's attachment or association to them. Repetition may function within narrative, but because of the prevalence of the "singulative" (i.e., one act of narration for each significant event) in mainstream fiction, its presence is more marked in nonnarrative films.[14]

Experimental films provide the richest field of examples of repetition as an artistic device. The strongest current in the European and American avant-garde has been nonnarrative. Fernand Léger's *Ballet mécanique* (1924) uses several strong repeating motifs in a visual collage noted for its asymmetry and unconventional rhythms. Partially masked close-ups of a carefully made-up set of female lips are intercalated near the beginning of the film with an aerial view of a white straw hat with a dark ribbon around it on a black background. The lips may be connected to the repeated close-up eyes heavy with mascara as well as to the androgynous head seen, eyes closed, from profile to full face to opposite profile a bit later. The abstract stylization of these facial features contrasts in tone and content with another intermittently repeated image, a fat peasant woman carrying a load of wash on her shoulder up a flight of steps — over and over again, seventeen times.[15]

In *Dog Star Man* (1961), Stan Brakhage uses repetition to attain evocative effects similar to those produced in Léger's geometric analysis of woman as spectacle. Images of a man climbing a mountain alternate obsessively with others of a dog, internal organs, ice and snow, and blackness and whiteness. Other important experimental films that use repetition as a principal device include Dziga Vertov's *Man With a Movie Camera* (1929), Kenneth Anger's *Eaux d'artifice* (1953), and Peter Kubelka's *Unsere Afrikareise* (1961–1966).

Working between the abstract tendencies of the avant-garde and the predominantly narrative bent of Hollywood, a number of iconoclastic filmmakers have made repetition a haunting detail of their signatures. Perhaps the greatest is Maya Deren, whose first film, *Meshes of the Afternoon* (1943), virtually launched the American independent film movement.[16] In this film, which deals in a quasi-narrative manner with a woman's obsession, repeated images become the clue for figuring out what motivates the woman's suicide. Yet, as in the Quentin section of William Faulkner's *Sound and the Fury,* the sequentialization of images lays out only *potential* patterns of a psychological resolve. Luis Buñuel's legendary *Chien andalou* (1928) relies on the repetition of enigmatic images (the hand infested with insects, the bicycle-riding hermaphrodite) to tell a tale of desire and repulsion so universal as to be perhaps the statement of a condition rather than simply a story. In *India Song,* Duras uses repeated images of dancing couples, vacant interiors and exteriors of a colonial estate, and nonsynchronous voice-overs to tell the story of an illicit love affair in India thirty years earlier. Duras explains that what distinguishes this work from other works based on the same colonialist (autobiographical) material is the "discovery of a means of unveiling, of exploration . . . : voices outside the narrative." This discovery "permitted the story to slip into oblivion so it could be made available to memories of people other than the author: memories that would *get remembered* similarly to any other love story."[17]

Repetition also helps to structure narrative films. Let us recall that the most basic devices of film narration depend to some extent on repetition. For example, in order for the spectator to follow any action or interchange, especially one involving visual intricacy, the director must remind us who is where in the scene, who is speaking to whom; the shot–reverse-shot conundrum in dialogues is perhaps the most obvious case. Parallel editing — the intercutting of two actions to show they are taking place simultaneously — offers a similar case. A last-minute rescue scene, for instance, requires, by definition, a systematic repetition of shots of the victim and shots of the rescuer. In these cases, narrative information exceeds what is strictly needed to render the story.

But more specifically, repetition holds narratives together in a variety of ways. In Michelangelo Antonioni's *Blow-Up* (1966), repeated images of a public garden where the protagonist has glimpsed and photographed a couple — images that appear as flashbacks as well as in the remarkable sequence of gradual enlargement — prompt and motivate the eventual unraveling of the film's enigma. In Jean Cocteau's *Blood of a Poet* (1930), images of snow falling around and amidst a children's snowball fight and images of the poet regarding himself in an otherwise disjointed sequence of mirror scenes, repeated at irregular intervals, thematize the artist's quest for the origins of his obsessions. The dogged repetition in *Psycho* (1960) of close-ups on a packet of cash wrapped up in a newspaper, both before Marion's murder and after, lead the viewer, in a manner typical of Alfred Hitchcock's hermeneutical playfulness, to focus more on the conventional question of criminal detection (How will the thief be brought to justice?) than on the far more unsettling questions of family relationships and sexual identity. In Ingmar Bergman's *Persona* (1966), an entire dialogue between Elisabet and Alma is repeated verbatim, with the only difference being the reverse-angle set-up in the second run-through, in order to stress the virtual exchange of identities taking place between the two women.

Repetition reaches its apogee in the composition of Robbe-Grillet's films. In these works, it functions less to remind the spectator of a plot detail or to stress a thematic or ironic parallel than to evoke a feeling of déjà vu that pertains to a character or to suggest an obsession that becomes as haunting for the spectator as for the character. In *L'Homme qui ment* (*The Man Who Lies*, 1968), for example, a shot of a man holding two huge dogs at the end of a leash is repeated over and over. It appears first in a sequence connected with a car ride. As the headlights of the car swing around a curve, the man and dogs appear. Later, the same image recurs, but now out of chronological sequence. Like the squashed centipede in *La Jalousie* (1957; translated as *Jealousy*, 1959), discussed below, its meaning modulates as it is repeated; yet the image is not repeated for the usual purposes of emphasis or analogy. In *Glissements progressifs du plaisir* (Progressive slippages of pleasure, 1974), the heroine loses a shoe when she trips while walking along a beach in a scene that seems to be connected chronologically with what precedes and follows. Later, however, this same shoe reappears, at first associated with the beach and then in new contexts, such as inside a bell jar. The obsessive quality of the shoe becomes a sign of fetishism as the repetitions increase. Although its symbolic meaning remains obscure, the variously contextualized repetitions of the shoe suggest rather explicitly the shift from male desire prompted by the female in distress (when she trips on the beach) to, with the hallowing of the shoe in the bell jar, male fascination for, even idolization of, female passivity.[18]

Even in the most conventional narratives, I would emphasize, repetition is a key binding device. The rocking cradle motif of D. W. Griffith's *Intolerance* (1916) is an early example of the use of single images or short sequences for the purpose of "punctuation" or (much like chapter headings) rhythmic breaks and reprises.

Repetition is just one aspect of film's unusual capacity for drawing our attention to specific objects, and in this way again film resembles dreams. As Sigmund Freud explains in *The Interpretation of Dreams* (1900), the elements of a dream always appear in a mixed-up order, and events typically succeed one another without clear cause-and-effect logic. The job of the analyst is precisely to pay attention to objects that appear out of context in dreams and to see how the unconscious mind is working on them. One process that occurs in dreams is condensation. Freud shows, for example, how a crushed may beetle in a dream contains, in highly condensed form, a female patient's desire for greater potency from her husband (the aphrodisiac "Spanish fly" is made from crushed beetles) and her simultaneous disgust with her sexual thoughts.[19] The beetle is a condensation of the patient's conflicting feelings of sexual need and disgust.

Condensation and repetition are linked in experimental fiction. In order for condensation to take place, some image must be repeated. The sewing needle in Stoltzfus's *Eye of the Needle* (1967), the association between eating and sexuality in Puig's *Rita Hayworth,* and the dynamite sticking out of characters' pockets in Sukenick's *Out* (1973), provide excellent examples of repetition and condensation. One of the most sustained instances appears in Robbe-Grillet's *Jealousy.* The image of a centipede, repeated with increasing frequency in a series of scenes strikingly similar to Freud's case involving the crushed beetle, serves to gather together the narrator's obsessive thoughts. The centipede is killed by Franck, the man suspected by the narrator of being his wife's lover, in a scene suggestive of sexual prowess. The sound made when the centipede is squashed is similar to the crackling sound made by A..., the wife, when she combs her hair. These sounds, in turn, are similar to a third sound, which occurs only within a fantasy of the narrator, that of the crackling fire engulfing the car Franck and A... are in after it crashes and bursts into flames.[20] The squashed centipede is thus a condensation of the narrator's suspicions, fears, hopes, and desires.

Through condensation and repetition, a film may also draw our attention to a seemingly unimportant object (e.g., a door) in order to lay the groundwork for a climax (where, say, the lover walks out on the heroine), or to establish a visual association (with the heroine's grief, for instance, over the departed lover). Elsewhere, I have shown how important the "life" of objects is in cinema, how their dynamization by means of camera work places objects on a par with human beings.[21] But the power of objects can also be demonstrated by a more commonplace phenomenon that occurs even in our waking consciousness. Memory is frequently triggered by a familiar but long-forgotten object. An attitude, mood, or even an entire stage of life, seemingly buried in the unconscious, can be brought back to the conscious mind in an instant by the look, smell, or feel of an object. Marcel Proust's *Remembrance of Things Past* is a demonstration, on a vast scale, of this phenomenon. As Marcel, the protagonist, dips a small cake into his tea, the associations he makes with the taste and smell engulf his consciousness and transport him into a euphoric past.

Like fiction, film also uses its ability to focus on the isolated object to suggest a character's memory process. Ben Stoltzfus cites one of the most celebrated examples of this device: the French actress's recollection of a past German lover as she stares at the arm of her Japanese lover in *Hiroshima mon amour* (1959). Duras (who wrote the scenario) and Alain Resnais (who directed the film) manage to show how the twitching of the Japanese man's hand (in the present) is similar to that of the dying German (in the past) — so much so that the association, we infer, in the actress's mind calls up a nexus of memories that she thought had been safely relegated to oblivion. The associative sequence thus puts into motion the powerful subplot of the actress's past, which, subsequently visualized for us more extensively, we are constantly forced to compare to the present.

The Word, the Image

The basic theme of this collection, taken up by every one of the writers, is the relation between words and images. Before they can address the question of how their writing has been affected by the impact of cinema, they must address this fundamental relationship. Robbe-Grillet reminds us of a point that semioticians have insisted on frequently: the "ineradicable presence" of the film image. Whereas literary language is always imbued with temporal interrelations conferred on it by grammatical tenses, film language has no such built-in code. In film, we are always in present time.[22] Sukenick focuses on the constant movement and the irreversibility of film images to explain the special role movies have played in the development of his artistic consciousness. For Sukenick, the discontinuous, yet relentless quality of film narrative has led to a unique kind of composition, a special sort of "performance" in which imitation of the world is secondary to a form of "visual thinking."

For Pasolini, the screenplay has a special mode of existence because it functions in two semiotic universes at the same time: first in the world of language, then in the world of (potential) images, those of the film to be made. It is in this sense that Pasolini defines the screenplay as a "structure that wants to be another structure." The screenplay thus throws another light on cinema's mixture of word and image because it is a verbal structure whose visual realization is always postponed: You cannot be sure what the images in a screenplay will look like until the film is produced.

Puig shows how the traits of cinematic narration require the spectator to engage in a "third reading," a reading not only of signifier and signified of verbal origin but also of visual signs and their configurations. An important advantage of this tripartite activity is the opening thus afforded into the realm of connotation. Modern novelists have delved deeply into this area by constructing stories in which the signifiers are not all neatly tied into the main plot. In the well-made nineteenth-century tale, every event and character action contributed clearly to the present or potential movement of the plot; in the twentieth-century work of fiction, it is common to encounter a seemingly floating signifier — "floating" because it is not tied to a referent. A good — almost literal — example of the floating signifier is the leaflet marked "Elijah" in James Joyce's *Ulysses*. It is seen at various points by Dubliners as they make their way through the city. Its fluttering over the Liffey is described in some detail. Yet it is never pinned down to a single place or character, never assigned a specific function. Perhaps it is a sign of Leopold Bloom's symbolically prophetic character in the story; perhaps it is a commentary on how lightly the Irish take divine ways.

There are many other examples: the skywriting airplane in *Mrs. Dalloway* (1925), which ties together various strands of action that are taking place simultaneously; Benjy's drooping flower in the finale of *The Sound and the Fury;* the person who throws open the window and sticks his head out just before Joseph K. is executed in *The Trial* (1925); the Martinville steeples that Marcel sees as he arrives in Combray in Proust's *Remembrance of Things Past.* In varying degrees, each functions to heighten the dramatic impact of the scene in which it appears; yet in each case a precise meaning cannot be assigned to the image.

Modern filmmakers have followed the novelists' lead in using images with no clear referents in order to force spectators to engage in free association — or, using Wolfgang Iser's terminology, to broaden the reader's "horizon of expectations."[23] Duras, in this connection, claims that she was never able to assign a specific meaning to the white rectangle that she uses again and again in *Aurélia Steiner,* also known as *Aurélia Vancouver* (1979). She knows that it has something to do with the extermination of Jews during World War II, which is when Aurélia Steiner's story begins. But the rectangle has no denotative relation to the events of the Holocaust. It is suggestive of absence, and hence of genocide — or, rather, of the decree that led to the attempted suppression of an entire race. Other connotations of the white rectangle include a hole, emptiness, the blank page. It also suggests a bare space in which no action takes place. It was derived in part from her reaction, as she explains, to a scene in Elie Wiesel's *La Nuit* (1958; translated as *Night,* 1960). The image that came to her mind in response to his description of a thirteen-year-old boy's three-day agony at the end of a noose was that of a white rectangle. The utter inadequacy of such an image, for conventional purposes, to signify or indicate *anything* is a measure of the extraordinary abjection Duras felt when reading *Night.* The rectangle exemplifies an extreme case of connotation and indicates the potential power of signification held by images in general.

In a manner that neatly clears the way for a deeper consideration of the relations between film and literature, Burroughs declares that, in fact, the difference between word and image is minimal. Pointing to the prevalence of montage in modern novels (i.e., the juxtaposition of words or phrases outside of strict temporal or causal sequence), he goes so far as to assert that "the written word is an image." To be sure, differences persist between the literary sign (word) and the film sign (image plus sound). But if you go along with Burroughs and think of each work of art as a conglomeration of signs, then you discern systems and conventions that films and novels have in common.

Beyond the signifying differences between the two arts, then, a common ground for mutual influencing and reciprocal borrowing can be established. However, it is important to make clear one's formal and historical assumptions when arguing for such influences or borrowings. Robbe-Grillet, for example, claims that the use of the realist novel of the nineteenth century as the model for cinematic excellence has stifled the cinema and has led to film work that ignores the expressive potentials of the medium. According to Robbe-Grillet, the connection between film and novel is a connection with the *modern* novel. The codes and conventions of representationalism, which many artists still practice and enforce in the twentieth century, must be ignored. Indeed, in Robbe-Grillet's view, cinema is a great art because it gives us the "real world." By that, he does not mean that its screen is some kind of window onto the world but rather that it is a medium dealing with time and space perception with limitless possibilities for distortion. It can thus lead us all the more easily into the usually hidden world of dreams, fears, and anxieties. Filmmakers such as Federico Fellini, Bergman, and Hitchcock have already broken ground in this area. But Robbe-Grillet complains that mainstream cinema is structured, industrially and institutionally, in a way that disallows attempts at discovering new means of expression and thus continuing this development.

A specific example will make Robbe-Grillet's point clearer. In the cinema today, we expect synchronization between the images of an action and the sounds of that action. Only "background" music adds sound that is not strictly synchronous with actions being viewed; yet it, too, follows certain codes of illustration that reinforce the dominant mood or action of the scene (suspense, romance, adventure, and so forth). When we encounter a scene in which, say, an actor's lips fail to correspond to the words we hear, we as viewers have to make a certain adjustment. Something is being expressed besides the words of dialogue we have grown to expect. Norman Bates stares into an in-frame space at the end of *Psycho* as a voice of his "mother" chatters on about being seen, about what people might think, and about how much they know. In the last part of *Hiroshima mon amour*, the French actress, who has told her story of taboo love and public humiliation to her present-day Japanese lover, is seen washing her face frenetically in an attempt to get rid of the memory as a voice-over says in a triumphant, mocking tone, "I told our story. I was unfaithful to you tonight." Cinema clearly has the potential for revealing the innermost states of men and women. Robbe-Grillet wants filmmakers to experiment further and, like the classic modern novelists, to take more risks.

Kluge, who is better known as a filmmaker than as a writer, would agree with Robbe-Grillet's critique of contemporary film practice. Like Robbe-Grillet, though perhaps with different motives, he argues for applying the same principles to the sound track as to the image track. If images can be linked suggestively or opposed violently through montage, then sound can be, too. According to Kluge, written intertitles are another device ripe for experimentation. Although they may seem at first glance a throwback to the early days of silent cinema, they have a special potential. Unlike voice-overs, they cannot be projected over the image of any person. Because of their affinity with literary language, they encourage the spectator toward increased participation, particularly as he or she tries to discover the link between these titles and the events of the film. Today, a number of experimental filmmakers are using the intertitle in innovative ways, including Yvonne Rainer, Jean-Luc Godard, and Michael Snow.

Sukenick provides useful background to the impact that cinema has made on his generation by explaining how the electrosphere denies the eternal time of the nineteenth-century novel. Whereas nineteenth-century novels such as *Pride and Prejudice* (1818) often adumbrate values that are woven into a seemingly eternal texture of right or wrong choices, today's art cannot stake such a claim on universality. Events in the electrosphere happen too fast and overtake one another at much too rapid a pace for the public to accept such an illusion. A new sensibility is required, one that makes the connection between visual and verbal systems as obvious as the television image. An important consideration along these lines is the use of the word in cinema as primarily an *oral* manifestation (further discussed in Pasolini's essay).

Burroughs shows that the elaborate system of rules for screenwriting can easily be applied to novel writing. Or, put another way, novelists can study how innovative films have challenged the conventions of cinematic storytelling and, by applying the lesson to their own narrative art, learn to tell stories more dynamically. At the level of technique, then, cinema has passed along to the novelist a whole new battery of storytelling devices. Temporal distortion, radical shifting of perspective, montage — these basic techniques that grew out of the film editing process and the spatio-temporal nature of cinema — are now stock-in-trade for the modern novelist.[24]

Radical shifts in temporal perspective can perhaps best be seen in Faulkner's novels. *The Sound and the Fury* (1929) narrates the collapse of the Compson clan by describing events on four nonsuccessive days. In the first two sections, Benjy's and Quentin's monologues, time shifts erratically from the present to various obsessive moments in the past without the least narrative marker to indicate the time frame or why exactly the shift has taken place.

Multiperspectivism can be seen in Proust's great novel, *Remembrance of Things Past*. Marcel, the narrator, adopts three different perspectives on his life and then melds them into a single voice. He is at once the child growing up, the adult looking back as he tosses and turns in bed, and the old man, now a writer, trying to put all the events into some kind of order. Multiperspectivism allows Proust to narrate an event, such as Mlle. de Vinteuil's profanation of her father, as if from multiple vantage points.

Virginia Woolf's use of multiperspectivism in *To the Lighthouse* is different from Proust's in that her narrator remains in control, opening and closing the diaphragm, so to speak, through which various characters view the events in the story. With Lily Briscoe, one of the characters in *To the Lighthouse*, Woolf achieves an exquisite meshing of perspectives, such as the scene in which Lily, who is painting, thinks back to a day she spent with Mrs. Ramsay ten years before and recalls her suppositions about Mrs. Ramsay's reactions to Mr. Ramsay's marriage proposal.

Perhaps the best example of perspectival montage is Joyce's *Ulysses*, because this novel deals not only with the external actions of Leopold Bloom, Stephen Dedalus, and other characters, but also with internal events: their random thoughts, reactions, and fantasies relating to everything going on around them. These events, internal as well as external, are juxtaposed in a piecemeal fashion to create a jigsaw narrative in which we skip back and forth between characters, inside and outside of characters, with a concern not so much for the continuity from one thought or one piece of dialogue to the next as for the ironies generated by such gross discontinuities.

Puig's essay exemplifies well the common goals of film writers and novelists. Because he had originally wanted to be a screenwriter, his experience of being led "back" to novel writing provides an example of interart cross-fertilization. The set of aesthetic expectations held by the young film writer were actually realized by the accomplished novelist. Puig describes, in particular, the process by which the scriptwriting evolved, for him, into novel writing. In his effort to express his ideas in script form, he automatically began using novel-writing devices. He discovered in a cinematic ambition a plenitude of novelistic expression that he had never tapped. (Indeed, one might claim that Puig's novels are unique precisely because of the way he has transmuted the feel of cinematic action into novel form.) In spite of the much-acclaimed visual appeal of cinema, Puig found that he needed more narrative space. And, ironically, it was the novel that afforded this space.

Note that Pasolini, an accomplished writer as well as filmmaker, would quarrel with Puig on this score. In his essay, Pasolini suggests that the screenplay, not the novel, opens onto boundless space. It is the written notation of a graphic space that will materialize only as the film is shot.

The rest of the writers join with a unanimous voice in declaring technique the most immediate means by which cinema affected them. Baumbach points to very specific, formal features of Godard's *Breathless* (1959): "its rhythm, its fragmentation, its hyped-up speed, its refusal to acknowledge conventional limitations." The riskiness, in fact, that Baumbach goes on to describe was a leading characteristic of French New Wave films, which probably had a more profound effect on this generation of writers than any other single group of films.

Stoltzfus hails cinematic technique by relating his writing experiments to Alexandre Astruc's call for the "camera-pen" (*caméra-stylo*). His novels demonstrate the extent to which even the most basic tenets of cinematic perception can lead to innovation in the novel. The title of his novel *The Eye of the Needle,* for example, provides a metaphor for the narrator's trained, steady gaze at central characters and objects, sometimes through a tiny opening such as a keyhole, a perceptual position strikingly similar to the camera operator's gaze through the camera lens. In *Black Lazarus* (1972), moreover, Stoltzfus uses a montage of moonlike gasoline company signs to suggest the ambiguities of traditional moon myths in light of the 1969 American moon landing.

The list of films that have influenced Stoltzfus is long and varied (see the Filmography). He has been impressed not only by the way cinema hurdles through space and time but also by the way it mixes history and fiction. Films that depict fictional events in a specific historical setting, such as René Clément's *Forbidden Games* (1952), have stirred his historical sense, making him as much aware of story context as of narrative technique.

Rules of the Game
and the Question of Verisimilitude

Curiously, mainstream cinema, the films we are accustomed to seeing coming out of Hollywood, is an exceedingly rule-bound art form, perhaps more constrained by convention than the novel ever was.

Burroughs stressed this fact in a lecture series, delivered to a group of young writers, that forms the basis of his essay. He points out, in the most candid manner conceivable, that success in Hollywood is directly determined by the degree to which the rules are followed. Condensing the film idea into a single sentence, advancing the action in each scene, constructing a plot with "plant" and "payoff," using telling details to establish characters, and creating a climax that jolts and relieves the audience — all these conventionalized devices can be identified in mainstream films and must be used in writing a screenplay that is intended to be commercially successful. The implication, of course, is that commercial screenplays, precisely because they are so rule-bound, leave little room for artistry. Burroughs was encouraging his listeners to consider techniques beyond the traditional ones, techniques that challenge the potentials of the film medium.

One might object to the self-assuredness with which Burroughs discounts the possibility of creativity in Hollywood. The set designers of the Busby Berkeley musicals, animators in the era of Walt Disney, music composers such as Max Steiner and Bernard Herrmann, the photographers and camera operators for Orson Welles and Hitchcock, and the canonizers of the well-made Hollywood film themselves, including Howard Hawks, John Ford, and John Huston — these are just a few examples of great Hollywood artists that even die-hard modernists and proponents of the avant-garde will acknowledge. Some of the writers whose essays appear in this volume, such as Baumbach and Puig, rejoice in the calculated complexity and easy lushness of Hollywood films; others (Burroughs, for example) are rather more reserved, doubting that any innovation can come out of an artistic practice so highly conventionalized. In any event, let us bear in mind that the two camps reflect an interpretive or ideological difference in attitude toward the American cinema. And only a minority of these authors would agree with André Bazin's "sociological" appraisal of American cinema's vitality and excellence of tradition: "The American cinema has been able, in an extraordinarily competent way, to show American society just as it wanted to see itself; but not at all passively, as a simple act of satisfaction and escape, but dynamically, i.e., by participating with the means at its disposal in the building of this society."[25]

Duras is one filmmaker whose works eschew the received ideas of cinematic practice. In *Destroy, She Said,* she juxtaposes voice-over conversations of one set of characters with the images of another set of characters. Long stillnesses create a mood of restlessness and uncertainty, just as they do in *Nathalie Granger.* In both of these films, it would be very difficult to show how each scene is advancing the action. One of the fundamental traits of Duras's cinema, in fact, is precisely the lack of an easily paraphrasable action. The personalities of Duras's characters, whose chilling hollowness reaches a kind of culmination in *India Song,* are never sufficiently defined to allow neat pigeonholing. One has the impression that these vague, seemingly alienated characters, rather than holding value in themselves as individuals, are elements of a composite male and female that Duras is inviting the audience to construct.

Duras's audience is perhaps very small in comparison with the public that regularly attends Hollywood films. Hers is a challenging cinema, in which the spectator is likely to feel discomfort before experiencing enlightenment. Perhaps most unnerving is the constant discrepancy between the flux of words and the flux of images. Duras rarely makes them mesh in the manner that mainstream cinema ascribes to life. Instead, they clash, obtrude upon one another, or introduce an unexpected dimension. Sound and image in Duras's films carry out in exemplary fashion the principles of the 1928 manifesto by Soviet directors (discussed below). They are separate coordinates, each forging ahead to create meaning and rarely lapsing back to mutual reinforcement. Instead, words and images react dialectically with one another.

In *Nathalie Granger,* as soon as the opening credits begin to roll by, we hear the high-pitched voice of a woman exclaiming, "Such violence in a little girl!" Later, these words are repeated in the sound track, but out of fictional context, and finally they are united with the image of the schoolmistress reporting to Nathalie's mother about the girl's behavior in school. This scene itself is a flashback, so that we must assume that the words heard earlier are a kind of echoing memory, perhaps passing through the mother's mind.

Destroy, She Said experiments more with spatial than temporal dislocation through sound and image. In one enigmatic scene, we see the two major female characters, Alissa and Elisabeth, making their first contact on the expansive lawn of the asylum where Alissa is recuperating after a miscarriage; but instead of the sound of their voices, we hear a conversation between two other characters, Max Thor and Stein. The effect is especially jarring because the men are commenting on the women's conversation, as though they are hearing what we cannot, in a mise-en-scène suggestive of the Marquis de Sade's works.[26]

What is blithely assumed in Hollywood aesthetics is not merely that verisimilitude is achieved only by following the established rules but, more significantly, that art has a responsibility to reflect life. Now, critics and philosophers since the beginning of time have pointed out that by the very nature of the signs we use to create artworks, these works can never be entirely faithful imitations of life. It is, in part, this deficiency that led Plato to banish the poets from his ideal Republic. One clearly established aesthetic principle that was associated with impressionism and symbolism and was in force in many parts of the artistic community at the time cinema came into being was that art achieves its effects through distortion, that meaning arises out of the rearrangement, not the reproduction, of bits and pieces of our universe. Cinema was drawn to representationalism by two powerful phenomena: One was the trend that ran counter to impressionism and symbolism, namely realism (and naturalism); the other was the overpowering verisimilitude of the photographic image. Coupled thirty years later with the technology of sound recording, the ever-recurrent notion about transcribing real life was compelling indeed.

It is for this reason that Robbe-Grillet implores us to reread the famous manifesto written in 1928 by Eisenstein, Vsevolod Pudovkin, and Gregori Alexandrov, in which the leaders of Soviet silent cinema heralded with caution the advent of sound.[27] They were concerned that cinema's ability to match voices to lips and to match sounds to actions would rigidify the art into a mere recording of events. Their fear, of course, was realized at the hands of many directors who, now that they were armed with the addition of sound effects, conceived their mission to be the bland transcription of "life." As Eisenstein explained in greater detail at a later time, sound has the potential for becoming the most dynamic element of cinematic articulation. Once we conceive of it as a separate element, not bound by any necessity to the person or object emitting it, then we may continue the work of analysis of the world that cinema should be committed to. In this sense, Robbe-Grillet claims that a primary function of cinema — as of all art — is to reveal the world to us. Such a revelation requires not recording what is before us but rather breaking it apart, examining its details, and putting it together in such a way that we do not accept reality but seriously consider its deficiencies and seek to change it. According to Eisenstein and Robbe-Grillet, cinema is uniquely endowed to fulfill this function.

Kluge fervently throws his support behind the project of tampering with the synchronous relation between lips and dialogue. He advocates creating a sound track independent of the image track. A precedent for this kind of sound/image play exists in the convention that inner speech is signified by voice-over and the absence of lip sync, as in the soliloquies of Laurence Olivier's *Hamlet* and in the examples already given from *Psycho* and *Hiroshima mon amour*. Furthermore, Kluge argues that the sound track should at times work *against* the image track. It is initially hard to imagine why a filmmaker might want to suggest one thing with an image and its opposite with the sound. But we need only consider the importance of negation in literary language to realize the potential of such disharmony. Cinematic discourse until now has seldom created structures of contradiction and negation. In *Deutschland im Herbst* (*Germany in Autumn*, 1978), the image track shows a man who is, quite obviously, alive, while Kluge's own voice-over describes the circumstances of the man's death and funeral. The effect is uncanny. In an analogous narrative situation in Billy Wilder's *Sunset Boulevard* (1950), we realize — but only at the end of the film — that the narrating protagonist is dead. Similarly, in Kluge's *Abschied von gestern* (*Yesterday Girl*, 1966), Christmas carols and other popular music associated with the home are played over images depicting the progressive loss of private shelter. In these examples, a contradictory relation between image and sound is used to predict a future event, to suggest the falseness of a present event, or to reinforce the image through blatant contrast.

Another film that plays with "negative" discourse is Robbe-Grillet's *L'Année dernière à Marienbad* (*Last Year at Marienbad*, 1961). We see a man trying to persuade a woman that they had met in Marienbad the year before. As he proceeds, insinuating more and more information, the woman's resistance seems to flag. We now see an image of her in her bedroom, doing more or less what the man says she was doing the previous year. Then, as her image huddles, full of anxiety, against the wall of her room, the man's voice suddenly says, "The door was closed now." However, we see that the door is open. His voice insists, "No! No! The door was closed."[28] As the image goes on contradicting him, we begin to doubt the truthfulness of everything he has said. By making the image track work against the sound track, Resnais and Robbe-Grillet manage to represent indirectly — and thus all the more dramatically — the woman's own doubts and hesitations about the man's version of the past.

The iconicity of film image and sound is not necessarily, then, to be enlisted in support of an aesthetic of realism. Instead, it is that special quality that allows cinema to make us see life more clearly. This quality is what Burroughs has in mind when he declares that "the language of film is the language of life."

Stoltzfus provides examples of great films whose ability to show us life more clearly and to reveal the world in greater depth has nothing whatsoever to do with the power of transcription. Godard's *Weekend* (1967), for example, makes a point about human brutality by exaggerating the carnage of car accidents during a highway melee. It is not simply that weekend traffic nullifies the pleasure of a day in the country but that today's slaughter on the highways is a small sign of the lowered esteem in which we hold the human body. A more interesting example, for historical reasons, is Jean Renoir's *Rules of the Game* (1939). Critics considered this film a failure at the time of its release because of an unmotivated death at the end of the story; yet this death later was seen as precisely the "nonrealistic" detail that the entire New Wave generation found so inspiring.

The finest example to come out of the New Wave along these lines is *Hiroshima mon amour*. Stoltzfus points to Resnais's daring combination of "fact and fantasy" in this film and implies that cinema had finally realized its full potential. Indeed, *Hiroshima* explicitly refutes the notion that truth is born out of documentary realism with the Japanese architect's refusal to acknowledge what the French actress has seen in the newsreels and in the museums of the bombed city. "You saw *nothing* in Hiroshima," he says as the film opens. "I saw *everything*," she insists. The entire structure of the action, moreover, refutes commonly held notions about the relative significance of different phases of momentous historical events. Instead of attempting to present us with a panorama of the bombing of Hiroshima and its aftermath, Resnais and Duras focus on a single Westerner's love experiences during the war and after. In so doing, the artists multiply a hundredfold the power of the unspeakable events themselves. The French actress, who believes at the beginning of the film that her dead German lover is safely buried in the past, is forced to heed her own words: "Why deny the obvious necessity for memory?" And the passion that she had thought was also lost she sees rekindled with her Japanese lover — to the point of confusing him with the dead German — so that, in the end, she and her lover are no longer mere individuals but rather crossroads of history, subjectivities that have been uncompromisingly riddled by earth-shattering events: "Hi-ro-shi-ma. That's your name," she says to him, to which he responds, "That's my name. Yes. Your name is Nevers. Ne-vers-in-France."

Innovation, Avant-Garde

In the previous section, I stated that it was curious that mainstream cinema is so devoted to its rules. I used the word "curious" because the inspiration gleaned from the cinema by novelists (and painters and dramatists, too) is based on a perception that goes quite beyond the rules. It is as though the film industry had turned out an Aladdin's lamp, worn and broken down to all appearances, that modern artists instinctively knew how to rub the right way. For out of this machine of manufactured illusions has been drawn a group of artistic techniques that virtually define twentieth-century formal innovation: montage, cross-cutting, collage, time shifting. In a sense, the attention to technical invention urged by Robbe-Grillet is already a characteristic of a large number of innovative writers. Sukenick specifies three techniques that he learned from years of movie-going. Collage, first of all, is the basic technique of assemblage that cinema shares with many modern visual forms and is perhaps derived from the assembly-line production mode of modern industry. Elements of unlike origin, texture, or rhythm are yoked together in order to produce unusual results. As in the collages of Kurt Schwitters and Pablo Picasso, the assemblage connotes a positive embrace of the totality of the modern industrial world. Or, more recently, in the flatbed constructions of Robert

Rauschenberg, objects are juxtaposed with an uncanniness close to, yet distinct from, the aesthetic aims of surrealism in order to initiate "a shakeup which contaminates all purified categories."[29]

Improvisation, Sukenick's second technique, is a method of creating, composing, or performing without a prewritten script. He speaks of it as less intrinsic to film than the other techniques because of the cumbersome machinery required just to get image onto celluloid and then to project it. The improvisation of Godard's early movies, inspired in part by the cinema verité technique of documentary, has had a lasting effect on writers. The energy and speed so much admired by Baumbach have their origin in improvisation.

The third technique is arbitrary form. Within this category, Sukenick includes the chance devices and experiments with randomness that go back to Stéphane Mallarmé. Related to the generative process Stoltzfus describes in his essay, arbitrary form prevents the artist from giving in to received ideas and hackneyed formulas. It forces the artist to go beyond accepted categories, "to de-fab the pre-fab," as Sukenick puts it.

There is another type of cinema, often categorized as avant-garde, that has a more complex relation to contemporary literature than does the traditional film. Avant-garde filmmakers, like the experimental writers I have been referring to, distill from the formula film certain devices that tend to reveal, rather than conceal, the operation of the cinematic apparatus itself. In the early days of cinema, this experimentation was scarcely distinguishable from the development of the medium in general. Technical experiments, such as those of Georges Méliès, were part and parcel of the evolution in film language that led to the narrative film. Avant-garde filmmakers of the 1920s, such as Jean Epstein, Abel Gance, Germaine Dulac, and Luis Buñuel, continued dedicating themselves to technical experimentation, thus forming a major bifurcation from the mainstream development of narrative film that would reach its apex with the Hollywood productions of the 1930s and 1940s. American "independent" filmmakers carried on the underground experimentation of the 1950s and 1960s, and today, with the hegemony of the Hollywood style significantly weakened, there are a good number of avant-garde filmmakers at work throughout the world, some of whom are mixing film with other plastic and temporal forms like video and dance.

•

I do not mean to say that the "well-made" story film has become obsolete. In fact, in the hands of accomplished artists, this form can always have inspiring results. It is a highly elaborated version of this form that Borges had in mind when he developed the screenplay for *Les Autres* (The others, 1974). He had made a bet "not to attempt to muddle the story and then to reproduce this muddlement on the screen," but rather "to confront the story as a 'natural object.' " The formula plot, then, became an object of interest in itself.

While film form developed along at least these two very different lines, with literary form bounding off in still other new directions, critical understanding of narrative form within the academy also underwent some significant changes. The serious study of narrative fiction began offhandedly in the modern era with Henry James. His "prefaces" were to become the groundwork for the writings of many influential critics of the 1920s and 1930s, including Percy Lubbock, Ramon Fernandez, and Joseph Warren Beach. During roughly the same period, the Soviet Vladimir Propp was collecting folk tales in an effort to discover their common "moves" and thus to abstract their basic patterns. Several decades later, certain French critics, very roughly grouped under the rubric of structuralism, developed descriptive and predictive models of narrative acts and action by using the linguistic laws established at the beginning of the century by Ferdinand de Saussure.

The Anglo-Americans, Soviets, and French had in common an interest in discerning rules of composition in narrative fiction that would enable them to read an author's work with greater authority or, by applying the rules to the works of several authors, to distinguish in purely textual terms how one author's work differs from that of others. Semioticians A. J. Greimas and Claude Bremond simultaneously expanded and condensed Propp's research to formulate laws according to which *all* narrative actions could be categorized; Tsvetan Todorov has written "grammars" of particular works to show how formulaic the storytelling is; and Gérard Genette writes a theory of narrative that derives from an expansion of the basic parts of speech — subject, predicate, object — along with its moods and voices.[30]

The semiotic approach to narrative analysis, although fruitful when applied to classic works of literature and film, curiously founders when applied to the avant-garde. This is partly due, no doubt, to the fact that many avant-garde forms reject narrative as such. As reflexive structures, they refer us not so much to a coherent fictional universe as to their own generation and composition. Another reason the semiotic approach fails when applied to the avant-garde is the dependence of the approach on pattern and prediction. Nothing is more contrary to the spirit of avant-garde film and fiction than the notion that the analyst will be able to predict the artist's moves or that the artist is working within easily recognizable conventions.

One definition of the avant-garde might be a corpus of works whose structures are designed precisely to hinder critical analysis — be it through a semiotic approach or any other. Semiotics appears manifestly inadequate mainly because it has claimed itself to be a science of *all* texts.

But most modern critics believe the avant-garde can be deciphered. They believe, indeed, that its forms hold meaning. One way to analyze the avant-garde is to define it precisely against the norm of classical narrative. Roland Barthes's term for the avant-garde was "writerly," which he defined as possessing structures and sequences that are not composed according to the prevailing codes of fiction (codes that manage the "readerly" text). The reader of the "writerly" text must enter into the creative process to make sense of the text.[31]

This negative definition of the avant-garde is particularly useful when applied to film because classical Hollywood cinema reached its greatest peaks so quickly and became in so short a time a monolithic model of representationalism to be contended with. Yet such a definition begs the question of analysis. We still must ask what avant-garde films are about. Even if they reject narrative (at least in its traditional forms), their images and sounds present some sort of comprehensible material.

Let us return to experimental fiction to consider the qualities it shares with avant-garde film. Much experimental fiction eschews narrative; and its effects on the reader are strikingly similar to experimental film's effects on the spectator. Avant-garde film and fiction share an iconoclastic attitude toward the received ideas about their respective art forms. Duras, whose acclaim as a filmmaker is beginning now to rival her reputation as a novelist, states that it is only when she arrives at a point in a film where its problematics cannot be resolved by the conventions of mainstream cinema that she feels she is truly engaged in filmmaking. Exemplary films, for Duras, often capture the constant mobility of the medium in order to immobilize it. An example is Stuart Pound's *Codex* (1979), which has a sound track by Philip Glass that, according to Duras, beats "with a metronomic regularity and becomes all regularity and presence." As with the very long films of Andy Warhol, such as *Empire* (1964) and *Sleep* (1963), film becomes the temporal medium for investigating time itself.

Another way to explore what experimental film and fiction have in common is to consider both as investigations of reflexive form. Avant-garde cinema has always laid bare the devices of film work itself. No attempt is made to cover over the materials and machinery that have gone into making the films' images and sounds. The films are thus reflexive in that their form reflects the apparatus that brought them into existence. Burroughs sees this element in all successfully constructed films and novels. He emphasizes not so much the departure from norms as the necessity for reflexivity, especially in creating a climax. The novelist casting about for a dynamic ending for a story need only look back over the elements of his or her text. Thus, in what some critics, invoking Aristotle, might call simply organic form, the novelist "manufactures" a climax "with the materials of the novel itself."

A good example of the reflexive film is Michael Snow's *Wavelength* (1967). With the camera focused from a distance on a side wall of a loft, where a snapshot is pinned between two windows, Snow zooms in very slowly, to the accompaniment of an electronic tone gradually rising in pitch. Toward the end of this forty-five-minute zoom, there is the sound of pounding on a door, followed by an apparent murder and then a telephone call. But these "events" remain around the borders of the frame, with the sounds often brought in off-camera. They never ruffle the steady, intractable forward movement of the zoom-in. By this time we can see that the snapshot is a picture of the sea. The film ends as the rectangle of the snapshot overflows the dimensions of the movie screen. *Wavelength* is reflexive because of the way it forces us to attend to the movement of the camera. This unwavering, yet barely perceptible, motion becomes far more compelling than the brief "climactic" struggle. In fact, it is precisely because the narrative elements are overshadowed that the film becomes reflexive in yet another way. It is like a declaration of freedom from narrative, a manifesto in favor of using cinema to investigate the properties of light, sound, and movement.

In fiction, a good example of reflexivity is Baumbach's *Reruns* (1974). The narrator, far from guiding the reader through a sequence of interconnected events, appears dazed from the outset by the trauma of writing. A sometime filmmaker, he uses dreams, movies plots, and free associations, without any causal connectives, in order to draw the reader's attention to the very process of fabrication. We can never be sure whether a scene is "really" taking place or being dreamed or fantasized. The movies the narrator describes have such an uncanny resemblance to the presumed events of the narrator's life that, at one moment, the two become indistinguishable: The narrator and an anonymous woman who had been sitting on his lap in a movie theater are being ejected from the theater just as figures on the screen who resemble them are walking down a dark corridor exactly like the one they are led along. The narrator actually sees himself on the screen, at which point the woman he is with is transformed into one of his lovers, Anna. With "real" events and screen events hopelessly entangled, the narrator begins a new chapter in which he announces his decision to become a comedian. The reflexivity of *Reruns* comes mainly from the breaks in the illusionism we expect to be maintained consistently by the narrator. By transgressing the conventional barriers between remembered account, dreams and fantasy, and interpolated movie, Baumbach's narrator draws our attention to the artifices of his fiction.

In his essay, Baumbach says that reflexive fiction should not be thought of as tricky or as an experiment in form for its own sake. On the contrary, he claims that the more an artwork deals with the resources of its own medium, the more authentic it is. Sukenick also praises reflexive writing, claiming that it surpasses similar effects of self-consciousness in the other arts. Its greater concreteness and at the same time its supple abstraction make writing "more self-conscious even than thought in the mind."

Yet for all their similarities of effect, filmmaking and writing in the avant-garde mode are very different in their means of engaging the spectator and the reader. Cinema, many would argue, has been more innovative than writing in this regard. Owing largely to the necessarily discontinuous process of editing any film, cinema presents fragments that must be assembled in the mind of the viewer. In contrast, traditional literature has for centuries encouraged a reading process based on imaginative identification. The reader is transported into the fiction, losing all sense of his or her present existence, participating vicariously in the action and identifying with the protagonists. Thus, as a means of expression, cinema was more open than literature to casting off the representational, or illusionist, aesthetic.

It was Bertolt Brecht who first developed a practice, in the theater, aimed at breaking down this illusionism. He forced the audience to adopt a clear, critical stance toward the action on stage by inserting in his "epic dramas" elements that reminded the audience that they were in a theater watching an artificially produced fiction. This method of distancing the viewer, what Brecht called the *Verfremdungseffekt*, or "estrangement effect," found its way readily into experimental film practice. With the adoption of numerous techniques aimed at estrangement, film has created a new, ideal spectator, one who asks questions and welcomes aesthetic challenges. In this way, film has become more open than literature to breaking illusions; it has managed, according to Sukenick, "to break the usually hypnotic relation between medium and viewer that amounts to a form of mind control."

The purpose of the estrangement effect is not merely to titillate the audience, however. It is a primary means of stimulating the viewer to take part in the dynamic process of producing meaning. In order to do this, according to Stoltzfus, "the audience must participate in the montage, assemble the images, play with them, and experience the re-creative freedom that produced the work in the first place."

Kluge places tremendous importance on the role of the spectator. In his films, not only must the viewer read written titles, thus keeping active the cognitive as well as the perceptual apparatus of the brain, he or she must also exercise the imagination necessary to make the leap from signifying configuration to sense. This task, Kluge insists, is not easy. How often have we found our minds wandering in the midst of a film, with the effect that our brains register the images and sounds but we do not construe their meaning? Film viewing, far from being a passive indulgence, requires concentration.[32]

Godard's *2 or 3 Things I Know About Her* (1966) uses estrangement techniques to engage the spectator and destroy, in Pasolini's words, "the 'grammar' of [the] film" before we know what it is. The narrator, speaking in a whisper, opens the film by situating the time and place of the action with deceptive precision (August 19, metropolitan Paris) and coyly introducing us to the main character. We are immediately tipped off that this narrator will function in an unusual manner when he introduces the protagonist first as Marina Vlady, the name of the actress playing the lead role, and then as Juliette Janson, the name of the leading female character. In the film, Godard acknowledges his indebtedness to "old man Brecht," as he is affectionately referred to, by having the actress quote a dictum of the great dramatist: "To speak as though citing truths."[33] This character is therefore seen as both a fictive being and a real-life actress.

By blurring the distinction between actress and fictional personage, Godard conflates art and personal history. He goes further in this direction by posing questions to Vlady through a hidden microphone — questions that she, after some reflection, responds to spontaneously from a personal perspective. She remains both inside and outside the character of Juliette.

The narrator in *2 or 3 Things I Know About Her* presents the fiction but refuses to perform the explanatory function of the ordinary storyteller. He throws off the viewers' expectations, for example, by referring to profilmic elements (those elements that lie outside the fiction). "Here's how Juliette," he says, "at 3:37, watched someone page through one of those objects which, in journalistic jargon, we call a magazine. And here's how, about 150 frames later, another young woman, her counterpart, her sister, looked at the same object."

With barriers broken between actress and character as well as between narrator and action, Godard goes on to rechart the line between spectator and fiction. In the film, he repeatedly uses a cinema verité–inspired technique whereby a character breaks out of the fiction, looks directly at the camera lens, and speaks to the audience during a tight close-up. These sudden miniconfessions suggest a new relation between the character, usually a minor figure, and the audience. For example, there is Paulette, the modest, ill-confident beauty salon worker; still in character though no longer "in" the story, she addresses the audience directly in a wonderful, heart-to-heart tone.

In addition to the unique position of the spectator in cinema, another striking difference exists between experimental filmmaking and writing. According to Duras, the position of the filmmaker is diametrically opposed to that of the writer in the sense that the writer can never reexperience his or her work in the manner open to the filmmaker. Duras stresses how the *réalisateur* (one of the French words for director) can assume the role of the spectator in order to "read," or "realize," his or her film. Viewing becomes a universalizable activity; verbal reading can never function in that way. Instead, according to Duras, the writer descends into an inner obscurity in which he or she confronts an entire consciousness to be expressed. This encounter is not reexperienced by a reader; the reader merely witnesses the results. The filmmaker's job begins where the writer's leaves off. And because filmmakers deal with visualization, they can share (and hence foresee) what the spectators will see.

Art, Ideology, Taste

Cinema has been heralded since its beginnings as an art uniquely endowed to provide escapist entertainment for a socially alienated audience. From a historical viewpoint, cinema seems to have played the same social role in the early twentieth century that the novel played during the eighteenth. Susan Sontag notes this fascinating parallel in her book *Against Interpretation* (1961). She points out that the content of the two forms in their infancy was also profoundly similar: sententious moralizing, stock characters of sexual innocence and ruthless brutality, and a constant, suppressed voluptuousness.[34]

The escapism afforded by cinema was not confined to its early years, however. Baumbach and Sukenick attest to the power it held over them and members of their entire generation. Movies offered respite from the oppressively value-laden institutions within which children spent most of their time: family, church, school. "We came to the movies," recalls Baumbach, "without the resistances we brought to those agencies of culture that were foisted on us for the good of our souls." Classic Hollywood cinema combined the quotidian with the ideal — the viewers saw objects and scenes that they encountered in their everyday lives together with highly idealized movie stars and situations. The vast industry of fan magazines and star reportages attests to the awe and fascination the public has for Hollywood personalities. The viewers' initial uneasiness at seeing their own streets and habitats projected onto the huge screen, as reported by many early commentators, was quickly replaced by a feeling of supreme comfort

— the security brought on by viewing the familiar. This scandalized amazement followed by mollification is in line with the reactions exhibited by primitive people in experiments in which they were introduced to film: At first, they feared that the cinematic apparatus had robbed them of their spiritual counterparts, the images on the screen, but that fear soon disappeared.[35]

Achieving a dynamic relation between art object and public, where demands can be satisfied as completely as possible, has always been a primary aim of Hollywood cinema. Although the gradual familiarity of film images that took over the film-going public may have resulted entirely from psychological factors, the growing standardization of movie content resulted from the industry's careful measuring of public taste. And as with all questions of taste, the industry was as much responsible for forming it as it was involved in interpreting it. Public taste, in other words, is the product of a circular process by which surmised tendencies are reinforced by particular contents. Once a predilection has been discerned, its standardization is a fait accompli. Hence, we see, for example, the repetitiousness of Hollywood plots and Hollywood's tendency to capitalize on fads, from "big-boom" science fiction stories to fantastic adventure plots like that of Steven Spielberg's *Raiders of the Lost Ark* (1981) and its sequels.

As Burroughs points out, the underlying logic of this state of affairs is very clear: "What has made money will make money." This axiom encourages studios to stick to the tried-and-true formula rather than experimenting with a new twist or a new technique.

Duras accuses the movie-reviewing establishment of complicity in this taste-making process. She claims that reviewers devote more space to discussing big-budget films than low-budget films, even if the films are potboilers. Money impresses everyone, from the public to the critics. But, Duras laments, the critics are responsible for pushing this ethic on the public.

What happens when a filmmaker wishes to challenge public taste? As a mass art, cinema has the potential for influencing and even manipulating public taste and public opinion. Many critics would argue that films reflect dominant public views rather than challenge them and thus act as a means of legitimating the ideologies of the group or class in power. Here again an analogy can be drawn with the history of the novel. In the nineteenth century the codes of realism prevailed in novel writing, encouraging the public to believe, first of all, that conditions as described in the novels were the exact replica of things as they were and, second, that these conditions were part of the natural scheme of things. A similar ideology can be seen in Hollywood cinema of the 1930s and 1940s. With a few notable exceptions, the Hollywood codes presented a "reality" in which middle-class, capitalist values prevailed; few challenges were successfully made to dominant attitudes about racism and sexism.

When European directors, shortly after World War II, began resisting these directions in cinema, their efforts were often stymied. As Puig reports, the Italian neorealists' attempts to create a new, politically engaged cinema met with tremendous resistance on the part of producers and critics. Even before and during the war, Roberto Rossellini, Vittorio De Sica, and other Italian directors were working with Cesare Zavattini and other scenarists to forge an aesthetic that opposed many of the underlying assumptions of mainstream cinema. Determined to present the reality of the peasants and urban poor in a new way (hence, they were called neorealists), these artists embraced direct methods of recording, including live (nonstudio) sound and handheld cameras, in an effort to strip cinema of the glamorous patina with which Hollywood had covered it. "Things are there," proclaimed Rossellini; "Why manipulate them?"[36] Masterpieces of human struggles and everyday plights — what might be called "docudrama" today — such as De Sica's *Bicycle Thief* (1948) and *Umberto D* (1952), Rossellini's *Open City* (1945), and Luchino Visconti's *La Terra trema* (1948), opened up to cinema a new expressability that was distinctly tinged by the war experience of an exhausted Europe.

As Puig's account reveals, however, no sooner had the neorealist aesthetic been formulated than it was seen — and attacked — as too rigid. Whereas one large faction of the postwar generation insisted that the camera had to leave things alone, to record reality and no more, another growing faction demanded that the camera go *beyond* mere externals. Thus was created, among the postwar directors who would herald the New Wave in France — Antonioni, Fellini, Robert Bresson, Resnais, François Truffaut — what one critic has called a "cinema of scars," one that "seeks no longer to grasp the situation, but its trace, no longer the outside world, but its internal reflection."[37]

Pasolini and others straddled this opposition, rejecting the neorealists' docudrama style yet holding to a notion of the film image as bearing not simply the "impression" of reality, but reality itself. For Pasolini, the controversy over image, sign, and concept being hotly debated by the semioticians was a red herring. Championing an aesthetic based on what he calls the "code of codes," Pasolini considers the film image to be nothing more or less than a *piece* of reality that has magically been lifted onto the screen.

Puig does not admit as readily as Sukenick and Baumbach to an explicit influence of cinema on his writing. He reveals in his essay, however, two important motifs of his novels that derive from his early contact with filmmaking. On the one hand, we see clearly his utter fascination with the artifacts and documents of ordinary life, from hair clips and tablecloths to diaries and newspaper articles. Like the neorealists, he revives for our century a "slice-of-life" aesthetic with a distinctly documentary twist. On the other hand, in his manipulation of these objects of everyday existence, we can detect not only an artist schooled in the technique of modernism but, in particular, his fascination for the processes of subject formation in the era of late capitalism — how, in other words, characters like Toto and Juan Carlos, Molina and Valentin get the ideas that they *seem* to be born with. In Puig's novels, mass media and mass psychology intermingle to such a degree that one seems always to be the future embodiment of the other: Movies are seen to determine character; psychology is seen as the trace of so many "alienated languages."[38]

The example, then, of Puig's complex embrace, partly negative and partly positive, of postwar Italian cinema may be taken as an emblem of future writing in this film age. Just as Rossellini and De Sica challenged the assumptions of studio production; just as Godard, Resnais, Bresson, and Truffaut challenged formulaic plots and stock characters; just as Antonioni and Fellini challenged the expectations of minimum and maximum load in cinematic expressivity; and just as today's generations of directors, inside Hollywood now as well as outside, continue questioning not only the conventional handling of the cinematic apparatus but also the subject formation fostered by such handling, so Puig and other contemporary writers have been able to use the aesthetic insights of the filmmakers in order to launch challenges against the engrained assumptions of their own craft. Have these writers and directors managed, through their innovation and against the tremendous odds laid down by the critical and industrial establishment, to change public taste either in their own countries or around the world? It is difficult at this point in time to make a definitive evaluation.

By being attentive to the innovations in each other's craft, filmmaker and writer remain open to the kinds of changes that are likely to condition cinema and literature in the twenty-first century. It is as though each segment of a book or a film were a minimal unit — what I would call the virtual text — of another great text that cannot be constituted in any medium. Barthes suggests that film — either the single frame or the enlarged photogram often used in movie publicity — functions somewhat in this manner, being "the fragment of a second text whose existence never exceeds the fragment."[39] The modern world offers virtual texts in every possible medium — dance, video, drama, music — as well as in every realm of the electrosphere we inhabit, from the strident discourse of advertising to the intimate details of personal life. Openness to the processes in the other arts as well as to these other natural and artificial "languages" will allow filmmakers and writers of the future access to virtual texts that, although at first foreign or rough in intonation and texture, may revolutionize their arts.

Notes

1. Erwin Panofsky, "Style and Medium in the Motion Pictures," *Critique* 1, no. 3 (Jan.–Feb. 1947); rpt. in Gerald Mast and Marshall Cohen, eds., *Film Theory and Criticism*, 3d ed. (New York: Oxford University Press, 1985), p. 215. Panofsky's idea that technology "gave rise to the discovery and gradual perfection of a new art" was challenged by some early theorists. André Bazin, for example, argues that the art had *imaginatively* existed since ancient times and that although it depended on certain inspired putterers for its actual technical assembly, "the cinema owes virtually nothing to the scientific spirit." Bazin, *What Is Cinema?* trans. H. Gray (Berkeley: University of California Press, 1967), p. 17.

2. Arnold Hauser, *The Social History of Art,* vol. 4, trans. S. Godman (New York: Random House, 1951), p. 239.

3. Stein's awareness of cinema is made clear in, among other places, her essay "Portraits and Repetition," in *Lectures in America* (New York: Random House, 1935), pp. 177–78. For further discussion of Gertrude Stein as a postcinema novelist, see Keith Cohen, *Film and Fiction* (New Haven: Yale University Press, 1979), pp. 109–26 and passim; and Bruce Kawin, *Telling It Again and Again: Repetition in Literature and Film* (Ithaca: Cornell University Press, 1972), pp. 108–10, 117–31, 136–53 (rpt. Boulder: University Press of Colorado, 1989). Dos

Passos's consciousness of camera technique is most evident in his use of the term "camera eye" for the intermittent interior monologues sprinkled through *U.S.A.* (1937) and in the montagelike composition of the newsreel sections of that novel. For further discussion of Dos Passos and film sensibility, see Claude-Edmonde Magny, *The Age of the American Novel,* trans. E. Hochman (New York: Frederick Ungar, 1972), pp. 105–23.

4. See Plato's *Meno,* 81–85, and *Phaedo,* 73–74.

5. "Aleatory" refers to chance; in literature aleatory experiments, beginning with Mallarmé's "Un Coup de dés jamais n'abolira le hasard" (A throw of the dice will never abolish chance) Paris: *Cosmopolis,* 1897; rpt. Paris: *Nouvelle Revue Française,* 1914), a prose poem whose form and substance foreground chance, signal the writer's desire to get outside the confines of rational processes. Such experiments, frequently practiced by symbolists and surrealists (cf. André Breton's "automatic writing"), are intended to put the writer in touch with forces or with material that ordinarily he or she could not access.

   For more information on the cut-up method, see William Burroughs and Brion Gysin, *The Third Mind* (New York: Viking, 1978), pp. 1–8, 42–60.

6. Julia Kristeva, "Postmodernism?" *Bucknell Review* 25, no. 2 (1981):139.

7. Sergei Eisenstein, *Film Form,* trans. J. Leyda (New York: Harcourt, Brace & World, 1949), pp. 48–49.

8. The relationship between film and conceptual thought, though a rather rarefied topic, has been addressed — or at least toyed with — by a number of theorists. Here is a partial list: Hugo Münsterberg, *The Film: A Psychological Study* (New York: Dover, 1970; orig. pbn. 1916); Elie Faure, *Fonction du cinéma* (Paris: Gonthier, 1964; orig. pbn. 1953); Eisenstein, *Film Form,* esp. "The Cinematographic Principle and the Ideogram" and "A Dialectic Approach to Film Form"; Béla Balázs, *Theory of the Film: Character and Growth of a New Art,* trans. E. Bone (London: Dobson, 1952); Bazin, *What Is Cinema?* esp. "The Ontology of the Photographic Image" and "The Evolution of the Language of Cinema"; Jean Mitry, *Esthétique et psychologie du cinéma,* vol. 1 (*Les Structures*), chs. 3–5 (Paris: Eds. Universitaires, 1965); Rudolf Arnheim, *Film as Art* (Berkeley: University of California Press, 1966) and *Visual Thinking* (Berkeley: University of California Press, 1969).

9. Eisenstein, *Film Form,* p. 105.

10. Christian Metz, *Language and Cinema,* trans. Donna Jean Umiker-Seboek (The Hague: Mouton, 1974), and *Film Language: A Semiotics of Cinema,* trans. Michael Taylor (New York: Oxford University Press, 1974), chs. 3–5.

11. John Locke, *An Essay Concerning Human Understanding* (1690).

12. Cf. Bazin's essay "The Myth of Total Cinema," *What Is Cinema?* pp. 17–22. Bazin's subtle argument is that cinema as myth has existed in people's imaginations since earliest times, but just as the myth of Icarus — the man with wings — had to await the invention of the internal combustion engine to fall to earth (i.e., to be demythologized), so cinema had to await the industrial and scientific fervor of the nineteenth century to be transported from the imaginary into the real world.

13. As with film and the thought process, the relationship between film and dreaming has been addressed by a number of critics. See, among others, André Malraux,

Esquisse d'une psychologie du cinéma (Paris: Gallimard, 1946), orig. in *Verve* 3 (1939); Susanne K. Langer, "A Note on the Film," in her *Feeling and Form* (New York: Scribner, 1953), pp. 411–15; Jacqueline Rose, "Paranoia and the Film System," *Screen* 17, no. 4 (Winter 1976–77):85–104, rpt. in C. Penley, *Feminism and Film Theory* (New York: Routledge, 1988), pp. 141–58; Roland Barthes, "Upon Leaving the Movie Theater," *University Publishing* 6 (Winter 1979):3–6, orig. in *Communications* 23 (1975):104–107; Thierry Kuntzel, "The Film Work," *enclitic* 2, no. 1 (Spring 1978):39–62, orig. in *Communications* 19 (1972):25–39, and "The Film Work, 2," *Camera Obscura* 5 (1980):7–69, orig. in *Communications* 23 (1975):136–89; and Christian Metz, *The Imaginary Signifier,* trans. C. Britton, A. Williams, B. Brewster, and A. Guezzetti, (Bloomington: Indiana University Press, 1982), esp. chs. 6–10 and 19–23 (orig. pbn. 1977).

14. Cohen, *Film and Fiction,* pp. 118–22. Cf. Kawin, *Telling It Again and Again.*

15. See Standish Lawder's valuable analysis of *Ballet mécanique* in *The Cubist Cinema* (New York: New York University Press, 1975), pp. 65–70, 117–67, 209–59.

16. David Curtis, *Experimental Cinema* (New York: Dell, 1971), pp. 65–66.

17. Marguerite Duras, *India Song* (Paris: Gallimard, 1973), p. 10 (from Duras's opening *Remarques générales*).

18. See David Bordwell's discussion of "parametric narration" for a fascinating explanation of how repetition and other stylistic devices motivate narrative structuration. Bordwell, *Narration in the Fiction Film* (Madison: University of Wisconsin Press, 1985), esp. pp. 274–79.

19. Sigmund Freud, *The Interpretation of Dreams,* trans. James Strachey (New York: Avon, 1965), pp. 324–26.

20. Alain Robbe-Grillet, *Two Novels:* Jealousy *and* In the Labyrinth, trans. R. Howard (New York: Grove Press, 1965), esp. pp. 113–14.

21. Cohen, *Film and Fiction,* pp. 109–13.

22. Cf. Roland Barthes, "Rhetoric of the Image," in *Image-Music-Text,* trans. S. Heath (New York: Hill & Wang, 1977), pp. 44–45.

23. Wolfgang Iser wrote, "One might simplify by saying that each intentional sentence correlative opens up a particular horizon, which is modified, if not completely changed, by succeeding sentences. While these expectations arouse interest in what is to come, the subsequent modification of them will also have a retrospective effect on what has already been read. This may now take on a different significance from that which it had at the moment of reading." Iser, *The Implied Reader* (Baltimore: Johns Hopkins University Press, 1974), p. 278.

24. Cf. Cohen, *Film and Fiction,* pp. 123–206.

25. Bazin, "La Politique des auteurs," in Peter Graham, ed., *The New Wave* (New York: Doubleday, 1968), pp. 143–44.

26. The narrative situation in most of the Marquis de Sade's works is a dialogue among two or more male and female "libertines." The character more or less in charge, such as Dolmance in *Philosophy in the Bedroom* (1795), describes the positions he wants the characters to assume, and they follow his directions. Thus, the spoken

dialogue of a character becomes the narrative description of action. Action and description are subsumed in dialogue.

27. In Eisenstein, *Film Form,* pp. 257–59.

28. Alain Robbe-Grillet, *Last Year at Marienbad,* trans. R. Howard (New York: Grove Press, 1962), p. 125.

29. Leo Steinberg, *Other Criteria* (New York: Oxford University Press, 1972), p. 91.

30. A. J. Greimas, *Sémantique structurale, recherche de méthode* (Paris: Larousse, 1966), trans. *Structural Semantics* (Lincoln: University of Nebraska Press, 1984); Claude Bremond, *Logique du récit* (Paris: Seuil, 1973); Tsvetan Todorov, *Grammaire du Décaméron* (The Hague: Mouton, 1969); Gérard Genette, *Discours du récit,* in *Figures III* (Paris: Seuil, 1972), trans. *Narrative Discourse* (Ithaca: Cornell University Press, 1980).

31. Roland Barthes, *S/Z,* trans. R. Howard (New York: Farrar, Straus & Giroux, 1974), pp. 3–6 and passim (orig. Paris: Seuil, 1970).

32. A fruitfully complex analysis of "spectatorship" has emerged in recent film theory out of the intersection of cinema, psychoanalysis, feminism, and a neo-Marxist critique of consumer culture inspired by the Frankfurt School. See, for example, Laura Mulvey, "Visual Pleasure and Narrative Cinema," *Screen* 16, no. 3 (1975), rpt. in Mast and Cohen, *Film Theory and Criticism,* pp. 803–16; Stephen Heath, "On Screen, in Frame: Film and Ideology," "On Suture," and "Body, Voice," in his *Questions of Cinema* (Bloomington: Indiana University Press, 1981), pp. 1–18, 76–112, 176–93; Kaja Silverman, *The Subject of Semiotics* (New York: Oxford University Press, 1983); Mary Ann Doane, "The Voice in the Cinema: The Articulation of Body and Space," *Yale French Studies* 60 (1980):33–50, and "Woman's Stake: Filming the Female Body," in C. Penley, ed., *Feminism and Film Theory* (New York: Routledge, 1988), pp. 216–28; and Metz, *The Imaginary Signifier,* chs. 3–5.

33. Jean-Luc Godard, *2 ou 3 choses que je sais d'elle* (Paris: Seuil, 1971), p. 20.

34. Susan Sontag, *Against Interpretation* (New York: Dell, 1961), pp. 242–43.

35. Edgar Morin, *Le Cinéma ou l'homme imaginaire* (Paris: Gonthier, 1956), p. 16.

36. Cited in Marie-Claire Ropars-Wuilleumier, *De la littérature au cinéma* (Paris: Armand Colin, 1970), p. 114.

37. Ibid., pp. 126–27.

38. Marta Morello-Frosch, *"Betrayed by Rita Hayworth,* or the New Art of Narrating Films," *Review* 4–5 (Winter–Spring 1971–72):52–55. For Morello-Frosch, cinema becomes an instance of "alienated language" to the extent that it functions, as in Manuel Puig's novel, as a substitute for meaningful communication among the protagonists: "This type of language is external, totally foreign, to human life concerns."

39. Roland Barthes, "The Third Meaning," in his *Image-Music-Text,* p. 67.

Part 1

Up Against Cinema

William S. Burroughs, 1914–   1

ailed by Norman Mailer as "the only American novelist living today who may conceivably be possessed by genius" and by his close friend Jack Kerouac as "the greatest satirical writer since Jonathan Swift," William Burroughs is by far the most controversial American writer of the contemporary period. Whereas Henry Miller's scatological novels gained him a reputation for obscenity and Robbe-Grillet's object-oriented fictions gave rise to furious critical debates about narrative minimalism, Burroughs's writing, like that of Gertrude Stein, has remained staunchly on the margins of the modern canon and outside the academic curriculum. Unlike other enfants terribles of modernism such as Arthur Rimbaud and Guillaume Apollinaire, Burroughs cultivates nothing of the childlike nor chants a lyricism of the urban experience. Quite to the contrary, his work is marked by an incredible lassitude, a vision of degradation and destruction that has a clear thematic kinship with the works of such early modernists as T. S. Eliot and William Butler Yeats.

What makes Burroughs's works initially inaccessible, however, is that his literary forebears were outside the Anglo-American tradition. Though his satire may be compared to that of Swift, or to the paintings of Pieter Breughel and Hieronymus Bosch, his aesthetic temperament is most similar to the Marquis de Sade and to those later rebels, the surrealists, who reclaimed Sade's works as one of the fountainheads of modernism. In Sade we find the same combination of relentless descriptions of polymorphous sexual acts and a dubious moral mission. But whereas in Sade sexual coupling becomes the metaphor for individual liberty, in Burroughs it is a metaphor for human need and vulnerability. The boys in Burroughs's works who leap on one another and quiver in instantaneous orgasms suggest an image of the human condition according to which we are all and nothing but body — body that is, on the one hand, in constant need of animal satisfaction and, on the other hand, constantly liable to become prey to that animalistic need in another.

The other dominant metaphor Burroughs uses to signify this dreadful dilemma of need is drugs. Opium, hashish, and other mild hallucinogens have inspired and been the subject of a good deal of literature since the mid-nineteenth century, and they have functioned as the passkeys to a realm beyond that of the immediate senses. They were part of the romantic period's program of enriching one's experiences, for example, and integral to Rimbaud's "systematic deregulation of the senses." But in works of Burroughs and other contemporary authors, drugs become the sign of a dead-end dependency, a wrong turn that leads not only to disillusionment but also to physical degeneration. This subject, we know, comes directly out of Burroughs's private life: He was addicted to heroin for at least thirteen years, and after his cure by means of apomorphine treatment he dedicated himself fairly systematically to spreading the word about the destructive nature of that drug and the horror of chemical dependency.

Burroughs first won critical attention, mainly of the sociological type, with his novel *Junkie: Confessions of an Unredeemed Drug Addict,* published in 1953 under the pseudonym William Lee. It deals, in extraordinary clinical detail, with the harrowing experiences of a man addicted to heroin and his attempts to break the habit. What raises the novel above a mere autobiographical case study is its portrayal of shady characters from the drug underworld and the equally sinister narcotics agents.

With *The Naked Lunch* (1959), Burroughs entered the literary limelight at the national level. Celebrated by people like Mary McCarthy and John Ciardi as a masterful depiction of consciousness at the limits of rationality and panned by other critics as cheaply sensational, the novel takes us into the same world of hard drugs and down-and-out users as *Junkie,* but the literary style of *The Naked Lunch* is markedly original. Burroughs was evidently influenced a great deal by the film medium. (His essay is remarkable in this connection; it insists that human experience is composed of mental processes that can be best revealed in cinema.) Not since Joyce and Dos Passos has the montage technique been put to such extensive literary use. Yet unlike Joyce and Dos Passos, Burroughs uses the technique not simply to illuminate characters' consciousness or to show ironic parallels among seemingly disparate events and situations. Rather, he employs montage to effect radical shifts at every level: in time, in space, and in subject matter.

One of the most talked about aspects of *The Naked Lunch* is its chronicling, direct and indirect, of the Beat movement, of which Burroughs had for years been a major figure. Like Kerouac and Allen Ginsberg, Burroughs is intent on reflecting in his work a certain generational attitude toward mainstream consumer society. In this context, drug addiction becomes simply one of the more obvious ways of "dropping out" of a social game plan that others questioned but were frustrated in their efforts to reform. It is these drop-outs and reformers whom Ginsberg eulogized as "the best minds of my generation" in his long poem, "Howl" (1956). As we know from chroniclers of the period, experimentation with drugs was one of the Beats' means of sustaining their infamous shiftlessness. Yet the world of *The Naked Lunch* is a far cry from the happy-go-lucky bohemianism of Kerouac's *On the Road* (1957).

The technique that Burroughs and his collaborator, Brion Gysin, developed, which most nearly approximated film montage, was the cut-up method. They took pieces of writing from a wide variety of sources and randomly cut them into strips, which they then haphazardly juxtaposed with one another. Although the resulting clashes were not always used as is, the important fact of composition was that chance was allowed to govern a great deal of the creative process. Furthermore, Burroughs had little concern about plagiarizing; the idea was that any and all preexisting texts were fair game to be put into the cut-up mill, the more diverse the better. More than anyone else's writings, Burroughs's novels demonstrate graphically the intense intertextuality of any written text — that is, its dependence on all texts that have already been written, be they literary texts or "texts of society," such as clichés, urban myths, proverbs, or the jargon of subcultures.

After *The Exterminator,* a collaborative anthology of cut-up experiments written with Gysin in 1960, Burroughs published two novels that made extensive use of the method — *The Soft Machine* (1961) and *The Ticket That Exploded* (1962). With *Nova Express* (1964), he further elaborated the method through the use of the fold-in, a means of increasing the juxtapositional possibilities in a single text by folding pages over to make them line up in new configurations. The fold-in permits Burroughs to go beyond the conventional limits of the science fiction genre, for example, and was the method he used when describing the surreal landscapes of Minraud in *Nova Express.*

> The grey smoke drifted   the grey that stops
> shift   cut   tangle   they   breathe   medium
> the   word   cut   shift   patterns   words
> cut   the   insect   tangle   cut   shift
> that   coats   word   cut   breath   silence
> shift   abdominal   cut   tangle   stop   word
> holes.[1]

He also used this type of cross-cutting to add dimension to the consciously farfetched plot of interplanetary gang warfare: "Electric storms of violence sweep the planet — Desperate position and advantage precariously held — Governments fall with a whole civilization and ruling class into streets of total fear — Leaders turn on image rays to flood the world with replicas — Swept out by counter image —."[2] Here, the cinematic effect is quite clear. As he says in his essay, what he sees in his mind before beginning to write is like a film, so it is not surprising that the various cutting and pasting methods, which at first may strike us as totally arbitrary, yield results that Burroughs can relate to the film process. He insists that such experiments "put you in touch with what you know and what you don't know you know."

One of the upshots of the cut-up method is the virtual banishment of story as we ordinarily think of it. Whereas *Nova Express* and *The Ticket That Exploded* maintain a rough plot within the conventions of science fiction, *The Wild Boys* (1969) and *Cities of the Red Night* (1981) do not. Their action is episodic, the focus switching from one group of characters to another and the narrative stance shifting from first person to third person without apparent logic. Although the use of cut-ups in these novels does not produce the surrealistic effects seen in *Nova Express,* it does lead to a notably rough texture and to extraordinary leaps in space and time. *Cities of the Red Night* includes what might otherwise pass as a conventional plot about the disappearance of a certain Jerry Green. His parents engage the narrator and several others to try to find Jerry. However, the adventures recounted in the novel take us from a British colony of the 1920s located somewhere in the East to an expedition to the New World in the early eighteenth century. Except for the repeated references to the quest for the lost Jerry — a conventional narrative pattern — nothing connects one chapter to the next. A Spanish section is about Kiki, one of Burroughs's omnipresent characters (based on a real-life friend), and his job as a waiter. Another section details the ancient rites of transmigration of souls practiced by the people of Tamaghis, one of the cities of the red night. In the end, the novel resembles more a log of a series of unholy archeological digs than a quest narrative.

The plot of *The Wild Boys* is even more vague. Purportedly about the takeover of the world by packs of wild boys who know no law and who are bent on killing everyone in sight, the novel consists of descriptions of strange encounters between various characters: Mark's treatment of Johnny's "crabs"; an anonymous wayfarer's meeting with the "Frisco Kid" in Nome, Alaska; Farja's ritual coupling with Ali; and so on. These encounters are at certain points linked together by scenes of a penny arcade, and the events narrated often blur into the images shown on the various peep show machines in the arcade. *The Wild Boys* presents a picture not so much of a takeover as of a timeless world in which human interaction has been reduced to lust and ethical values have disappeared entirely.

As Burroughs details in his essay, he has worked a good deal on commercial filmscripts and experimental films. It is on the basis of his film work that he delivered a series of lectures at the Naropa Institute in Boulder, Colorado, which forms the basis for his essay. Although he never fully engaged in a Hollywood production, his film experiences enabled him to gain critical insight into the aesthetic stakes of scriptwriting and, in particular, to understand how radically different this kind of writing is from that of the novel.

Burroughs emphasizes in his essay the dual imperative for the scriptwriter to be both cognizant of the "rules" established by Hollywood and able nevertheless to ignore the rules in order for the resulting film to be moving. ("A moving film must move," he says.) His most extensive remarks relate to the construction of the plot: the use of flashback, the hook, the one-sentence summary, the telling detail, the plant, the payoff, and so on. He also gives useful advice on musical accompaniment and dialogue. Perhaps his most original and suggestive remarks have to do with future experimentation in cinema and its effects on the human brain. In the last pages of his essay, Burroughs proposes a national institute that would perform experiments on the relation between REM sleep and moving pictures, the relation of dreams to the movies, the cinematic reproduction of brain images, and other processes, the results of which would yield "more knowledge about the process of life."

Burroughs has no illusion, however, about the likelihood that such an institute would be created. More than most contemporary writers, his attitude toward the establishment is clearly hostile and cynical. He is convinced that the only research on cinema and the brain likely to be funded would be the kind of mind-control experiments conducted by the Central Intelligence Agency. In all of his writings, literary and cinematic, Burroughs launches a clear-sighted attack against every type of authoritarian control, every structure of mental straitjacketing. In his mythology, "Hell consists of falling into enemy hands, into the hands of the virus power, and heaven consists of freeing oneself from this power, of achieving inner freedom, freedom from conditioning."[3] Destruction of the whole apparatus of control and degeneration begins for Burroughs with the attack on the words upon which seemingly rational institutions are based. Institutionalized language — including all of its professional jargons — must be parodied, circumvented, short-circuited, and reshuffled. The vocabulary of cinema, along with the cut-up and fold-in techniques, provides a key means of liberation from the rigidly canonized models of logical and linguistic coherence.

Notes

1. William Burroughs, *Nova Express* (New York: Grove, 1964), p. 58.
2. Ibid., p. 59.
3. Burroughs, quoted in Eric Mottram, *William Burroughs: The Algebra of Need* (Buffalo, N.Y.: Intrepid Press, 1971), pp. 25–26.

William S. Burroughs

Screenwriting
and the Potentials of Cinema

On Techniques of Temporal and Spatial Distortion

Consider a film as a slice of time with which you can do anything you want. You can speed it up, slow it down, run it backwards, flash back, flash forward, scramble, overlay, underexpose, overexpose, and you can also feed in audience reaction. The standard product simply presents a sequential narrative, which is actually an arbitrary form with a beginning, a middle, and an end. It's really as arbitrary a form as the sonnet. But it is what the audience is accustomed to seeing.

Here we have a time segment; say it's five minutes. And I can move around in it. I can smell the flowers, touch the bridge, hear the stream. And I can also randomize it. Now, instead of consciously moving in the time segment, you can simply hold it in your attention. What you have here is a section of film, a piece of time, a five-minute walk. And you can speed it up — you can do five minutes in five seconds, zip around the block; you can slow it down to five hours. So, you can flash back, flash forward, overlay, and superimpose — all by the process of memory. And you can randomize the time segment or split it into fragments.

Now, you can apply contemplation and concentration techniques to this time segment. Let your mind rest on it without effort or direction and see what you actually see, feel, taste, touch; think about your time segment. Don't push at all; just leave your mind on that whole time

This essay is an edited version of five lectures Burroughs delivered June 10 and 12, 1975, and July 20, 22, and 25, 1977, at the Jack Kerouac School of Disembodied Poetics at the Naropa Institute in Boulder, Colorado. The Naropa Lecture Series constitutes a significant exploration into contemporary poetic theories and practices and a continuous investigation of the relation between literature and other arts.

segment like you were concentrating on a flower or any object. Just let your mind look at it. Now, hold your mind on this time segment, allowing your attention to move away on lines of association but always bringing it back to the time segment. This is more or less the exercise of concentration or one-pointedness: keeping your mind on one point. . . .

Now you can try some more advanced time travel. Go back in your mind seventy-five years ago to June 10, 1900. Now, don't try to decide or improvise what you will see; just go back and look around and see what you actually do see. Put your mind back there and look around. A lifetime reporter gave me a hint about time travel: He said you need a peg to hang it on; that is, a coordinate point to line up on, like the sightings you use in flying a light plane. Line up on cobwebs and see the morning dew seventy-five years ago.

You can apply this exercise to writing. Look at your movie sets. You can move your sets and characters around in time, speed up, slow down, etcetera. Try the contemplation exercise on your characters and sets. Let your mind rest there. Don't push; don't improvise; don't put words in your characters' mouths. Let them talk — and act. Just observe and contemplate. The less consciously contrived your characters are, the more real they will be. Now, of course, it is ultimately *you* who are talking; but if you just leave your characters alone and let them talk, you're putting yourself in touch with your own subconscious perception of these characters, and they'll come through a lot clearer.

If you do that — for maybe ten or fifteen minutes — suddenly a character will start talking on its own. You'll find this exercise puts more reality into your characters than if you were to try, consciously, to decide what they were going to say and do, using the very small part of the mind that is the conscious, logical, sequential part.

In 1959 Brion Gysin said that writing was fifty years behind painting. He applied the montage technique to writing, which had already been used for fifty years in painting. As you know, painters had the whole representational position knocked out from under them by photography. There was, in fact, a photography exhibition around the turn of the century entitled "Photography: The Death of Painting." Well, painting didn't die, but it did have to get a new look. I mean, painters couldn't go on painting cows in the grass. So painters turned first to montage. Now, montage is actually much closer to the act of perception — certainly urban perception — than representational painting is. You take a walk down a city street and put what you have just seen down on canvas, whether you've seen a person's form cut in half by a car, bits and pieces of street signs and advertisements, reflections from shop windows. In short, you've seen a montage of fragments. And the same happens, of course, with words. Remember that the written word is an image.

Brion Gysin's cut-up method consists of cutting up pages of text and rearranging them in montage combinations. But if you apply the montage method to writing, you're accused by the critics of promulgating a cult of unintelligibility. Writing is still confined by the sequential, representational straitjacket of the novel, an arbitrary form that's far from the actual facts of human perception and consciousness. Consciousness is a cut-up, and life is a cut-up. Every time you walk down the street or look out the window your stream of consciousness is cut by random factors. Brion Gysin applied this process to text, using a pair of scissors, and provided writers with a new way to touch and handle their medium. These first cut-ups were published in *Minutes to Go* in 1960.

The method had not been used before in writing, but, as I mentioned, montage had been used in painting for about fifty years. It has been used even more extensively in music — John Cage and Earl Brown, for example, applied randomness to their music. Earl Brown would give one of the musicians in his orchestra a choice of three scores, so that every performance was different.

Randomness has also been used quite extensively in military strategy. In fact, what I would call the cut-up method was a basic factor in the strategy of the Air Force during World War II, as explained by John von Neumann in *The Theory of Games and Economic Behavior.*[1] He enunciated the principle of Minimax. That is, you assume that the worst has happened and then act in such a way that it is of minimal assistance to the enemy. Suppose you've got three flight plans. Now, suppose the enemy knows your three flight plans; the worst has happened. But, just before flight you flip a coin or use any random method to decide which flight plan you're going to use. Even if the enemy knows you're going to do this, that knowledge doesn't do them any good because even you don't know beforehand which flight plan you are going to use. Something new is usually the application of something that has already been used, perhaps for some time, in another area.

I've done quite a few experiments in cutting up film with my friend Anthony Balch. In fact, we released a film called *The Cut-Ups* in 1968. It was shown to Nicholas Roeg, who adopted quite a few of the ideas for his film, *Performance* (1970).

Of course, cut-ups have also been used in films. The line between film editing — what goes on in the cutting room — and any random process is a very thin one. So if you consider all film editing to be film cut-up, the method is rather standard in films. However, I consider the two processes to be different.

Any product or invention is standardized by mass production, and this standardization of the product discourages further experimentation. Take, for example, the motor industry. Because it can sell — or rather it could up until a few months ago — as many cars with internal combustion engines as it could produce, it didn't want to know about jet-turbine engines. Of course, the turbine engine is better, more efficient. But why bother with a better product if you can sell what is already in production? This consideration also applies to the film industry: So long as it can sell westerns, gangster movies, spectaculars, musicals, all the standard Hollywood products, why experiment? "What has made money will make money" is a Hollywood axiom. Anything new is a gamble that the big studios don't want to take. In consequence, the surface has barely been scratched with regard to experimentation with the film medium. Now, the flashback, of course, is an old device, but the flashforward is a quite recent device and is still rarely used. Inventiveness, to use B. F. Skinner's phrase, has not been reinforced by the studios.

I've made a number of cut-ups on tape recorders by actually cutting and resplicing tape. This process is laborious and time-consuming if you're working with standard tape; but movie tape, which is much larger, is easier to use. A simpler method than cutting and resplicing is to record for any length of time and then spin the tape backwards and forwards on the recorder, cutting in new phrases at random. Where you cut in, of course, the old words are wiped out and the new words are cut in, seemingly at random. I have experimented with tape recorder cut-ups over a period of years, and I've frequently been surprised at how often the cut-ins fall in appropriate places and how much of the new recording makes perfect sequential sense. So just how random are these cut-ins? Well, consciously, of course, I don't know where in the message already recorded I am stopping the tape to make a cut-in. But because we know so much more than we are aware that we know, on some level I probably do know exactly where in the original recording I am cutting in. The cut-ups put you in touch with what you know and what you don't know you know.

Anthony Balch and I applied the cut-up technique to films by taking a section of film, cutting it into segments, and then rearranging the segments. Now, this process differs from film editing, since you cannot foresee the result, and you will get new images and words and meanings just as you do in cutting up words. This method is simply an extension of the text cut-up. You can cut the film into sections of a minute or you can cut it into one-frame sections. Working with single frames means quite a splicing job, but the results are interesting. We did this once, and the film disintegrated after being run through the projector several times. But I would like to see further experiments in scrambling film in this way.

When working with film cut-ups, you can edit the film and choose the most effective sequences, just as you can with tape and text cut-ups. However, in our film cut-ups, we did not edit the material. We just cut up film sections and rearranged them. When our film cut-ups were shown in London, the manager of the theater said that in all his forty years' experience he had never seen so many people come to the box office furious, demanding a refund of their money, nor so many people express congratulations and approval. After one week, he asked Anthony to withdraw the film, and it hasn't been shown publicly since.

That is one experimental device — cutting and scrambling film segments — but there are many others that you can use in films. And a surprising number of them have not been used. Of course, there are time experiments. You have all seen films sped up, slowed down, and run backwards. But now consider applying these techniques to comparatively immobile subjects. Slowing down the frames of a face that is not moving gives a curious expression of statuesque immobility. This technique could be used to advantage, I think, in science fiction films. Speeding up the frames of a face produces strange seismic twitches, and running the film of an immobile face backwards is quite disorienting. You know that something strange is happening, but you don't know what it is.

Speed-ups, slow motion, and running film backwards have been technically possible since the beginning of motion pictures, and one cannot but marvel at the lack of imagination exhibited by conventional filmmakers. They have had the ability to control time, yet in their films, for the most part, they have turned their backs on slow motion and pratfalls for eighty years.[2]

Methods of Engaging the Audience

There are many simple experiments aimed at capturing the viewer's attention and many variations and extensions that can be derived from each. I suppose some of you must have tried the following experiment; if you haven't, it's quite a lot of fun. You select a film to be shown on a television set, cut the sound track, and substitute a recorded sound track from a similar film if you want. For example, you take one western, cut the sound track, and substitute the recorded sound track from another western. I've seen people watch such an experimental film for five or ten minutes before they realize there's anything amiss with the sound track. The sound track determines for viewers what they're seeing; that is, they mentally alter the image track to fit the sound track. Now, you can do the same thing with your own film images and sound tracks. If you add machine-gun sound effects to a picture of people running to catch a bus, the audience will assume that the people are running from the machine guns. And if one person stumbles and falls in the film, the audience will assume that he has been shot.

Here is another simple experiment that has been performed. I don't recall the director's name.[3] At any rate, he filmed a well-known actor between acts, when his face bore an expression that was quite neutral. The actor wasn't acting; he wasn't doing anything. Then he inserted several scenes in front of the frames showing the empty expression on the actor's face. The first was of a baby in a cradle; then somebody in a coffin; and then an accident victim lying on a street. He showed this sequence to an audience and asked them what the actor's expression meant. Well, they said he was expressing love for the baby, he was feeling sorry for the person in the coffin, and he was horrified at the sight of the accident victim. You see, the viewers supplied the expression. The actor, of course, was not reacting to the scenes in front of him. All of the scenes had been artificially inserted.

This very simple experiment in audience reaction is susceptible to many variations, since you can arrange any context. Precise experiments can easily be carried out with an 8-millimeter camera, a few subjects, some test pictures, and selected audiences. You can show your audience pictures, preferably pictures to which they will have strong and varied reactions. They can be still or moving pictures. For instance, you can photograph an audience and then show the pictures to another audience and ask them to guess what the first group of people were watching. Or you can film an audience's reaction to a disorienting variation of a sound track. For example, the audience may be watching what they think at first is a normal television program, but you've inserted your own prerecorded sound track that you've arranged so that it is progressively more inappropriate and outrageous. In other experiments, you can insert overt sex scenes in a totally different type of film or you can have the schoolteacher in a western lapse into four-letter words. Then, with a video camera, you can capture the moment when your audience finally realizes there's something a bit strange about the film.

Audience reaction to films involves the whole complex mechanism of perception, and, as I pointed out, what viewers see is conditioned by what they expect to see, which in turn is determined by the sound track and by context. Let's go back to the experiment of splicing scenes in front of shots of an actor's face, where the audience supplies the appropriate expression — love, grief, horror — an expression that is not there. You can carry this experiment further. Put your actors in situations in which their faces show very definite expressions. Photograph expressions of people making love. Photograph expressions of people playing poker, committing a murder, or simply relaxing in a friendly context. Now, shift the scenes around so that the orgasm faces appear at the poker table; the friendly, relaxed faces are murdering someone; and the poker faces are situated in what would normally be a friendly, relaxed context. How far will the audience go in altering the expressions to suit the context? At first, I thought that orgasm faces at the poker table might be carrying the experiment too far; but after looking at the expressions in some photos in sex magazines, I decided that the new context wouldn't be so outrageous after all. Murderous and sexual expressions, of course, are quite interchangeable.

Well, those are some simple experiments in audience interpretation, reaction, and perception. Of course, they could be carried much further with psychogalvanometers or with any reaction detectors. With encephalographic equipment, you could establish an exact correlation between sound and image and the physiological and psychological reactions of the audience.

You can also observe the reactions of subjects who do not know that they are being observed and do not know that they are reacting to an environment you have created. The simplest form of this experiment can be carried out with a tape recorder. You walk down a street and record the street sounds and conversations. Now make the same walk playing back the tape that you have just recorded in the street. What is happening? As long as you adjust the sound level to that of the new street sounds and you move quickly and unobtrusively, adjusting the volume as you go, people hearing the tape will not detect that they are listening to prerecorded sounds. They will think they are hearing actual street sounds and scraps of conversation.

You are throwing a whole, unreal environment around the people you pass, and consciously or unconsciously, they are reacting to this environment. You are tampering with the so-called reality of the people you pass. You are affecting them without their knowledge.

Now, you can also photograph their reactions if you hide the camera and tape recorder. Or you can do a spectacular, using whole truckloads of hidden equipment and covering one street for hours, days, or even months. Then you select the most interesting material from the footage you have taken.

Let's also consider some experiments in deliberately upsetting and deranging the audience. The results could ultimately break down preconceived notions and make way for new film forms. These experiments could take the form of the double bind, as set forth by Gregory Bateson and R. D. Laing. With the double bind, people are subjected to a set of contradictory statements or attitudes expressed by authority figures: "Pay close attention; this is not important." "This is serious; I am joking." And so forth. A simple form of the double bind in film would be friendly and unfriendly words and faces alternating at rapid intervals. If you wanted to make those at one-frame intervals, it would be quite upsetting to watch, I think. "Yes. No. I love you. I hate you." This is basically alternating current. You can carry the experiment much further with friendly faces and unfriendly words; unfriendly faces and friendly words; lynch mobs uttering benedictions and singing lullabies and angelic, kind faces screaming threats and insults. An extreme form of the double bind is the alternation of sex and violence; you soften the audience with pornography and then hit them with a nightstick until they realize there is no sex theme and no theme of violence at all, just images.

Anyone with a movie camera can play God; he can slow time down, speed it up, run it backwards, and he can literally stop the sun in the sky. So he might as well use his prerogative as God to invent, create, and experiment with the film medium.

Devices for Successful Screenwriting

For centuries artists have been asking themselves and have been asked by those who, as they put it, work for a living, "Exactly what are you doing and why?" What socially useful function does art serve? We are not in a position to answer that question and to stop apologizing for our existence or to take refuge in the untenable vacuum of art for art's sake. Recent research into dreams and sleep has demonstrated that dreams are a biological necessity for all warm-blooded animals. Deprived of REM sleep, that is, dream sleep, animals and humans show all the symptoms of sleeplessness, no matter how much dreamless sleep they are allowed. And the relation between dreams and art is very close. In fact, you could say that a dream serves as a model for creativity. So, if art serves somewhat the same biological function as a dream and is equally necessary (and, in fact, no culture has been found, no matter how primitive, that does not have some form of artistic expression) — if it serves a definite purpose — then it can be judged on how well it serves that purpose.

Now, it would seem that the sound film is a relative newcomer to the artistic scene. But this is not so, since the whole concept of the sound film is implicit in painting and picture writing, and before that, way back in the first warm-blooded animals, in the form of dreams, for dreams are in fact, talking films. Now, all warm-blooded animals dream; cold-blooded animals don't dream — at least those that have been tested so far don't dream. Certainly one of the functions of art — and I see this as sort of an evolutionary function — is to objectify some implicit process of perception (in the form of a book, painting, or film) so that we see something that we have been seeing without knowing it; that is, when it's put in front of us, we realize, "Well, I have been seeing this without knowing it."

Yet to call the attention of the public to what they themselves see every day is in some cases to invite the most vindictive and scurrilous hatred. At early exhibitions of abstract art, the viewers would sometimes attack the canvases with their umbrellas. They were so annoyed at having abstract paintings presented as art when they were used to paintings of cows in the grass. In the Middle Ages, people living on the seacoast probably knew that the world was round, but they said they believed the earth was flat. To say or demonstrate, at that time, that the world was round could have resulted in the most drastic penalties, due to the teachings of the Church. That's precisely the function of art, to jar the viewer or reader into awareness of what he is actually aware of already on some level, no matter how uncomfortable the revelation may be. So, science has been acting in concert with art, since the function of both is to make the viewer or the reader more aware of his own perceptions.

At first, motion pictures were simply something that could be done, a trick; and that was enough in the beginning, since people were impressed just to see this done. The locomotive coming right for the audience made people shriek and shrink away — but not for long. Soon the public became tired of movies being simply demonstrations that people and objects could be made to move on screen, and later actors talked. And they talked too much at first. But long before the advent of the sound film, the public demanded a story in the movies they watched, and the screenwriter came into being — a writer, as we will see, quite different from the novelist. At first, the screenwriter was often the director as well. Some directors required only a few notes on the back of an envelope to shoot a scene. But as time went on, the license of film to present anything on screen, no matter how poor the quality, began to wear out. Take a look at some productions from the 1930s and see what writers and directors could get away with in those days in the way of creaky plots and banal dialogue. The screenwriter has become more and more important; the screenplay is now the first step in making any film. Until the producer has a screenplay — whether it's done by a screenwriter or by the director — the picture cannot be budgeted and cast.

Writing for film is quite different from any other form of writing. It is unlike writing a novel, although at first glance it may seem the same. George Bluestone quoted D. W. Griffith as having said, "The task I'm trying to achieve is above all to make you see."[4] And Joseph Conrad, in the preface to *The Nigger of the Narcissus* (1897), stated, "My task which I am trying to achieve is, by the power of the written word, to make you hear, to make you feel — it is before all to make you *see*."[5] However, it is quite a different kind of seeing. When you read a novel — that is, if the writer is good — you *are* seeing a "film," but you are seeing it in your own mind. There's quite a difference between seeing it on the screen and seeing it in your mind.

When I was teaching creative writing I came to doubt whether any technology of writing could be taught. Perhaps "creative writing" is too vague and too general. But there is a very definite technology for writing filmscripts, and it can be taught. Perhaps attempting to write a filmscript is one of the quickest ways to find out if you are cut out to be a writer, if writing could be your profession, because there are standards by which you can judge your success. The tests of successful novel or poetry writing are not nearly as clear. If a man is called upon to build a bridge and the bridge falls down, there's something wrong with his viewpoint and his blueprint. But if his blueprints are never put to the test of actual construction, he might spend a lifetime doing something that he is not cut out to do.

The test of a successful screenplay is what the film looks like on screen, not what the screenplay looks like on paper. That is, beautifully written sentences don't mean anything so far as a filmscript goes, because the script isn't to be read, it's to be put on the screen. Is it a good film according to the rules of film structure? And if it violates those rules, are the violations justified and valid? Novel and short-story writers may assume that they know how to write filmscripts. But they may find, as I did, that they have to learn how to write filmscripts just as an airplane pilot would have to learn how to fly a helicopter. I found that some of the filmscript ideas I had that I thought were new were not at all new and also were not good. When I wrote *The Last Words of Dutch Schultz* (1970), I knew nothing about writing filmscripts. There are a lot of ideas in that book that are not viable for a film; whatever it may be, it is not a viable filmscript. For example, I thought that mixing black and white and color was a good idea. Well, it's not; it's been tried — in *If*. . . (Lindsay Anderson, 1969), for example — and it doesn't work very well. Now, just because something's been tried and doesn't work doesn't mean that it couldn't work — just that it hasn't worked to date.

Another technique in *The Last Words of Dutch Schultz* (one that I suggested for *Junkie* when I was working with Terry Southern, who's an old hand at writing scripts) was to use the same character playing several different roles. Now, of course, Southern did that himself in *Dr. Strangelove* (Kubrick, 1963), where Peter Sellers played three parts; but I meant the same person who is recognizable as the same person. For example, a snotty doctor who refuses to write a narcotics scrip and calls the police would be played by and recognized as the same actor who plays a narcotics agent. Terry said, "No, no, no; it's just going to confuse the audience." And you don't want to confuse the audience, not if you're writing a commercial filmscript.

But didn't I just say that the function of art is to increase awareness even if the audience is made to feel uncomfortable? Well, I'm talking now about a commercial script, and before you're really able to jolt the people in an audience you need to know how to please them. Rules are made to be broken, but not to be disregarded.

Now to consider characters further. In a film, you can't describe your characters as you can in a novel. A film doesn't describe; it *is*. You can't say, "George is an old man." You have to show him as an old man. It's a good idea to have a dossier on each of your characters including all of the traits you can think of, even if you don't intend to show all these in the film. That is, you should make a sort of composite picture of each character, his habits, etcetera. It will give you a much clearer idea of your characters and how to handle them.

Here is a scene from *Junkie* that shows the lack of fear in one of the characters. The scene takes place in the Angle Bar, and Whitey, who is six feet, three inches tall and weighs two hundred pounds, all bone and muscle, with nasty, white pig eyes and no more control over his aggression than a baboon, is stomping up and down the bar, sweeping people's change into his big, dirty hand. So all up and down the bar the customers sit hunched over, trying to disappear into their bar seats, as they surreptitiously pocket their change. Only Roy, at the end of the bar, leaves his change on the bar. He's characterized, then, by something he doesn't do — by the fact that he doesn't remove his change. And that establishes Roy's character, that he is the one person in the bar not afraid of Whitey. In other words, you want to establish a character as quickly as possible in terms of something he does or says.

Another example: Here's a fluffy blonde ruffling a boy's hair as she intones, "I love you, anyhoo, but where have you been and stuff?" Well, she's the kind of girl who says "anyhoo" and "and stuff." She's characterized by what she says. Beware, young man, there she is ten years from now fat as a pig, sitting on her chintzy pillows with an asthmatic Pekinese dog, gin bottles hidden all over the house. Supper is canned tuna soufflé; she got the recipe from the evening news. Now, she has served the tuna soufflé one time too many, and he says, "I'm gonna kill you and stuff." And he starts chasing her around the house with a boning knife.

Now here's another man succinctly defined by one action. He's the real-life proprietor of a bar in Paris, one of the nastiest people in the city. His bar is called Lips, and only certain people can get in. You know the type. The lucky ones are in the front room, and the Americans and the tourists, "the scum of the earth," as he puts it, are upstairs. So here's a young American coming down from the second floor, and the proprietor bars his way to the sanctum of the front room, which is reserved for politicians, journalists, and French writers. So he stands there in front of the guy and just raises an eyebrow — doesn't say a word — and the young American stammers something about going to the toilet. Slowly, like an old dog roused from sleep, the proprietor moves out of the way. You see, it's all in that arched eyebrow. You need his permission to go to the john in his trap. Just that one silent shot shows the whole character of the man. He could be a secret agent in this film, and the gauche young man, who is with the Central Intelligence Agency, will get him back later.

Filmscript writers, with their emphasis on movement, tend to set up some sort of separation between words and action, forgetting that words *are* action, that there's no distinction whatever between action and words. Whether your character is delineated by a raised eyebrow, by leaving his change on the bar, or by saying "anyhoo," the point is that you define the character by something he does or says, something only that character would do or say.

Dialogue is supposed to move, and these days the rules say it's supposed to be short. But these rules are not always valid. When the talkies first came in, characters in them made long speeches. Then the line between plays and films began breaking down. Now the trend is for very short dialogue — the shorter the better.

But whether they give their characters long speeches or short, writers need something called "an ear for dialogue." John O'Hara had it; F. Scott Fitzgerald didn't and neither did Ernest Hemingway. Having an ear for dialogue simply means that the writer keeps his ears open and derives much of his dialogue from what people actually said at some time in his hearing, maybe years ago. Once you've got a character saying something in his very own words, you can elaborate. As you write dialogue and read it aloud, your ear will tell you whether or not it is right. When I started doing readings and was using mostly dialogue material, I learned that if dialogue doesn't sound right read aloud, it isn't written right. Similarly, if it sounds wrong, then it isn't exactly what your character would say.

List your characters and ask yourself, "What is each character doing at this moment of the picture or what might the characters be doing?" If you're concentrating on the main characters in the scene, you'll tend to forget that other characters could be brought in. What are they doing? Are they just sitting around? You need to think about what will be seen on the screen at all times.

Screenwriters are preoccupied with action — what is being done and said — and I think they fail to realize that what someone does not say or does not do may tell more about his character and advance the action further than what he actually says or does. I gave the example of Roy leaving his change on the bar. Here's another example: The camera picks out a corpse, the face eaten by rats. A man passes with a briefcase. He glances casually at the corpse with a slight purse of his lips, indicating distaste. These shots tell you something about both the character and the setting: that the man has no compassion and that corpses are commonplace at the time the scene unfolds. Then we see an armored band roaming city streets, twenty-dollar bills lying in the gutter, and the people glancing down at the money but walking by.

Now, this tells you something more about the setting: that it's some future time when money is worthless.

Look at some of the differences between a novel and a screenplay. There is a different way of seeing and also a different appeal. That is, the filmscript must appeal to a much wider audience than the novel. Also, those people who have bought a novel are already predisposed to be interested. A box-office failure reaches many more people than even a best-selling novel.

Still more important is the gap between the screenplay and what appears on the screen as a finished film. Now, a writer writes a novel the way he wants it, and there it is; the publisher, in some cases, may want some rewriting, but generally the writer does not have his work heavily edited. But rewriting is almost always required in a filmscript, which brings us to the most important difference between a novel and a screenplay: A screenplay is not a finished product. It is a stage in a process involving many artisans other than the writer. There are as many as thirty stages. When you're writing a filmscript, you have someone looking over your shoulder and saying, "Well, the studio doesn't like that; we don't want it." And you may come back from lunch to find someone else's idea right in the middle of your filmscript. As they say in Hollywood, good filmscripts are not written, they are rewritten, sometimes as often as five or six times.

Kerouac always said that the first version is always the best. I don't find this true in novels, but he did, and that's a perfectly valid way to write a novel. But no one can write a filmscript that way. The first version is usually only to get your ideas out there where you can see them. Then you can stand back and look, and you can see that one of the scenes you liked so much just does not belong in the film, and that certain characters have to be changed or combined with other characters. (This sort of hybrid character, made of two or three characters squashed together, occurs all the time in filmscripts.)

The director may request one kind of a rewrite: "This is a good script, but it simply isn't the type of film I can make." A change of actors may necessitate another kind of rewriting. For example, you may have good dialogue, but if your actor can't say it, what good is it? Or, you may have written a part for a specific actor, and in the middle of the film, or long before your script is finished, a different actor replaces the one you had in mind.

Now let's consider some of the rules for writing screenplays. How do you begin? The first step is to write your film idea in one sentence. It's very important to be able to say in one sentence what the film is about, both when you are writing a so-called original screenplay and when you are doing an adaptation from a novel or a play. What is *The Great Gatsby* (Brenon, 1926, Nugent, 1949, and Clayton, 1974) about? Poor boy, rich girl. *Panic in Needle Park* (Schatzberg, 1971) was described as Romeo and Juliet on junk. Now, this one-sentence run-down can be put in other ways, such as, "What if . . . ?" "What if a Jewish boy married an Irish girl?" That was *Abie's Irish Rose* (Sutherland, 1946). The "what if" always contains the seeds of the difficulties that will animate the film. Remember, when there is no trouble, there's no action; and when there's no action, there's no film. Or you can put it this way: "What is the hero or heroine trying to do, and who or what is keeping him or her from doing it?"

After you have your film idea down to one sentence, you can expand it to three or four pages, giving the barest outline of the film. This is the film idea. The next step is to write a film treatment of thirty pages or so; then a film synopsis; and finally a screenplay. Shooting the script is generally left to the director now, and the director generally doesn't want the writer telling him what camera angles he should use. In fact, after they have the screenplay, most directors prefer not have the writer on the set at all.

How do you generate a screen story? You use the old Hollywood springboard — the one-sentence summary — and pray there's water in the pool. I learned about Hollywood in just three days. Terry Southern and I had gone there trying to sell the script for *The Naked Lunch* to someone named Chuck Barris, and we were met at the airport by a Daimler and a saluting chauffeur. Two days later the studio's decision about our script was spelled out for us in Hollywood language. When our Daimler shrank down to a two-seater, we knew the studio didn't like this script and it was time to move fast. They'd already frozen our bar bill.

So you run the film backwards to the springboard. Now you pick a topic that interests you. Then you try to view the topic from unique angles.

This one-sentence procedure is even more useful if you're adapting a novel into a film. With an original screenplay, you're already thinking in screen terms, and you will probably have started with a topic and a question. But when you consider a complex novel with a lot of subplots and mysterious, unexplained incidents, it may not be so easy to cook it down to the springboard question. Many novels are about a number of different things, so you really have to simplify the novel to one sentence or your screenplay will flounder.

The summary is also what sells a film to the viewer, whether on the billboard or by word of mouth. What is this film about? It's about a shark that bites people in two. The movie is all very realistic — and it's enough to scare people out of the water.

A related film device is the running gag. This is a motif that goes through the film to a final payoff. All running gags must pay off. Do you remember the man in *Hellzapoppin* (H. C. Potter, 1941) who kept carrying a plant around, trying to give it to one of the actors? The plant keeps growing; it grows into a tree over the course of the film. Or do you recall the girl nobody knew who kept coming in and out of the party? She's finally revealed to be the assistant producer's girlfriend. Now, running gags are not always comic; they can be simply a recurrent motif, like the tapping of the blind man's cane in *The Informer* (Ford, 1935). Very often the running gag is a mannerism of an actor, like George Raft flipping the coin.

There's an expanded version of the one-sentence summary known as the Weanie or the McGuffin or the Switcheroo. It summarizes the mainspring of the action, the secret formula that everyone is looking for, or the plans. All of Hitchcock's movies are based on Weanies. Here's an example of a Weanie. It's a film idea that I used in a column in *Crawdaddy*: "What if a sure, painless cure for drug addiction were discovered? And then, what if not only the Mafia and the pushers but also the narcotics agents and the Central Intelligence Agency tried to stop this cure?" So you have not only the pusher but the clean-cut agent as well trying to block the cure for addiction, which would put him out of business. Of course, the Weanie is not used for all types of films; it's mostly in serials, mysteries, westerns, and *all* spy pictures.

Now to consider the plant and payoff. This technique is used in all films and in all novels. Someone said that if you show a dagger on the wall in the first act it should be used for killing somebody in the last act. That's the plant and payoff. The plant is something to which your attention is called, perhaps at the beginning of a film. The payoff occurs when that thing becomes important later on. The plant should not be telegraphed. That is, when people see the plant, they should not know what is going to happen; they should not know what the payoff is. The running gag, rather similar to the plant, must also have a payoff.

In a film, the camera can zero in on the plant. You can't do that in a play. Of course, you can also zero in on a plant in a novel, but you do it with words. Fake plants are confusing to the audience and will always be resented. That is, if you focus in on something and there's no payoff, the audience is going to feel, quite rightly, that they've been cheated. Your plant cannot be too obvious, but it has to be obvious enough that the audience will remember it. There's a very fine line there. The payoff should always elicit a sense of surprise recognition: "Yes, that's just right, and I see it now at the payoff." If you see a plant before the payoff, you can, of course, avoid the payoff, as when a man remembers the sound of the ticking watch he heard that morning and then realizes there's a time bomb in the room. And, of course, the plant can be verbal. It can be a sound. It doesn't have to be purely visual.

The plant and the payoff also happen all the time in real life. Something you noticed, you don't know quite why, becomes important later. To give an example: I was living in New Orleans about twenty-five years ago. I was thinking about going into raising ramie; that's the hardest fabric known. I went looking for information about ramie, and I happened to walk into the office of a lawyer by mistake. He was the same lawyer my wife hired much later to defend me when I was in jail on narcotics charges. So he was the one I was really looking for, not this lost cause of ramie.

Another example is relayed in a book written about his illness by a man who had leprosy. Before telling you the example, let me say that leprosy is hardly contagious at all. Doctors don't know just how it is transmitted, but it's difficult to catch. Well, years before the man found out he had leprosy, he was riding his horse when it ran away with him on it. It took him to the gates of a leprosarium.

If you learn to recognize and use plants and payoffs in writing and film, you will also learn to recognize and use them in so-called real life. The screenwriter cultivates, as a matter of necessity, marginal thinking, because he's always looking for a new slant on his material. Marginal thinking helps you to solve many problems. If you're just dealing in sequential logical thought, you won't make it as a screenwriter, because you'll never come up with a new angle.

The flashback. Some people feel that the use of flashback destroys the illusion that the characters are real people in the immediate present. However, I don't think films could get along without flashbacks. A purist would say that the less you use flashbacks the better, that flashbacks do not happen in real life. Well, they do.

There are many types of problems in films that have never really properly been solved. One is how to show the passage of time. You know the old techniques of showing calendar leaves blowing off the wall and of showing the seasons changing. Both are very old and not very good, but it's hard to think of new techniques. If time is that which ends, which is my definition of time, then time is always limited. Thus, to show the passage of time, you can show anything running out — water, food, junk, oil, whatever — you need only show the process of running out. For example, say a guy cleans his apartment every two weeks; so you film the apartment dirty, then the apartment clean, and the apartment dirty again.

It is also difficult to show dreams, thoughts, and fantasies. You would think that film could show these abstractions, but they're very hard to convey. I had some experience attempting to do so in the *Junkie* script, and I found that the difficulty is that showing abstractions on film violates reality. A film *looks* real; to cut in something that isn't real is sort of disturbing, because it's artificial. That is, you're not actually screening a thought or a fantasy, you're constructing it and inserting it.

Climax and relief are very old devices. And films can't do without them. You've got to pick the audience up and let them down. If you hit them with one climax after another, the audiences get bored, and they won't sit still for it. Take the horse's head in *The Godfather* (Coppola, 1972) — you can't have a horse's head on every page in a novel, and you can't do it in every scene in a movie. You remember the scene in *Jaws* (Spielberg, 1975), in which teenagers put a fake fin in the water. Though it's meant as a joke, the people at the beach panic. Well, the teenagers' joke is actually about as funny as talking about a bomb on a plane or about malpractice in a hospital. But it's still a relief in comparison to the real thing. So the audience unwinds and relaxes as a result of that scene.

Now, relief doesn't always follow a climax. The filmmaker can simply shift to a different scene. For example, after a noisy, exciting car chase, the film may cut to birds singing as the hero and heroine wake up in the car in the early morning.

A purely episodic treatment doesn't work very well in films. You need some kind of climax. And there's such a thing as too much tension in the climax. There can also be too much relief if the climactic action goes on too long. You always have to remember that in a commercial film you're dealing with a segment of usually about ninety minutes.

The alternation of tension and release seems to happen in real life, too: A crisis in life is often followed by some sort of relief. Either you've solved the crisis or the whole situation has changed. Once you see this mechanism, it will teach you not to let the release put you too far off guard, since there's always another crisis on the way.

And this brings us to the finale of the film. The important thing about a finale is that it should wind the film up. Ask yourself what you want the audience to carry away from your film. What should the audience feel as they walk out? The finale should be impressive, and it should be positive. A very great error is made when a finale doesn't look like a finale. If the audience isn't quite sure the show is over, there have probably been too many or overemphasized climaxes prior to the finale. I remember an endless Japanese movie. I thought, "This has got to be the finale; he's committing hara-kiri." Then, "This must be it; she's on her deathbed;" and so on. But each time, the film continued. Of course, a conventional finale can be redeemed by a last-minute twist that the audience doesn't expect. Frederick Forsyth is good at that. I just read his novels *The Day of the Jackal* (1971), *Dogs of War* (1974), and *The Odessa File* (1972), and they all had little twists at the end that redeemed rather conventional windups.

Standard Rules and the Potentials of the Medium

Here are some standard rules for screenwriting. A moving film must move. Anything that slows down the action has to be cut. Every scene must either advance the action in some way or tell us something about the characters. Now, let's consider what can and cannot be done in film by differentiating between these rules, which are often put in dogmatic terms, and the devices, or tools, that allow you to use best the potentials of the medium. I'll give you examples of both rules and tools.

Dwight Swain cites a film writer who once told him, "In this business, 'Can you do it in a hurry?' counts for a lot more than 'Can you do it good?' "[6] That is, the ability to see the film potential in any situation and see it immediately is the scriptwriter's most highly valued skill. Swain also calls creativity "the major tool in [the scriptwriter's] craft-kit."[7] "The creative person," he says, is someone who is "conditioned to make multiple responses to single stimuli."[8] Show him a candlestick and he can come up with ten different ways of murdering someone with it. The creative filmscript writer is always juggling situations, moving them around. Take a newspaper story that has potential as film material: How many different slants can you think of on that particular story? There are exercises, tools, that I think are very useful. One is to leave a film two-thirds of the way through the picture and devise five alternative endings. Then go back and see if the writer has done as well as you have. Of course, you can do the same with novels. If you keep your eyes and your mind open you could can come up with two or three film plots every day, actually. Some of them will be good and some of them will be very bad indeed. The source may be newspaper stories, overheard conversations, novels, films, dreams, fantasies.

Now, here's an example of some film ideas I came up with. I was reading a book called *The Ultimate Athlete* (1975), by George Leonard, and he was talking about his experiences with the civil rights movement. He describes a revolutionary technique, which I'd never heard of before, that was devised by a mathematician named Michael Roseman. The technique is, very simply, to use all of the facilities of a university or any other institution to bring it to a grinding halt. For example, everybody takes out all the books they can from the library. Everybody crowds into the study hall; they've got to expand the study hall. Everybody goes into the gymnasium. Leonard says he "can imagine no institution . . . that could survive being used to the full."[9] Now, this could become a film idea with the old "What if?" formula: There are three thousand people in jail in New York on looting charges. What if they all demanded jury trials, a demand that is certainly within their rights? They'd have the courts of New York tied up for twenty years. The whole system finally breaks down, and you have a massive confrontation. It could be a Stanley Kubrick spectacular. It's just a question of keeping your eyes open for ideas. This frame of mind is itself a tool.

"Dreams and memories . . . cannot be adequately represented in spatial terms. . . . [A film's] spatial devices . . . cannot render the conceptual feel of dreams and memories. The realistic tug of the film is too strong. . . . Proust and Joyce would seem as absurd on film as Chaplin would in print."[10] That quote is from George Bluestone. He's got some very sensible things to say in other connections, but this is a dogmatic, purely arbitrary opinion as to what films can and cannot do.

Bluestone also talks about the problems of turning a novel into a film, beginning with the difference between the imaginative seeing that you experience in a novel and the seeing of an actual visual image in a film. As you read a novel and see the action of the novel, you are not in the purely passive position of a viewer. In performing the act of reading, you are also performing the mental act of translating what you read into pictures, words, sounds, and so on. And, of course, different readers will see different pictures and will have different concepts of the characters in the novel. But once the novel is on the screen, whoever the viewers are, they're all seeing the same movie with the same actors. Of course, there'll be some differences in what the viewers notice or what interests them, but they are seeing the same movie. And they do not need to use their imagination to perform any act at all; they need only sit there and watch the screen. So, says Bluestone, the act of reading a novel involves symbolic thinking, which is peculiar to imaginative rather than visual activity.

Now, I would say that, more accurately, reading novels and watching films involve different and incompatible types of visual activity. Some filmscript writers are reluctant to admit that any visual activity exists apart from watching the screen. They are afraid that people will eventually learn how to make their own films in their own heads, just as some doctors are afraid a great cure-all will be discovered and put them out of business.

But the imaginative activity that takes place when you read a novel is certainly visual, in part. You are seeing the scenes and characters of the novel. It would, however, be difficult to carry on such imaginative activity if you were watching a film at the same time. In other words, it's visual activity in both cases, but the two activities are quite incompatible. A film aspires to provide maximum distraction.

Citing Virginia Woolf's statement, "All this, which is accessible to words, and to words alone, the cinema must avoid," Bluestone goes on to claim that "the rendition of mental states cannot be as adequately represented by film as by language."[11] Well, you have to avoid rendering mental states or else find an adequate way of representing them; otherwise, you're going to end up with a debacle like the film version of *The Great Gatsby.*

> Gatsby believed in the green light, the orgiastic future that year by year recedes before us. It eluded us then, but that's no matter — tomorrow we will run faster, stretch out our arms farther. . . . And one fine morning —
> So we beat on, boats against the current, borne back ceaselessly into the past.[12]

The whole charm and point of this novel lies in the prose, which is not really translatable. I don't say it's impossible, but a way hasn't been found to translate passages like the end of *The Great Gatsby* into film terms.

Now, what about the problem of the voice-over? This device violates the dogma that a film has a reality or at least creates the illusion of reality, of real people in real situations in the immediate present. Where is this voice-over coming from? And what is the voice-over doing? In this case, obviously, it's reading a novel. The narrator in a novel from which a film is made is, generally speaking, an unmentionable subject for the film itself. As in *Junkie:* What is Lee doing collecting material for a novel? The novel should not be referred to in the film. So a voice-over is really no solution. And if you try to take those sentences and turn them into little pieces of film, it just doesn't look like anything.

The scriptwriter has to come up with something seemingly new. One way of accomplishing this is with the hook, the striking scene at the beginning of a film that is meant to immediately involve the audience and pull them into the screen. It shouldn't be too striking, unless you're prepared to follow up with things that are even more striking; otherwise the film will never live up to the hook.

Now, crises can be too far apart or close together. Either way is bad. If you get too many crises piling up, people soon get very tired of them. They get apathetic. And if there are not enough crises, then the action drags.

The flashback and flashforward. Consider Lewis Herman. He's pretty hard-core. His rules are hard and dogmatic and apply strictly to commercial films. "Realism is often killed," he says, "with still another popular device, the flashback. . . . The flashback impedes motion. . . . Flashbacks fritter suspense."[13] You see, the audience wants to know what happens next, not what happened before. According to Herman, "It is the motion picture's task to create . . . the illusion . . . that the shadows . . . on the screen are real people undergoing real experiences, *in the immediate present.*"[14] In other words, the audience has to believe what they know to be untrue. They must maintain this illusion to maintain their interest in the film. And the flashback, he adds, does not occur in real life. Well, as I've said, it certainly does occur in real life. Herman doesn't even consider the flashforward, which, I suppose, he would think further violates this illusion of immediacy.

But both flashbacks and flashforwards occur all the time in real life, and it's pretty difficult to write a film without the flashback. I would say that flashbacks actually happen every second. Every time you perform a simple action, say, like drinking water, you're activating a whole network of associations of the millions of times in your life you have performed this action and the contexts in which it was performed. Now, can these associations be represented on screen? Anthony Balch and I did some experiments in which we tried to do exactly that, and I'll discuss them later.

Of all these rules, then, some of them, under the heading of tools (or devices), are valid, and some of them are arbitrary. But you do need to know the rules and the reasons behind them.

Adaptation

No doubt several alternative and successful filmscripts could be based on the same novel. If you took the actual filmscript of *Jaws* and tried to turn it back into a novel, with no reference to the actual novel and just the filmscript as your given material, you would most likely end up with a very dull novel and also quite a short one. In translating a filmscript into a novel, you have to take the same liberties with your material as a scriptwriter takes with a novel. Because there's less to go on, you can write more novels from filmscripts than filmscripts from novels. "Beware of too many characters" — that's one of the rules of scriptwriting. It's a pretty good one, because if you get too many characters, people can't keep track of them. A mistake scriptwriters often make when turning a novel into a filmscript is shoving several often completely incompatible characters into the same persona. Conversely, when turning a filmscript into a novel, you can take a character and split him into two or three characters. You could alter your characters and make them more complex or you could introduce unexplained incidents.

Joseph Wambaugh started out as a cop and ended up a multimillionaire writer of best-selling novels about cops. His novel *The New Centurions* (1970) is written according to the best-seller formula: Write something that people know something about and want to know more about. For some reason, people always want to know about cops. A lot of them are cop lovers, I guess. Well, in the novel the reason for Kilvinsky's suicide is never apparent. He is described as a mysterious and secretive man. But in the film (*The New Centurions,* Richard Fleischer, 1972) he is turned into a very simple character played by George C. Scott, and the reasons for his suicide are as obvious as Hollywood can make them. It's a drastic, surgical simplification of a character. You have only an hour and a half in a film, so every word must count.

There are all sorts of transitions between novels and filmscripts. I wrote a script from a science fiction novel called *Blade Runner* (1982).[15] This novel is set in a future time when medicine has gone underground because some professor or theoretician has demonstrated that medical advances, in the long run, lead to more illness; by saturating the population with antibiotics, their natural resistance is lowered, so that epidemics can break out at any time. So the premise of the book is that no medical service will be extended to anyone who does not first agree to be sterilized. Those who refuse are serviced by underground doctors who are supplied with medicine and instruments by blade runners. Well, I turned this into a filmscript, and Kubrick made it into a spectacular that would be filmed in the ruins of Manhattan devastated by health act riots. (Filming those riots alone would cost five million dollars.) On Rudy Wurlitzer's advice, I dropped the idea of producing this lavish and impractical film. He said, "You've got twenty million dollars to spend already — and you'll have to tear down New York for this film." So I'm now turning the script into a novel with another title.

It often happens, with a science fiction novel or any novel, that the filmscript idea is quickly developed to a point where it has little or nothing to do with the novel. So why bother to keep the original title or pay for the idea? Steal anything in sight. In this case, the novel was simply a springboard. After all, the work of other writers is one of a writer's main sources of input, so don't hesitate to use it; just because somebody else has an idea doesn't mean you can't take that idea and develop a new twist for it. Adaptations may become quite legitimate adoptions.

Short stories are frequently made into films. Take two examples of really horrible adaptations: Hemingway's "The Snows of Kilimanjaro" (1936) and "The Killers" (1927). Just as I blame Christ for the atrocities committed in his name, so I blame Hemingway for letting Hollywood butcher his work so that he could go around shooting animals and catching marlins. Now, "The Snows of Kilimanjaro," to my mind one of the better stories in the language about death, has a great ending: a phantom plane and the pilot pointing toward the snows of Kilimanjaro. And what happens in the film? A real pilot flies in with penicillin. Boy! It was the worst film ever based on one of Hemingway's works. "The Killers" is a beautiful short story but simply is redundant as a film. Exactly enough information is conveyed in the story; in the film, the question of why the killers are after the former prize-fighter is simply not interesting — it's sort of tacked on.

Generally speaking, though not always, good movie adaptations are made from bad books. I think this is partly because screenwriters feel they can take any liberties with second-rate books. The fatal sentiment, "We're gonna make a classic, B. J.," doesn't develop, which is good because such "classics" are, generally speaking, bad films that don't even make money, like *The Great Gatsby*. That's what happens when Hollywood sets out to make a classic.

The Informer is much better on the screen than it is as a novel. The film version is actually, of course, a new creation developed under Ford's direction. The same is true of *The Treasure of the Sierra Madre*

(Huston, 1948). After seeing the film, I read the book, and the book just doesn't come up to the film.

Experimentation and Subliminal Perception

How successful has the underground art film been as an alternative to the commercial film? All the rules that I've discussed are aimed at doing a commercially viable film. Experimental films, which presumably are not concerned with commercial viability, have an entirely different set of criteria. For example, in the experimental films that I did with Anthony Balch, we were trying to expand the awareness of the audience by experimenting with the film medium. It's been said that the conscious, logical part of the mind is like the tip of the iceberg that appears above the water. What we were trying to do was jar people into an awareness of the area under the water by actually showing them mechanisms of perception that, of course, go on all the time. And we succeeded to some extent.

By making explicit the fragmentary nature of consciousness, we managed to arouse and upset the audience, just as viewers were upset by the first exhibitions of abstract paintings. I don't think these films shown at the present time would produce such strong reactions because the experiments developed have now been used in commercial films.

In our experimental films, we also went back to the basic premise of film: the retention of the image. Film is based on the fact that you retain an image in your mind for one-tenth of a second, so that images that are actually still, when presented in sequence, will seem to move. And we showed this by having a delayed image. You see someone reaching for a glass, and you also see the one-tenth-of-a-second lag — sort of a shadowy figure — behind that. This is actually what is happening all the time in film.

There's another type of cinema that would seem to offer a possibility for alternative film, so-called cinema verité, where you ignore the process of filming as much as possible. Instead of roping off a street to cut off any random intrusions, you leave the film open to chance encounters.

Cinema verité seems to me to be an ideal testing ground for getting synchronicity into films. It's a very important part of our experience and has not really been shown very precisely in films. Here's an example of an exercise I've given to students. Just take a walk around town, keeping your eyes open, observing what you see. Then come back and write down what you have just seen, paying particular attention to what you were thinking when you saw each thing. These thoughts are intersection points — those points where your stream of consciousness intersects with so-called objective reality. It is at these points of intersection that you will observe the process of synchronicity. Exactly what were you thinking, feeling, remembering when somebody dropped a plate, for example? Very often you'll find yourself saying, "Now, that's something that hasn't been used in films."

The observation of synchronicity, I think, could lead to a whole new film language. For example, in 1968 in Chicago I was asking myself what the role was of a certain cult leader — who shall remain nameless — and just then a police car passed, which told me, in the language of synchronicity, "He's a cop." When people first start noticing synchronous events, they think they're going crazy. I've had people come up to me and say, "Every street sign says something to me." "Of course," I say; "Who else is seeing the signs?" Remember, you don't see everything on the street; you see what you want to see, what means something to you.

However, even if you accept synchronicity as a fact, how can this process be represented on the screen? What actually happens in your mind, and how could this event be effectively transferred to the screen? Take the man walking down the street: How did the cult leader come into his mind? He can't remember exactly. We're in difficulty right away with a script full of holes. Well, you can shoot your film that way, showing a script actually full of holes and whirlwinds of word and image, but that's very hard to do. Or, you can show it as a sort of animation: the music-box routine where tinsel figures revolve in time to the sound track. The cult leader's picture appears on the screen, and then the police car . . .

With cinema verité, you can show the random intrusions as they actually happen. Of course, you're not going to do that unless you can conceal your photographic equipment. I think that cinema verité filmmakers are too eager to work with no script at all. They get to the filming location and then just sort of mill around. If you have a very definite script, but one that is still open enough that you don't rope off the streets, you might get some interesting encounters.

Of course, art films have much less circulation than commercial films. But if they're good, the devices used in them are sooner or later absorbed into commercial films. None of those devices, though, are altogether satisfactory, because we can't as yet photograph thoughts or feelings directly. A film shows surfaces. It doesn't show what people think.

Anthony Balch and I used another device to bring up the whole matter of identity in a film called *Bill and Tony*. We showed Anthony's face projected onto mine and mine onto his. When his face was projected onto my face, the image looked like him. Then we switched the voices around, so that sometimes I had Anthony's face and my voice and sometimes his face and my voice, and so on. It was all done with projections. Now, this technique, which can only be done with color, not black and white, could be used for all kinds of Jekyll-and-Hyde effects, as well as for horror stories.

A lot of what passes for historical fact may be, in fact, distorted. History — a lot of it — is simply rumor and hearsay. You can carry the walk exercise that I mentioned when talking about synchronicity much further with film and sound. Anthony Balch and I got some interesting intersections that way. For example, I was across Piccadilly, and Anthony was filming from the other side of the intersection. I had stopped under one of those news banners, but it was above and behind me, so I couldn't see it. I raised my hat to Anthony just to acknowledge that I saw him; but when the film was projected, just as I raised my hat, the words "Sir William" could be seen on the news banner.

As soon as you start an exercise in synchronicity, even the walk exercise, you'll begin to notice all these intersections. In this instance with Anthony, we had the minimal film context: director, photographer, and actor. Now, what if there's only one person involved and he's director/photographer walking around with his camera? Say, a Coca-Cola truck passes, and that reminds him of a T-shirt with "Cocaine Is the Real Thing" written on it. Now, you could splice in a chorus line of T-shirts to indicate that this association had been made. Of course, you haven't solved the problem of photographing an event that occurs in the brain. You have simply indicated the event with contrived surface images. Unless you have some way of differentiating between the association and the actual event, viewers will get very confused. They will think that people are dancing around in cocaine T-shirts on the street. All devices for indicating mental associations are hard to use; it's hard to make them not seem contrived.

So, with synchronicity we have pinpointed a process that goes on all the time, but we have not found a precise way to indicate it in film terms.

Now, Hollywood has always been a money-making industry dedicated to the proposition that what *has* made money *will* make money. Even if that hasn't always proven true, Hollywood still believes it. So, experiments in film have not been reinforced. When directors have used new techniques, they have tended to keep them to themselves; that is, if a director's got some little trick for doing something, as a rule he doesn't tell people about it. There is a basic incompatibility between experimentation and producing a commercial film. It's hard to stay under budget with a film using conventional techniques; there's simply not enough time or money to try new techniques that might not work out. It isn't the time to get too experimental.

Ideally, an institute for pure cinema research would be set up so that filmmakers and others could perform experiments in film techniques without having to consider immediate uses for the techniques — as has been done with physics and the natural sciences. No doubt, many of the discoveries of such an institute would be counterindicated for public performances, and the institute would have to use volunteer test audiences. The actual performance before an audience is very important, since it's the basic test of any film device. I think one of the important subjects that could be studied is time. Filmmakers still haven't come up with a new way to indicate the passage of time, insisting that the actual experience of time cannot be photographed. Why can't it? I think it can and has been photographed. In the famous massacre scene on the Odessa steps in *Potemkin* (1925), I'm sure Eisenstein was using some of these time tricks.

In *The Writer and the Screen* (1973), the author discusses some of the time tricks that are in use today.[16] Let's say we want to show a man getting dressed. The length of time it takes for him to dress would be, say, ten minutes. Well, that's too long for the film; so we reduce the film segment to three minutes. In other words, we want three minutes that will give the impression of ten minutes. The audience will believe that they've seen everything the man has done getting dressed while we've actually shown only part of the sequence. For instance, a close-up shows his hands putting on the first shoe and beginning to tie its laces. We cut to his face and show its concentrated, immobile expression. In a scene like that, the filmmaker is probably using slow motion on the face; it definitely gives you a sense of more time passing. Now, suppose his face were speeded up. Would the contrary be experienced? We don't know. That film experiment would have to be carried out with test audiences. Would the audiences think the screen time was shorter than it actually was?

The subliminal image, which has been outlawed, could also be reevaluated experimentally. A subliminal image is an image that is on the screen at the borderline of conscious perception. The idea is that any suggestion at that level would act directly on the unconscious, and people would have a tremendous compulsion to go out and buy Coca-Cola or whatever was shown. Well, the question is open. I know that Anthony Balch, who actually ran a theater, tried this, and he said it didn't work at all. The advertising industry was terrified of the whole thing, since it could make them look like sinister manipulators of the public mind. Very bad PR. I don't know if any experiments have ever been carried out to find just how effective subliminal images are.

Say you have a film in which there is no danger on the screen — for instance, some bland documentary about happy peasants; at the same time you show horrible images of death and violence on the subliminal level. Would the subliminal images affect the audience? Would they experience any uneasiness or anxiety? Would they suspect that their feelings were the result of a film trick?[17]

Waking suggestion is a very different thing. That can easily be done on the screen, too. It simply means that while your attention is engaged on one point, a suggestion is made from another. Say I was giving a lecture here, and at the same time voices were coming from microphones positioned in the audience, repeating suggestions at my voice level. If you were paying attention to the lecture, you wouldn't hear those suggestions consciously, though you would immediately hear them if I stopped talking. In other words, they're not at the subliminal level at all; they are simply at a level that is above the noise level around you.

Let's suppose a film does use horrible subliminal images. Would the film continue to produce anxiety on repeated showings? Or suppose the horrible subliminals were shown to the audience at a conscious level. Would doing so completely dispel their subliminal effect? Questions like these can be answered only by experimentation.

I mentioned earlier a recent discovery showing the biological necessity of dreaming for all warm-blooded animals. Dreaming can be seen as a creative act and a talking film. In fact, we can infer that art, in some form, is a necessity for the human, since no tribes seem to exist without some artistic expression.

Some precise experimentation could be carried out on the relationship of dreams to film. Swain writes, "The effective story fools audiences by its use of desire and danger to manipulate tension in the viewers. It poises them for action and then relaxes them according to a preplanned pattern."[18] People attend films, in part, because they find this ebb and flow of tension stimulating and pleasurable. One wonders to what extent this ebb and flow reflects the cycles of sleep and a balance of REM sleep. In fact, during dreams the whole organism is actually poised for action. The brain waves are about the same as in the waking state; blood pressure, heartbeat, and respiration rates go up, just as they would in waking life in response to danger or an interesting situation, even though the body is motionless. I see a parallel between the movie viewer, who is sitting passively in his chair and is stimulated to a not unpleasant extent by his identification with the action and the actors on screen, and the person who is dreaming. Relief is ensured by a change of scene and pace that is relaxing and reassuring, like the cycles of sleep in which there is no awareness of danger. The ebb and flow on the movie screen might actually reflect what happens in sleep. We could also experiment to see the extent to which those deprived of REM sleep could find an acceptable substitute in watching films. And further, we could investigate whether people have recurrent dreams that could be used as models for filmscripts. In other words, could films do your dreaming for you? And to what extent do they do this already?

In view of the fact that films are still the best working model for dreams, it is certainly a cop-out to say that films cannot show us thoughts and feelings directly just because filmmakers haven't been able to do so thus far. No doubt the technical potentials already at the disposal of the film industry have been deliberately neglected, but new technologies could arise in a context of pure experimentation. If we cannot yet photograph experiences, thoughts, fantasies, dreams, it may be that we do not yet have equipment sensitive enough to do so. You see, if we had microphones that could pick up subvocal speech. We could represent at least the sound track of thought. Imagine cameras that could pick up mental images. Innovations of this sort may not be so far away. They get us into a top-secret area that has to do with experiments in behavior modification. Researchers are already capable of stimulating the brain electrically, as shown by José M.R. Delgado in *Physical Control of the Mind* (1969). By stimulating certain areas of the brain, scientists can create anxiety, hatred, pleasure, sexual desire, or what have you.

Now, the reproduction of brain waves is quite within the range of the research that's going on now. The Central Intelligence Agency is said to be developing a brain-reading machine that, so far, can read only reactions but would later by able to read context as well. As with electric brain stimulation, you could produce anxiety but not the context of the anxiety — that is, the actual pictures people see in their minds, which would be different for each person. But with more precise knowledge, that might be possible. For example, I think films could eventually be produced directly in the mind by brain stimulation. Years ago, experiments were conducted in Norway in which researchers conveyed words directly into the brain by an electronic field. By analogy, visual images could be simulated in a test subject's brain, thereby breaking down the line between film and reality. The test subject would be an active participant in what his brain waves told him were real events. William Walters, who wrote *The Living Brain* (1953), told a story years ago about a woman who had an epileptic aura that she was visited by a personable young stranger with whom she had sexual relations, which were not only visual but also tactile; in other words, it was a completely real experience produced simply by stimulation of a certain brain area.[19]

Such experiments as I've been discussing would help us to gain more precise knowledge about films and exactly how they work, which would, in turn, give us more knowledge about the process of life. All film techniques do occur in real life. So if, as I've said, the function of art is to increase awareness by showing us what we're doing all the time anyway, then learning more about film processes will teach us more about ourselves. And perhaps we will eventually learn to make up our own movies right in our heads.

Notes

1. John von Neumann with Oskar Morgenstern, *The Theory of Games* (Princeton: Princeton University Press, 1944).

2. "Pratfalls" is a theatrical term referring to sudden spills (literally, falling on one's buttocks), associated with slapstick comedy. — ED.

3. Burroughs is referring to Lev Kuleshov, a Russian director of the 1920s. There are many different accounts of the images Kuleshov actually used in this famous experiment. —ED.

4. George Bluestone, *Novels Into Film* (Berkeley: University of California Press, 1961), p. 1.

5. Joseph Conrad, *Three Novels by Joseph Conrad* (New York: Washington Square Press, 1970), p. 7.

6. Dwight V. Swain, *Film Scriptwriting* (New York: Hastings House, 1976), p. 3.

7. Ibid., p. 4.

8. Ibid.

9. George Leonard, *The Ultimate Athlete* (New York: Viking, 1975), p. 115.

10. Bluestone, *Novels Into Film*, pp. 47–48, 63.

11. Ibid., pp. 21 and 47.

12. F. Scott Fitzgerald, *The Great Gatsby* (New York: Scribner's, 1925, 1953), p. 182.

13. Lewis Herman, *A Practical Manual of Screen Playwriting for Theater and Television* (Cleveland: World Pub. Co., 1963), pp. 66–67.

14. Ibid., p. 67.

15. *Blade Runner: A Movie* (Berkeley: Blue Wind Press, 1979) is a hybrid of novel and filmscript, narrative combined with camera directions. Burroughs's text is not to be confused with *Blade Runner*, a film directed by Ridley Scott in 1982 and based on Philip K. Dick's *Do Androids Dream of Electric Sheep?* (1968), presumably also the novel that Burroughs is referring to. Hampton Fancher and David Peoples wrote the screenplay for Scott's film. Burroughs's work was done before the film was actually made in 1982. —ED.

16. Wolf Peter Rilla, *The Writer and the Screen* (New York: W. H. Allen, 1973).

17. Other examples of subliminal suggestion include William Friedkin's alleged attempts in *The Exorcist* (1973) to induce viewers to lean left or right and Hitchcock's use of a red flash-frame just before the murders in *Psycho*. W. B. Key, in *Subliminal Seduction* (New York: New American Library, 1974), considers the uses of subliminal suggestion in advertising, from T-shirts to television commercials.

18. Swain, *Film Scriptwriting*, p. 79.

19. William Walters, *The Living Brain* (New York: Norton, 1953).

arguerite Duras, it might be argued, has succeeded at integrating film work with writing more thoroughly than any of her contemporaries. For her, writing and filming begin as two separate trajectories, but they soon intersect, become intertwined, and, mixed with her theatrical writings, fuse in continually surprising combinations. She wrote her first novel, *Les Impudents* (The impudent), in 1943, and by 1957 she had done a screen adaptation of another one of her novels, *Un Barrage contre le Pacifique* (1950; translated as *The Sea Wall*, 1967). Critics noted early on that her prose writings were imbued with a mysteriously cinematic quality. She was asked in 1959 by Alain Resnais, whose early success with *Nuit et brouillard* (*Night and Fog*, 1955) made him already a top-ranked director, to write an original scenario; the Resnais/Duras collaboration resulted in what is indisputably one of the masterworks of modern French cinema, *Hiroshima mon amour* (1959). Duras began to make her own films in 1969 with the film version of her *Détruire, dit-elle* (*Destroy, She Said*, 1969), followed by *Nathalie Granger* (1972) and *La Femme du Gange* (*Woman of the Ganges*, 1973). In a somewhat obverse manner to her novels, these films seem to forsake the most obvious aspect of the film medium, that is, its visual character, in order to concentrate on sound, silence, and oblique relations between sound and image. In 1975 she made what many believe to be her greatest film, *India Song*.

    Yet despite Duras's consistent productivity and growing renown both in France and abroad, she has been significantly marginalized by the critical establishment. Every aspect of her work that in another writer might be reason for lionizing is perceived to be flawed in some way. Her relation to the classical tradition of French narrative was tenuous from the start because of her interest in interior states that are not readily defined and interpersonal malaises that lack motivation. Her relation to contemporary experimental trends, such as the *nouveau roman,* has been equally problematic because her writing is not uniformly any one thing: She does not focus exclusively on the arrangement of objects, as Robbe-Grillet did in his first novels; she does not string together repetitive events and thus dissolve chronology, as Michel Butor and Claude Simon do; nor does she catalogue the obsessions and fantasies of characters at the preverbal level of consciousness, as Nathalie Sarraute did in her early work. Duras's novels were never taken up as a cause by the French political Left despite the fact that she belonged for a time to the Communist Party and has lent her support to nearly every progressive movement since the Resistance. Finally, her relation to "women's literature" has always been vexed. On the one hand, she has said that she does not perceive women's writing to be a special domain or enterprise and that she does not write *for* women — or for any other particular group. On the other hand, there are many traces in her work of a fertile and unique feminist consciousness: Her female characters are always drawn more fully and with greater complexity than her male characters; a persistent motif is a female speech hushed by cultural constraint; and — perhaps most striking of all in her work — silence, which is usually associated with women's passivity, takes on a powerful, subversive force.

Critics generally identify the writing of Duras's earliest period, preceding the unqualified success of *Moderato cantabile* (1958), as her formative stage. Her first novels, from *Les Impudents* to *The Sea Wall,* can be associated with the enthusiasm, predominantly seen among such existentialist writers as Jean-Paul Sartre and Albert Camus, for the tough, laconic style of American realists such as Hemingway and John Steinbeck. Claude-Edmonde Magny, in *L'Age du roman américain* (1948), identified the period between World War I and World War II as the Age of the American Novel because, among other reasons, American novelists succeeded in finding a style to express the anxiety and absurdity of an uncertain existence.[1] Dominant themes of despair and oppression during this period of Duras's work clearly link her to both the existentialists and their American forebears. However, the oppression is always tied to a certain kind of resistance — a resistance that has characterized all her later work. By its title alone, *Un Barrage contre le Pacifique* (literally "a dam against the Pacific") suggests this dogged opposition to a formidable, even super-human, force. Yet the crushing forces in Duras's work are not neces-sarily the power of nature (as in works of the naturalists) or the impersonality of a machine-run society (as in works of Franz Kafka) but rather the deleterious forces within each one of us, the negative capabilities attendant upon solitude and depression.

Among the techniques that will reappear continuously in Duras's works is the use of dialogue as an organizing principle. *Le Marin de Gibraltar* (1952; translated as *The Sailor From Gibraltar,* 1966) is recounted almost completely through dialogue. Duras has the ability to charge simple conversations with tremendous emotional impact. Dialogue can also be used to offset the more obvious interest of suspense. In *L'Amante anglaise* (1967), Duras relates the story through tape-recorded interviews with the three major characters. The entire intrigue, which is elicited by the circumstantial details we learn from the protagonists' words, is delayed, drowned in a sense, by the concat-enation of these words.

Fascination with dialogue led Duras to drama, the genre she used as a tool to effect the radical paring down of event and character in her novels and films. She partakes of and promotes a Brechtian trend in modern playwrighting toward neutral, passionless rendering of the dialogue by the actors. Rather than filling their lines with a prescribed emotional tenor, the actors are instructed to deliver them as though reading from the script in a sort of recitativo. The screenplay of *Hiroshima mon amour* (1959) suggests that the French actress, whose personal history constitutes a major fulcrum of the work, speak in the "flat, muffled, monotonous . . . voice of someone reciting."[2] In the play *L'Eden cinéma* (1977), the daughter, Suzanne, who along with her brother narrates the disastrous history of their mother's settling in the French colonies of Indochina, is supposed to render her lines "mechan-ically" or "as if being read."

Duras's work thus questions the relation between voice and passion. If in her early novels dialogue is charged with a high, emotional pitch, it is drained of evident passion in her later works. However, passion itself is by no means diluted or denied. On the contrary, the neutral recitativos become the principal indirect method of *implying* passion. The mechanical, automatonlike delivery suggests a posttraumatic state in which the individual has just begun to be able to formulate a verbal reaction. This situation is seen in such works as *Hiroshima; Destroy, She Said;* and *L'Eden cinéma.*

Moderato cantabile was the first novel in which Duras combined a number of her principal preoccupations in the sparse, lyrical, tightly structured form that would characterize most of her later work. Taking as her point of departure a prototypical act of passion, what the French call a *crime passionnel,* Duras fashioned a taut composition in the musical manner of theme and variation. As one of the characters, Anne Desbarèdes, waits for her son, who is taking a piano lesson, she witnesses the aftermath of a murder in a café. A man has shot his lover. But the identities of these two personages remain unknown and even the motivation for the murder remains largely a mystery for the duration of the novel. Duras is more interested in people's *reactions* than their actions. The crime of passion becomes the central motivating nugget for the major actions — such as they are — in the novel, yet these events bear not on the agent and victim of the crime, only on the witnesses. Chauvin, a man who was at the café at the time of the murder, shares Anne Desbaredes's curiosity. Together they reconstruct several possible scenarios for the unknown couple. And as they do so, their own passion is stirred. A faint past relation between Chauvin and Anne gradually comes to light through long conversations. But the novel never really establishes a connection between the past insinuated by Chauvin and the present.

The power of this novel comes from the indirectly evoked, gradually evolving feelings between Anne and Chauvin. As with most male-female relationships in Duras's work, fulfillment or consummation of those feelings is not possible. Through brooding dialogues they explore the implications of their relationship, but they never envision any deep communion. Scenes succeed one another elliptically; time does not proceed in a linear manner but rather circularly.

The dominant mood of the work is thus not one of action or even of strongly expressed emotions. It is rather a "medium-paced, singable" (*moderato cantabile*) composition, which yields nothing but malaise and awkwardness. According to Julia Kristeva, these qualities are "imposed on a troubled consciousness by the horror of World War II and . . . by the individual's psychic malaise due to hidden biological, familial, and interpersonal calamities." Whatever lyric residue might be detected in the form of this and other Duras works is subordinated to "the confrontation with the silence of horror within the self and in the world. Such a confrontation leads to an aesthetic of *awkwardness* on the one hand and to a *noncathartic literature* on the other."[3] These qualities mark most of Duras's production from *Le Ravissement de Lol V. Stein* (1964; translated as *The Ravishing of Lol V. Stein*, 1967) to her film *India Song* (1975). Her writing during the 1980s was increasingly autobiographical. The novel that became a best-seller both in the United States and in France, *L'Amant* (1984; translated as *The Lover*, 1985) is apparently a composite memoir of Duras's troubled adolescence and her early love affair with a Chinese man. In this work we glimpse for the first time the spiteful ill-will that she bears toward her mother. Even though Marguerite had obvious scholastic talents, her mother, a schoolteacher, set impossibly high standards for her. One day, when the headmaster told the mother that Marguerite was at the top of her French class, her first response was, "Well, what about math?"[4]

Duras's film work can best be approached by suggesting the technical parallels it shares with her literary work. The alternating long shot and close-up that establishes the basic rhythm of *Moderato cantabile* (as in the admirable modulation between dinner party and exterior settings in chapter 7) is a close relative of the device Duras used in *Hiroshima mon amour,* where a French actress's pent-up past is gradually released and juxtaposed dramatically with the present. Although she made film adaptations of her works, especially of her early novels, throughout her career (she finished the adaptation of *Moderato cantabile* in 1960 and of *The Sailor From Gibraltar* in 1967), Duras states quite clearly in one of the excerpts included here from her critical sketches, *Les Yeux verts* (Green eyes, 1980), that film work and novel writing are two very separate paths that never traverse the same territory. With the exceptions of direct adaptations, she considers that written texts are always different from film texts; the film *India Song,* for example, is, according to Duras, a wholly different work from the play of the same name. It is in no sense a filmed version of the written text, nor is the text a blueprint for the film.

One factor that led Duras and Resnais to achieve such a startling success with *Hiroshima* was their shared commitment to a certain notion of the past and to the importance of memory. All of Resnais's films are in one way or another about remembering. In the postwar period of the 1950s, remembering took on an obvious political tinge: Left-liberals and pacifists were intent on avoiding a repetition of Hiroshima and Nagasaki for fear that the next offensive use of nuclear arms could spell the end of civilization such as they knew it. Remembering Hiroshima became a significant activity intended, through the example of the past, to ward off another holocaust.

But the success of *Hiroshima* goes far beyond these shared ideologies. The film is a testament of the relevance of personal history in the midst of the most cataclysmic events of world history. The French woman's past love affair with a German soldier serves as a rallying point for a protracted meditation on the nature of repression, the power of oblivion, and the process of what Freud called "working through."[5] As the similarities between her past affair and her present one with a Japanese man dawn on the French woman, she begins to allow more and more of her past memories to resurface. We come to know this past just as intimately as we know her present. The two are intertwined as though within her head; and yet the film is not a mirror of her consciousness but rather a collage of past and present experiences whose net significance can be gauged only by seeing them juxtaposed starkly.

A certain culmination comes during the tea house scene, when the French woman narrates, in a near-hypnotic daze, the day on which her German lover was shot and, in particular, her realization, after she has thrown herself down on his body, that he was dead.

> The moment of his death actually escaped me, because . . . because even at that very moment, and even afterward, yes, even afterward, I can say that I couldn't feel the slightest difference between this dead body and mine. All I could find between this body and mine were obvious similarities, do you understand?[6]

Here the experience of death is imaginatively negated by the strong love the woman feels for the man who has just died. It is a moment of complete paroxysm, like the moment of the *crime passionnel* in *Moderato cantabile,* in which we are invited to explore those primordial regions of the human condition, such as the no-man's-land separating life and death. The film reaches its peak of emotional power here not simply because of the primal experience of the woman, but also because of the thematic parallel between this event and the more general "event" of post-Hiroshima mourning. As the love story unfolds out of the woman's past, we tend to lose sight of the reason for her meeting with the Japanese man — the film she is making on location, a Franco-Japanese documentary promoting peace by recalling the horrors of Hiroshima. The film opens, moreover, with a never-to-be-resolved argument between the two lovers about the extent to which the French woman can ever "see" what happened in Hiroshima. The Japanese man insists that no matter how many documentaries and reconstructions one might see, and no matter how accurately detailed these might be, one is always buffered from the actual horror of the bomb, which, as the film later points out, is gradually being forgotten if only because of the sheer numbing effect it has on people's minds.

In 1969, inspired perhaps in part by the student and worker strikes and demonstrations of May 1968, which led to a serious shake-up of the de Gaulle government, Duras took off on a new path by directing her own film, *Destroy, She Said*. Based on her theatrical piece of the same title, written in 1958, this film allowed Duras the opportunity to experiment with those techniques that she would further develop and refine in later films. *Destroy* is about Alissa, a woman recuperating from a miscarriage at an asylum in the country. Two men, Alissa's husband, Max Thor, and Stein, and one woman, Elisabeth Alione, have come to visit her, possibly to take her home. This is all that actually happens in the film. The action consists of minimal dialogues among the four protagonists, who speak to each other obliquely or, in a startling scene, behind each other's backs. In the male voice-over lawn scene, Max Thor and Stein converse off-camera about Alissa and Elisabeth, whom we see lounging on lawn chairs. Without making a direct statement about the subjection of women by the attitudes of men, Duras suggests, through the banal words the men exchange, that they seek to position and thus, through language, to regulate the women.

Destroy, She Said is a drama in which the very absence of physical action and lack of variety in setting and personage charge the spoken words with a tremendous force, at times bordering on the allegorical. Camera movement and angle, similarly, readily take on symbolic significance. A zoom-in, for example, on the reflected image of Alissa and Elisabeth before a mirror, staring at and inspecting each other thus cut off from the others, introduces the theme of alternative matriarchy.

It is nowhere more apparent than at the end of the film. When Alissa returns from the forest, which has taken on special meaning by this point, she mumbles a word that only Elisabeth understands. In order to explain to the others, Elisabeth says, "Destroy, she said." The single word in this context has a formidable connotation. It is as though Duras were suggesting that the world of male-female relations must be destroyed in order to reconstruct interpersonal relationships. At the same moment, the others hear a dull sound issuing from the forest. It turns into vague music. The film ends on this ambiguous note. One is tempted to see the forest music as some primordial call-to-arms for a newly formulated woman.

Duras's later films further explore the world of the socialized female. The most powerful perhaps is *Nathalie Granger,* in which a young girl, having exhibited an undue amount of "violence" at school, is being expelled. Her mother tries in vain to have Nathalie reinstated, but nothing can be done.

India Song returns us to the landscape of Southeast Asia to tell the story of French colonialists who are leading a decadent life amidst the misery of the indigenous people. Duras juxtaposes the dominant story line, which is centered on richly dressed bourgeois dancing across ornately decorated ballrooms, with an obscure story about a beggar woman who wanders along the Ganges. This figure, the principal focus of one of Duras's earlier works, *La Femme du Gange,* becomes the correlative of the ambiguous sound from the forest in *Destroy, She Said.* She has neither beginning nor end, but simply existence, and her existence seems to give the lie to the empty glitter of colonial life.

Marguerite Duras's works contain a very discrete group of themes and images: the mother who has been cheated out of her life's savings and left destitute in a lonely province of Indochina, the woman who has lost touch with the everyday world of dominant culture and now seeks a new beginning, the lovers who touch one another and talk to one another without ever really communicating, and the mother consumed by the love of her child. This recurrence of the same minimal themes is what Sharon Willis has called a "serial focus on the fragment." Duras employs the technique in order to stress loss and anomie, separation without reintegration. "In their refusal of textual boundaries — their intertextual recall and perpetual rewriting — the texts from the 1960s to the present resemble more one long narrative than a series.

They constitute a sort of inverted *A la recherche du temps perdu* [Proust's *Remembrance of Things Past*], substituting dispersal for recollection."[7]

She was invited in 1980 by *Cahiers du Cinéma*, a major French film journal, to write on the subject of her films and on cinema in general. The result was *Les Yeux verts*, a collection of memoirs, essays, meditations, and interviews from which the following pages have been excerpted. Duras touches on several themes of her works and on questions of commercial and artistic success. She reflects, moreover, on the double tug that writing and filmmaking have exerted upon her with varying intensity.

Notes

1. Claude-Edmonde Magny, *L'Age du roman américain* (Paris: Seuil, 1948), trans. E. Hochman, *The Age of the American Novel* (New York: Frederick Ungar, 1972).

2. Marguerite Duras, *Hiroshima, Mon Amour,* trans. R. Seaver (New York: Grove Press, 1961), p. 15.

3. Julia Kristeva, "The Pain of Sorrow in the Modern World: The Works of Marguerite Duras," *PMLA* 102, no. 2 (March 1987):140.

4. Marguerite Duras, *The Lover,* trans. B. Bray (New York: Pantheon, 1985), p. 31. Duras was born to French parents, both teachers, in Cochin China, the southern tip of Vietnam, where she spent most of her childhood. She was eighteen years old when she moved to Paris (1932).

5. Sigmund Freud, "Remembering, Repeating and Working-Through" (1914), in *The Standard Edition of the Complete Psychological Works* (London: Hogarth Press, 1953–66), vol. 12, pp. 147–56.

6. Duras, *Hiroshima,* p. 65.

7. Sharon Willis, *Marguerite Duras: Writing on the Body* (Chicago: University of Illinois Press, 1987), p. 3.

Marguerite Duras

Green Eyes (Les Yeux verts): Selections

The Movie Theater[1]

In the movie theater, the people are captivated, captured. You could say that they are prepared, that you have already a constituted public. Even so, you can hear people moving. Don't you hear them moving?

No, there's an effect of captivation. I think that your voice and the way it resounds over the images is something truly fundamental in this process. The audience is captured by a voice. You were saying that Aurélia Steiner calls out. That call can be formulated thus: "I write." It's impossible to see any difference. This text is a voice and this voice is a text. So, out of two things, one: Either the flux breaks down and the machine gets jammed or it doesn't break down and we're carried to the end. As it turns out, it doesn't break. There is a textual flux.

I don't think there's any hiatus, any blank space between the voice and what she says. When I speak, if you wish, I am Aurélia Steiner. What I pay attention to is less, not more. It's not a question of interpreting the text but paying attention to not distance myself from her, from Aurélia speaking. It takes an extreme attention, at every second, not to lose Aurélia, to stay with her, not to speak in my name. To respect Aurélia, even if she does come from me.

The Written Image

. . . In the book Aurélia Steiner,[2] *one can see the progression of each text leading toward the next. The night call in* Le Navire Night.

Translated by Keith Cohen from Marguerite Duras, *Les Yeux verts* (Paris: Editions de l'Etoile-Cahiers du Cinéma, 1981), by permission of the publisher.

Then the call across geography. Then through the caverns and then through time.

I see no equivalent to the space of the white rectangle of death. It's a space to fill in, to fill up, and it's the birthplace of Aurélia Steiner.

This place is in every life, and that's why that white rectangle has a universal value.

No. The Jewish place is what I cannot manage to resolve, to attach, even from afar, to any element of our life. The mystery that remains for me is just this: that there could be people who don't see it as I see it. I say at a given moment: "The place is empty except for your body." I hear: "The story is empty except for your death." The death of a Jew at Auschwitz, in my view, fills the entire history of our time — and the whole war.

You see the white rectangle as having something to do specifically with the Jews?

Yes: No other extermination in the history of the world was like that of the Jews — none. It was not a genocide. It was not a punitive order, an eruption of violence. It was a decree, a reflected decision, a logical organization, a meticulous, maniacal advance call for the suppression of a whole race. I remember for the *n*th time the existence of those stranglers, that Women Corps, Officers in Charge of the Strangling of Jewish Children. Similarly, there were the Teaching Corps, the Medical Corps.

What is mysterious is that image of the white rectangle, that hole.

It's also a page, a scene. Originally, it was my personal translation of Elie Wiesel's book, *La Nuit* [*The Night*]. He tells about the death of a little thirteen-year-old Jewish boy who was so skinny, so light, that he couldn't be hanged, about how he jiggled for three days at the end of his rope in the courtyard of the camp. That image, intolerable now and forever, I see this way: Under that child's body I see a white rectangle. It is tiled, perfect, bare; no one comes near the child during the agony. The border roads of Switzerland are also for me white rectangles. Jewish parents would take their children, at night, along these roads; they had them cross toward the Swiss soldiers and thus flee.

I believe I associate with the Jews a certain uneasiness[3] which for me is very powerful, which I see in full light, and before which I feel myself in a position of deadly sharp-sightedness. That uneasiness is

connected with writing. To write is to go looking outside oneself for
what is already inside oneself. This uneasiness has the function of
getting us to readjust to the latent horror scattered all over the world,
and I recognize that. It presents that horror as a part of its principle.
The word "Jew" tells at the same time of the deathly power that man
can bestow upon himself and its recognition by us. It's because the
Nazis didn't recognize this horror in themselves that they committed
it. This sense of uneasiness and déjà vu that I associate with the Jews
must have certainly started during my childhood in Asia. The quaran-
tine camps outside the villages, the endemic diseases like pestilence
and cholera, the misery, and the condemned streets of the plague
victims were the first concentration camps that I ever saw. So, I accused
God for it.[4]

*You describe yourself and your brother as "skinny, yellow" chil-
dren, racially different from your mother.*

Yes, we didn't have her skin color; we weren't bothered by either
heat or sun; we would always be running off to be with the children of
the villages out in the forests.

Criticism

I have the feeling that established film critics pay no attention to
movies unless they've cost a lot. Even if they say that a film is not very
good, if it's expensive they say so in three full columns. You can tell
how expensive a film was by the length of the article.

*It's true, I believe, that criticism today is entirely dependent on the
work of press agents.*

That goes for *Le Matin* and *Le Monde* — with the exception of
Claire Devarieux. Even *Télérama* now. The only exception: *Libér-
ation.* Today, when there are two pages on a film, you know that the
film's budget has gone over half a million. Very few critics came to
see *Aurélia Steiner.* Its budget wasn't big enough. I think they may not
be conscious of this trend (they'll be astonished to read that). But it's
true that they don't bother with inexpensive films. Maybe they figure
they'll see them when they are on vacation.

*It's absolutely true. People are far more impressed by money than
before.*

They are no longer discoverers of film. Except for Devarieux and Cournot, who are free and go to see everything, critics don't go to films anymore for the pleasure of seeing them.

There is perhaps a fatigue among critics. For one thing, there are a lot of movies. And then many critics have felt let down at one time or another by the so-called avant-garde or marginal cinema. I saw that happen with Siclier; he's really serious.

It's true. If you want to have some fun, imagine three or four established critics at a screening of *Aurélia Steiner Vancouver,* which cost about $7,500. It's unthinkable. I don't hold it against them, but they ought to double their forces. As film critics, how can they stand not seeing certain films that they know are important? It's hard to understand. There are some whose names I totally forget but who are always there, faithful to me whenever I publish anything, film or book. They try — like militants — to tear down whatever I do. Friends tell me their names, but then I forget them. They don't forget. They come to see; they read; they don't forget to. This has gone on for years and years now. Those people make it a matter of principle to hold onto their hatred, don't they?

Yes, it's a tradition.

It's to affirm their personality, don't you think? Because it seems to me that no one could hate with that constancy unless they had decided to hate in advance, before reading, before going to see anything.

Different Cinema

At this point the film [named below] says nothing. Its evolution is difficult to comprehend; it appears not to change, not to progress, not to advance, to be mobile only relative to itself, to an axis of immobility that it has supposedly imposed on itself during its whole development. Any change that occurs, whether apparent or real, is not external to the film. The film contains it. Thus, this immobility, this fixity around which it unrolls, retains it within itself, closes it in on itself. Nothing departs from it; nothing lightens its density.

I'm thinking at this moment of *Codex* by Stuart Pound, with music by Philip Glass.[5] The film is without past, without development. It pulses with the regularity of a metronome. It is only that: regularity and presence. The movement of the film, you could say, comes from Philip Glass. You could also say that the subject of the film is the movement that is implanted or transmitted to Pound's film by Glass's music. Even if from time to time the camera stops briefly on images of a woman's face, open doors, scenery, these shots blend together with the musical invasion. They advance with it, play a part in its circulation. You could even say that *Codex* is an example of a pure, intellectual cinema — intellectual in this case because of its image-sound simultaneity. It's simply that, an intellectual movement of image and sound — but of an exalted type.

The film does not unfold; it acts. Very quickly an accord is made between the film and you; you pass over to the other side, onto its border — that is, its axis remains the same, its field reaches you, and you in turn come under its force.[6] The film remains nevertheless in its orbit, chained to its steel axis, that of its writing. Compared to this enterprise by Stuart Pound, everything else is digression, loss of substance, loss of music, force, and space. When the bridge is thrown down between you and the film, it's your turn to be chained to the spiral, to the movement of immobility. The spiral acts on you as well, pulling you into its frequency, its irresistible and immobile thrust.

Hyères, Digne: the only places outside of money, the only places where there's a passion for cinema.

The Book, the Film

This morning I was forced to compare the ending of *The Vice-Consul* with a text I wrote years ago. I was wondering if I had taken this text from the ending of the book. So I reread a part of *The Vice-Consul*. The most extraordinary thing: I realized that I'd forgotten the book. I forgot it because cinema had passed over it, because I'd made the film *India Song*. I rediscovered the book with amazement and deep emotion; and while I was reading it, the India songs got lost.

Lol V. Stein has remained intact, shut up in the book, cloistered within. As for Aurélia Steiner Paris, the seven-year-old child, the little girl of the war and black towers, perhaps I had better not make a film about her either. Let her stay inside the book, like an absolute and untranscribable proposition. Infernal.

Solitude

People are too solitary in today's society. Saying it this way, though, doesn't mean anything. There are "uninhabitable" people whom everyone shuns precisely because they're not skilled at being alone. [. . .] Most people marry in order to get out of their solitude. Just to have someone to live with, to eat with, to go to the movies with. Solitude is foiled but not defeated. [. . .]

The woman in *Hiroshima* is alone, made solitary by the death of the young German soldier. She remains alone even in marriage and throughout motherhood. Anne-Marie Stretter[7] has a lover, but the raison d'être of a couple, an end to solitude, no longer exists between them. Despair has free rein here. Anne-Marie Stretter's solitude is permanent. When she dies, she dies alone. He won't lift a finger to prevent her from killing herself. And as for Aurélia Steiner, there is no solitude greater than hers.

You can always talk about future projects, about a future film, for example, and that talking won't hold up the film, the project. But a book that is coming into being is an inviolable space in danger of not existing. By letting a book be seen, looked at outside of yourself, you deprive it of something from inside yourself — once and for all. The book grows; and as it grows it is nothing but life, forced to exist, and it needs all of life's constraints — suffocation, pain, slowness, suffering, obstacles of every sort, along with silence and darkness. First it goes through the stage of disgust at being born, the horror of growing up and seeing the light of day. Once it does exist it bears no trace, nothing, of this first stage. But when it takes its first step it must do it alone, without any help whatsoever. You can't decide too hastily what the book will be, can't show off the mystery that hovers over its fate, or else you mutilate its future and, what's more, you chase away that mystery for good, leaving the book forever altered. You have to undergo this painful experience with the newly conceived book all the time it is being written. You develop a taste for this marvelous misfortune.

I'm talking about writing. I talk about writing even when I seem to be talking about cinema. I don't know how to talk about anything else. When I make films, I write; I write about the image, about what it should represent, about my doubts concerning its nature. I write about the meaning it should have. The choice of image that is then made is a consequence of this writing. For me, the writing of the film is cinema. Theoretically, a script is written for something that comes after. But not a text. At least with me, it's quite the contrary.

When I wrote *Aurélia Steiner Vancouver,* I wasn't sure I could shoot it afterwards. I wrote it with the good fortune of not having to shoot it afterwards. I just wrote it. Then, if I hadn't been given the $1 million to shoot it, I would have made a black film, an entirely black optical track. I have a murderous relationship with cinema. I began to do whatever was necessary to attain the *creative experience of textual destruction*. It's now the image that I want to get at, to boil it down. I'm at the point of envisioning a pass-key image [*image passe-partout*] that is indefinitely superimposable over a series of texts, an image that would have no meaning in itself, that would be neither beautiful nor ugly, and that would take its meaning only from the text that passes over it. With the image track of *Aurélia Steiner Vancouver,* I am already very close to the ideal image, the one that would be so neutral — seriously — as to spare me the trouble of creating a new one. Those who shoot miles of film images are naive and — have you noticed? — end up at times with nothing. With the black film, I would have attained the ideal image, that of an unabashed murder of cinema. That's what I feel I've discovered in my work over the past few years.

If in the film I don't find the text just as it was on the page — that is, as a written voice — then I start all over.[8] I began *Le Navire Night* four times. With *Le Camion* and *Aurélia,* I found the voice right off the bat. You see, I make no effort whatsoever to deepen the meaning of the text when I read it; no it's not at all like that. What I aim for is the text in its raw state, as one tries to remember a distant event, not actually lived but just "heard about." The meaning will come afterwards; it has no need of me. The reading voice alone will render meaning without my getting involved at all. Reading aloud is intended in the same way that it was intended for you alone, the first time, reading to yourself, without voice. There is a slowness, an unruliness of punctuation, as if I were undressing the words, one after another, to discover what lay underneath, the isolated, unrecognizable word, stripped of all roots, of all identity, abandoned. At times there's a space offered for a phrase to come. At times there's scarcely any space, nothing, just a form, but open, for the taking. Everything, though, must be read — I mean the empty space, too. Everything must be found. When you recite, when you listen, you realize how brittle words are and how easily they can turn to dust.

Notes

1. This section, as well as some of the subsequent ones, is in the form of a conversation or interview. Duras's words are indicated in Roman type; those of the questioner or other speaker are in italics. —TRANS.

2. *Aurélia Steiner* is the composite title for a written text and for three films. Each film has the same image track, but a different voice-over narrative, read by Duras herself, determines its title. Hence *Aurélia Steiner Vancouver, Aurélia Steiner Melbourne, Aurélia Steiner Paris.* The replication of similar but not identical names suggests that Jewish female identity has had various embodiments, in different parts of the world, and that it will continue being reembodied elsewhere. In one version, Aurélia is a woman who has survived the Nazi concentration camp at Auschwitz. —TRANS.

3. Duras used the French word *trouble,* which can be translated as agitation, confusion, uneasiness. —TRANS.

4. Duras speaks of God in another connection to comment on the scarcity of films dealing with that concept. Although the majority of films, she says, steer clear of it, "there are extremely rare exceptions, films like *Ordet,* for example, which use cinema to go to the limits of faith, which show through a film the crushing, unapproachable force of the idea of God." *Cahiers du Cinéma* 312–13 (June 1980):78. —TRANS.

5. *Codex* was the recipient of the Grand Prix at the Festival d'Hyères in 1979. Like Digne, mentioned later in this section, Hyères is the location of an important annual film competiton. —TRANS.

6. Duras seems to be describing throughout this passage an unusual relation between film and viewer by likening the film to a spinning object that exerts a force — like a magnetic field — on all who approach it. —TRANS.

7. A major character in *India Song.* — Trans.

8. Duras remarks at another moment that her work in cinema consists of avoiding film clichés: "When I can't manage to resolve my films in the traps of cinema, when they remain suspended like permanent questions, when I can't free myself from their thought, then I've made a film." *Cahiers du Cinéma* 312–13 (June 1980):91. —TRANS.

Alain Robbe-Grillet, 1922– 3

T itular head of a group of French novelists who write the *nouveau roman* (new novel), Robbe-Grillet became a well-known and controversial figure in France in the 1950s with the publication of his first novels, *Les Gommes* (1953), *Le Voyeur* (1955), *La Jalousie* (1957), and *Dans le labyrinthe* (1959). He became equally renowned in the United States following the translations of two of these by Richard Howard: *The Voyeur* (1958) and *Jealousy* (1959). Subsequently, Howard also translated the other two novels: *In the Labyrinth* (1960) and *The Erasers* (1964). Robbe-Grillet's collection of critical essays, *Pour un nouveau roman* (1963), translated in 1965 as *For a New Novel*, intensified the controversy surrounding what one critic called "objective literature"[1] by attacking the tacit assumptions of nineteenth-century novelistic form and ideology, which, as Robbe-Grillet charged, had been uncritically assimilated by mainstream twentieth-century writers. His essays specifically attacked certain "obsolete notions," such as character, story, the relation of form and content, and the writer's social commitment.

Robbe-Grillet gained further notoriety during the 1960s with the release of his first film, *L'Année dernière à Marienbad* (*Last Year at Marienbad*, 1961), directed by Alain Resnais. Early critics of his novels, who identified as "cinematic" Robbe-Grillet's careful, even obsessive, attention to objects and their arrangements, were not surprised by his move to the film medium. However, Robbe-Grillet has consistently denied any natural alliance between writing and filmmaking in his own work or in that of anyone else. For him, the two are entirely separate activities; each engages different sign systems and different internal histories, and hence they diverge radically from one another in their means of expression and in their production of ideology. What relation exists between his literary work and his film work must certainly have more to do with his manipulation of perspective (admittedly different in each medium) and his use of repetition and temporal distortion than with his much-heralded attention to objects.

As the following essay amply demonstrates, Robbe-Grillet considers cinema to be beleaguered by just as many unexamined assumptions about form and expression, albeit of a different nature and from a different source, as is the novel. Following a line of argument initiated by Eisenstein at the dawn of the sound era and echoed by major film theoreticians ever since, Robbe-Grillet calls for "a new cinema" (reminiscent of his call for a new novel), one that eschews the reductionist, conformist practices that became canonized around the 1930s. Rather than using cinema's ever-increasing technical innovation in the service of greater realism, filmmakers should pay more attention to those unwritten laws of the unconscious that, devoid though they may be of "sense" or "meaning," hint at how reality *might* be restructured. Although the underlying assumption of all forms of realism is that reality ought to be reflected "accurately," Robbe-Grillet contends, to the contrary, that the function of cinema — and of all art — is not to proffer some image of the world that we will smile in recognition of but rather to provide some blueprint for how the world might be changed.

Robbe-Grillet's novels and films do indeed invent a world that bears only superficial resemblance to the one we know. This is not to say that his works are some sort of autonomous linguistic or image structures without link to external reality, as some critics would describe the writings of Phillippe Sollers and other *Tel Quel* novelists, the so-called *nouveau nouveau romanciers*.[2] On the contrary, what resemblance there is in Robbe-Grillet's work to external reality is crucial. For he is working on and against the popular conceptions and misconceptions of everyday interpersonal relations and international power relations — what Roland Barthes calls "mythologies."[3]

Jealousy, for example, juxtaposes a play on the jealous husband and love triangle with a sardonic look at French colonialism in the era of its political and economic decline. Seemingly pointless descriptions of banana fields in a nameless colonial nation suggest the highly regulated inventorying performed under the aegis of an economic dominion that is just as unsure of itself as is the anxious narrator who watches his wife write letters to Franck, the man he suspects to be her lover. Objects are singled out not so much to provide the reader with some perfect portrait of a Caribbean or North African colony as to underline the severity of this double uncertainty, economic and emotional: the insistent song sung by the faceless native, the centipede squashed by Franck, the wife's long hair being combed relentlessly, the blue writing paper first seen on the wife's desk and later seen sticking out of Franck's pocket. These compositional methods result in an atmosphere that is rare in narrative fiction. Like certain travelogue films and documentaries about industry, *Jealousy* teems with motion and activity that are not human. Because all actions and situations, whether they involve human beings or not, are placed on the same level of significance, a whole scene can be created out of the sound of insects and a description of nightfall.

More important than the atmosphere created, though intimately linked with it, is the indirect revelation of the narrator's state of mind by what he describes. Repetition serves the purpose of signaling to the reader those objects that hold some special symbolic significance for the narrator. The crushed centipede, for example, is without significance in and of itself. But after the narrator repeats the description of the squashing over and over in a variety of contexts, the reader comes to conclude that, for the narrator, the act has an aura of virile performance ordinarily associated with the sexual act. We learn more about the narrator's state of mind from the following: When A... and Franck go to town together, the narrator is left to imagine what they might be doing. As the time arrives when they should be back, the narrator fixes on a presumably hypothetical automobile accident. The fantasy nature of this series of images is conveyed by the associational contexts that are supplied: the crash and the attendant conflagration are described amidst other actions we have already "seen," the combing of A...'s hair and the crushing of the centipede. As the insect's mandibles make a rapid reflex movement, "it is possible for an ear close enough to hear the faint crackling they produce." But immediately after we are given that information, we are told: "The sound is that of the comb in the long hair." Then, when the car bursts into flames, "the whole brush is illuminated by the crackling, spreading fire. It is the sound the centipede makes."[4] Thus, the sound of crackling unites these three events, making the imagined crash as real as the other two events. We are faced not simply with a metaphorical series (as one might expect, say, in a symbolist poem), but rather with the signs of an idiosyncratic mindset. The narrator's jealousy, which is, after all, the central plot nugget, has been merely suggested until now; no sign has been given of what action he might take as a result of that feeling. Now we have a concrete fantasy that explicitly embodies the narrator's desire for revenge and brings to the surface his wish for the death of the (supposed) lovers. Notice, however, that nowhere has the narrator confessed his feelings to the reader and nowhere has there been either a verbal interchange or the merest gesture to suggest that the narrator is on the verge of making an accusation and seeking vengeance. Instead, following a cinematic montage model, Robbe-Grillet juxtaposes three actions, each of which has its own emotional or sexual connotation, in order to convey a global feeling of vengeful, wishful thinking.

Another novel, *Projet pour une révolution à New York* (1970; translated as *Project for a Revolution in New York,* 1972), takes the clichés of student rebellion and sets them against a phantasmagoric view of New York at a time when covert drug deals and illicit sexual encounters are commonplace. Here the scenes of interpersonal agony are melded to the very beams and rafters that enclose the narrator's unnamed quest by means of "slipping signifiers," words and phrases that function simultaneously in two different scenes and hence make clear referential structuration impossible. The novel opens, for example, with the description of a door that the narrator has just closed behind him:

> The wood around the [door's] window is coated with a brownish varnish in which thin lines of a lighter color, lines which are the imitation of imaginary veins running through another substance considered more decorative, constitute parallel networks or networks of only slightly divergent curves outlining darker knots, round or oval or even triangular, a group of changing signs in which I have discerned human figures for a long time: a young woman lying on her left side and facing me.[5]

These human figures that the narrator at first merely "discerns" amidst the wood-grain patterns gradually and imperceptibly come to life; that is, they take over the narrative present:

The mouth, which has been wide open too long, must be distended by some kind of gag: for example, a piece of black lingerie stuffed between the lips. Besides, a scream, if the girl were screaming, would be audible even through the thick pane of the oblong window with its cast-iron grille.

But now a silver-haired man in a white doctor's coat appears in the foreground from the right; he is seen from behind, so that only a hint of his face can be glimpsed in profile. He walks toward the bound girl whom he stares at for a moment.[6]

The first passage suggests a film parallel in its meticulous, probing description — a virtual close-up — of the wood grain on a door. As in cinema, an anonymous glance is cast across a surface that, when inspected more closely, seems to reveal something not visible to the casual observer. This moving perusal of an object, in other words, a common device in cinema, becomes unusual and even disconcerting in the hands of Robbe-Grillet. Cinema characteristically constructs spaces by bringing together such camera moves. And such moves in Robbe-Grillet's writing have earned him his reputation as a cinematic novelist.

The second passage is more complicated. What passes at first as a static description suddenly comes to life. The "young woman" functions here as the slipping signifier. Although she appears at first as an example of the human figures discerned in the wood grain by the narrating "I," the "bound girl" now is part of an interactive scene with the silver-haired man. A mere decorative metaphor that appears on the periphery of the first scene thus takes center stage in the unfolding of the second scene.

The cinematic technique here evoked is one rarely used in films. It relies on the difference between the still image and the moving image. Chris Marker used the technique in *La Jetée* (1963), most of which is composed of still images of the world following some sort of nuclear devastation. The images are connected by lap-dissolves, a technique that involves the artificial fading of one image into another and reinforces the stillness of the images. Then, toward the end of the film, the voice-over narrator tells about a woman who remembers a scene at an airport runway. It is this scene that will bring back the past to her and to the other characters who, living a monotonous underground existence, have been deprived of memories and are thus incapable of reconstructing their history. As the camera slowly zooms in on a still image of the woman, her eyes blink and her head moves slightly. Rarely in the cinema has the spectator been more shocked by the fundamental feature of moving pictures, their motion. Motion comes to signify memory in this offbeat science fiction work; gradually other memories return to the characters and motion recaptivates the images.

The same process is at work in Robbe-Grillet's novel. The basic opposition is between stasis and movement. As static scene succeeds static scene, one gets the impression of a mind that cannot recall the linkage of events, as if the past were a disordered patchwork of clear-cut but fragmentary scenes. Every once in a while, as in the passage cited, the silver-haired man begins to move, temporality is reintroduced and a sudden dynamic integration of previously disconnected images begins to take place. The film parallel here is a telling one: In both media, time is signified by motion. When memory loss or the inability to organize past events needs to be expressed, static, disconnected images or descriptions can convey the message without any narratorial intervention.

Robbe-Grillet's films are interesting to view in light of the pervasiveness of cinematic techniques in his fiction and his insistence (like that of Duras) that film work is a separate, very different activity. Just as his novels show his dedication to the notion that traditional fiction-writing procedures are now obsolete, so his filmmaking amply demonstrates his contention that cinematic art is in need of constant innovation.

After his collaboration with Resnais on *Marienbad,* he went on to direct films himself, beginning with *L'Immortelle (The Immortal Woman,* 1963). As might be expected, the techniques of repetition and impossible referentiality that characterize his novels also make their appearance in his films; what differentiates the two bodies of work most clearly is the films' exploitation of the noncongruence of image and sound track. In *L'Homme qui ment (The Man Who Lies,* 1968), for example, the voice of the protagonist tells a story over an image track that not only fails to illustrate or act out the story but even blatantly contradicts it. *L'Eden et après* (The Eden and after, 1970) is composed of a vague story, narrated in voice-over, about people who meet at a café called L'Eden. But once we become familiar with the café setting, the image track leaps into scenes of a chase in the desert. The café itself is constructed of moveable panels whose placement differs — according to some symbolic ordering device, one suspects — each time the scene returns to the café, so that no shot of the café can ever be relied on to anchor us in a clearly marked space. And this regulated disordering of space reflects the distortion of time effected by constant flashbacks and flashforwards within the main and the interpolated stories. Robbe-Grillet has explained that the film's structure is actually ordered around an arbitrary sequencing key that resembles Arnold Schoenberg's twelve-tone row of musical composition.[7]

Like his novels, these films (as well as his others: *Trans-Europ-Express* [1966]; *Glissements progressifs du plaisir* [Progressive slippages of pleasure, 1974], *Le Jeu avec le feu* [Playing with fire, 1975], and *La Belle captive* [The beautiful captive, 1983]) take as their points of departure certain Western clichés and myths, which are then always intermeshed with images that recur throughout Robbe-Grillet's work: the broken shoe, the mirror, the shattered glass, and the woman with a dog.

An early defender of Robbe-Grillet's art, Roland Barthes, described in *Mythologies* (1972; orig. 1957) the process by which cultural objects and symbols, such as advertisements and flags, are imbedded with highly codified messages. The work of the individual in bourgeois society becomes that of *decoding* such objects in order to recover their latent messages.[8] Robbe-Grillet's work, which is patterned, like the films of Jean-Luc Godard, on just such ideologically pitched images and symbols, requires the same sort of multileveled reading. In his novel *La Maison de rendez-vous* (1965), for example, the signs of Hong Kong — Malaysian prostitutes, luxurious brothels, drug dens, and sleazy magazines — evoke not so much the geographical-historical place called Hong Kong as the moral depravity of all international communities that have been repeatedly looted of their indigenous traditions and suffused with layer upon layer of a glittery but empty culture of domination. The world that Robbe-Grillet thus presents is not an actual representation of Hong Kong. His invented world aims at shocking the reader into an awareness not of the vicissitudes of Hong Kong but of the harrowing processes of psychological subjugation practiced by the dominant cultures in advanced industrial societies. For this reason, the reading of a Robbe-Grillet text, be it literary or filmic, can never be "innocent"; his work is not traditionally "realistic." There is always a double process: First we see minutely described objects and scenes and then we are led beyond these signifiers to the messages the culture has injected them with. Reading Robbe-Grillet's texts, in other words, becomes a complex exercise of semantic and symbolic decoding within a universe highly charged with the stereotypes and predigested images of contemporary culture.

Notes

1. Roland Barthes, "Objective Literature" (1954), in *Critical Essays,* trans. R. Howard (Evanston: Northwestern University Press, 1979).

2. During the late 1960s and the 1970s a group of writers and theoreticians loosely associated with the journal *Tel Quel,* then edited by Phillippe Sollers and others, began gradually to differentiate themselves from the growing critical domination of the *nouveau roman,* a school they had championed earlier, by emphasizing the materiality of language and the suppleness and variability of the signifier even when considered independently of signified and referent. The signifier is the sensuous aspect of the communicating medium (written word, oral word, or image); the signified is the mental concept one forms upon apprehending the signifier; and the referent is the object or condition in reality to which the signifier and signified refer.

3. Roland Barthes, *Mythologies,* trans. A. Lavers, (New York: Hill & Wang, 1972).

4. Alain Robbe-Grillet, *Jealousy,* trans. R. Howard in *Two Novels by Robbe-Grillet,* (New York: Grove, 1965), pp. 113–14.

5. Alain Robbe-Grillet, *Project for a Revolution in New York,* trans. R. Howard (New York: Grove, 1972), pp. 1–2.

6. Ibid., pp. 2–3.

7. Alain Robbe-Grillet, *"L'Eden et après,"* lecture delivered at the International Symposium of Film Theory and Practical Criticism, University of Wisconsin–Milwaukee, November 20, 1975.

8. Barthes, *Mythologies.*

Alain Robbe-Grillet

For a New Cinema

The history of cinema is still rather short, yet it is already characterized by discontinuities and reversals. The majority of contemporary
films that now pass for masterpieces would have been rejected by
Eisenstein — and rightly so — as altogether worthless, as the very
negation of all art.

We should reread today the famous manifesto Eisenstein and
Pudovkin wrote in the 1920s on the sound film.[1] At a time when, in
Moscow, a brand new American invention was being announced that
would permit the actors on the screen to speak, this prophetic text
warned vigorously — and with extraordinary clarity of vision —
against the fatal abyss into which cinema was in danger of sliding:
Since the illusion of realism would be considerably strengthened by
giving the characters a voice, cinema could let itself be led down the
cowardly path of glib superficiality (a temptation that never stops
menacing us) and from then on, the better to please the multitudes,
could remain content with an allegedly faithful reproduction of reality.
It would thus surrender all claims to the creation of genuine artworks
— works in which that reality would be challenged by the very
structures of the cinematic narrative.

Now, what Eisenstein demanded, with his customary vehemence,
was that sound be used to create, on the contrary, new shocks: To the
shocks between sequences created by montage (which links, according
to relations of harmonic resonance or of opposition, the sequences to
one another) should be added the shocks between the various elements
of the sound track and still others between sounds and simultaneously
projected images. As one may have expected, good Marxist-Leninist

Translated by Sophia S. Morgan, January 1982.

that he was, he called upon the sacrosanct "dialectic" in order to support this thesis.

But Communist ideology — alas! — could not save the Soviet cinema (which today is one of the worst in the world) from falling into the snares of glibness. In fact, good old "bourgeois realism" triumphed everywhere — in the West as well as the East, where they simply rebaptized it "socialist." Eisenstein and his friends were rapidly subjected to the new universal norm: The montage of the visual sequences of their films (*¡Que viva México!* for example) was redone by the right-thinking bureaucracy, and all the sounds were made to follow obediently the recorded images.

Even in France, it was a theoretician of the extreme Left, André Bazin, who, merrily letting the dialectic go by the board, became the spokesman of illusionist realism, going so far as to write that the ideal film would entail no montage whatsoever, "since in the natural reality of the world there is no montage"! Thus, the numerous and fascinating forms of expression created in Russia and elsewhere during the silent era were summarily repudiated as if they were nothing but childish stammerings born of a merely rudimentary technique. Sound, wide screens, deep focus, color, long-duration reels — all of these have allowed us to transform cinema today into a simple reproduction of the world, which, in the final analysis, is tantamount to forcing cinema as an art to disappear.

If today we want to restore its life, its former power, and its ability to give us veritable artworks, worthy of vying with fiction or painting of the modern era, then we must bring back to film work the ambitiousness and prominence that characterized it in the days of silent film. And so, as Eisenstein urges, we need to take advantage of every new technical invention, not in order to subject ourselves even further to the ideology of realism but, quite the opposite, to increase the possibilities of dialectical confrontation within film, thereby intensifying the "release of energy" that is just what such internal shocks and tensions allow for.

From this point of view, the alleged realism of contemporary commercial films, whether they be signed by Truffaut or by Altman, appears as a flawless — totalitarian — system, founded on hackneyed, stereotyped redundancy. The least detail in every shot, the connections between sequences, all the elements of the sound track —

everything, absolutely everything — must concur with the same sense and meaning, with a *single* sense and meaning, and with good old common sense. The immense potential richness that is concealed in this stuff of dreams — these discontinuous, sonorous images — must be utterly reduced, subjected to the laws of normative consciousness, to the status quo, so that, at any cost, meaning may be prevented from deviating, swarming, bifurcating, going off in several directions at once, or else getting completely lost. The technicians on the set or in the various recording studios are there precisely to see to it that no imperfections and divergences ever occur.

But what is the significance of this will-to-reduction?[2] What it all means, in the final analysis, is that reality — and a living reality at that — is reduced to a reassuring, homogeneous, unilinear story line, a reconciled and compromised, entirely rational story line[3] from which any disturbing roughness has been purged. Plainly put, realism is by no means the expression of the real, of what is real. But rather, the opposite. Reality is always ambiguous, uncertain, moving, enigmatic, and endlessly intersected by contradictory currents and ruptures. In a word, it is "incomprehensible." Without a doubt, it is also unacceptable — whereas the first and foremost function of realism is to make us accept reality. Realism, therefore, has a pressing obligation not only to make sense but to make one and only one sense, always the same, which it must buttress tirelessly with all the technical means, all the artifices and conventions, that can possibly serve its ends.

Thus, for example, prevailing film criticism may blame a certain detective film for lack of realism, ostensibly because the murderer's motives are not clear enough, or because there are contradictions in the scenario, or because there remain lacunae in the causal chain of events. And yet, what do we actually know about nonfictional attempts to solve real crimes? Precisely that uncertainties — at times essential ones — always persist until the end, as do unsettling absences, "mistakes" in the protagonist's behavior, useless and supernumerary characters, diverging proofs, a piece or two too many in the puzzle that the preliminary investigation in vain tries to complete. . . .

Reality, then, is problematic. We run up against it as against a wall of fog. Meanwhile, our relation to the world becomes still more complicated because, at every moment, the world of realism presents itself to us as if it were *familiar*. We become so used to it that we hardly see it: It is our habitat, our cocoon. Yet, actually, we stumble against what's real with a violence we never get used to — a violence that no amount of previous experience can ever assuage — so that reality remains for us irremediably *foreign* and *strange*. The German words *heimlich* and *unheimlich*,[4] which both Freud and Heidegger have used, though in different but here overlapping contexts, give indeed an idea of this lived opposition — fundamental because it is inescapable — between the strange and the familiar. Both the psychoanalyst and the philosopher insist that the familiarity we think we have with the world is misleading (i.e., ideological, socialized). To acknowledge and explore (even to the point of anguish) the world's strangeness constitutes the necessary starting point for creating a consciousness that is free. And one of the essential functions of art is precisely that it assumes this role of revealing the world to us. This explains why art does not attempt to make the world more bearable (which undoubtedly is what realism does), but less so: because its ultimate ambition is not to make us accept reality but to change it.

It certainly does seem that cinema, simply by virtue of its signifying material, is a privileged instrument for this double adventure [of acknowledging and exploring the world's strangeness]. In the first place, moving pictures possess two essential characteristics (which realism in vain tries to forget): They are in the present and they are discontinuous. This ineradicable *presence* of the cinematic image can be considered undeniably in opposition to the complex game of grammatical tenses that the classical novel has at its disposal: No photographic code exists to let us indicate that such-and-such a scene is taking place in a past tense — be it preterit, perfect, or imperfect — or in the future, and much less in the conditional. When I see an event unfolding on the screen, I perceive it as if it were in the process of happening: It is in the present indicative.[5] But the continuity of this present-tense action becomes violently and unforeseeably interrupted each time there is a change of sequence, that is, each time the editing shears have cut the film in order to tack onto it (or replace part of it with) a different take. Between the last shot of sequence *n* and the first shot of sequence *n*+1, something has happened that has no duration in the film (i.e., whose filmic duration is nil); the camera has changed position and a gap of some duration has slipped into diegetic time.[6]

Paradoxically, the conjunction of these leaps — in space and in time — allows the splices of traditional editing to move past the spectator's eyes unnoticed. In fact, all it takes is the juxtaposition of two filmed gestures. Consider, for example, the foot of a person walking, shot twice at the same point in its cyclical movement — but each time from a different angle. When these images are spliced together, the spectator remains unaware of the temporal and spatial leaps (as well as the film cement) occasioned by the change of angle. Thus, the definition accepted by all filmmaking schools: Correct splicing is the one the spectator doesn't see! It is easy to judge how far we are — at the opposite pole, in fact — from the montage effects recommended and put into practice by Eisenstein.

Echoes of this academic definition of supposedly proper editing can be found at all levels of film production. Here let us briefly run over a few applications of this curious aesthetic. Good framing is the framing that the spectators will be unaware of; in other words, the one in which the borders of the frame play no role whatsoever. Good lighting: the one that seems the most "natural." Best camera position: the one with the least personality, the better to conceal the material origin of the shot. (Moreover, because the camera must disappear from view, mirrors become the bane of the camera operator's existence.) The best actor is the one who is not perceived as an actor, but only as a character. Etcetera. A certain theoretician of the sound track has even gone so far as to write that "the best film music is the one which the spectator doesn't hear."

All of this leads us to the following definition of realistic illusionism: The best film is the one whose narrative and plastic forms have the least existence and the least force, and in which only the diegesis — the story that is being told — is perceived by the public. Since, according to this view, the cinematic material is supposed to be perfectly transparent, the screen is nothing more than a window opened onto the world. But surely the window is opened only onto the world of realism and not the real world! — only onto the world of hackneyed familiarity and not onto the strangeness of the world.

In all of this, there is a fraudulence more serious still than the pretension of opening a window upon reality, and this is the substitution, from the outset, of reality by its ideological simulation — in other words, by realism, which after all is nothing other than the everlasting reproduction of the workings of the Balzacian novel. We know (I myself have said it a hundred times, but one must never pass up the opportunity of saying it again) that it was no accident that out of all the French novels of the past, it was Balzac's works that academic criticism chose as the mode, forever and ever, of the true novel. The Balzac of *Eugénie Grandet, Père Goriot,* etcetera, incarnates, in fact, a very special moment in our history — that very brief period that separates two revolutions (the 1830 revolution, which established the triumph of bourgeois ideas, and the proletarian revolt of 1848), a blessed period, one might say, unique in the annals of the bourgeoisie, when that class was happy and writers could embrace, in all good conscience, the values of society. Balzac never asked himself a single question about his own writing, any more than the social class to which he belonged ever questioned the legitimacy of its own power. To write a novel was then as "natural" and proper as possessing land or a factory.

Only a few years later (from 1848 on), this would no longer be true: Flaubert expresses brilliantly the loss of naiveté in the practice of writing. And a while earlier, in the age of Diderot, for instance, this was not true either: Note, in particular, the questioning of narrative in *Jacques le fataliste*. The Balzacian narrative (that is, bourgeois realism) would thus persist in the minds of the guardians of order as if it were a privileged form: It belongs to that all too brief paradise lost. And, quite naturally, when cinema learned to speak, it was the Balzacian model, as the absolute ideal of every narrative, that prevailed as well. Which explains why they wanted from the start to install in cinema a faultless continuity, a rigorous causality, and an unequivocal meaning — everything, in short, that in the novel is implied by the use of the preterit tense: a guarantee of the coherence, truth, and stability of the world, and of the necessity of the laws that govern it.

It is difficult, as we have seen, to imagine a signifying material more poorly suited to such a task. For our academics, therefore, there was an urgent need to force this potentially too modernist medium to efface itself to the greatest possible degree: The present-tense image, the links of montage, the professional actors, the camera eye, a sound track independent of the visual sequences (produced separately, out of multiple, heterogeneous, simultaneous components, variously combined) — all these things had first to be disguised, camouflaged as much as possible, as if they were so many shameful blemishes, in order to arrive at the well-known results.

But now it is our turn to go against this kind of system: first of all, to restore to its rightful place the fundamental need of every art — that is, the need to allow the stuff and matter of the medium and the creative labor that has gone into the work to become visible without shame or disgrace. And should there be a need to work against, to fight against, the material conditions of the medium, let this be an open struggle, carried out before the public, not behind its back. And if it is possible to make a connection between film and the novel, let it be a connection with the modern novel (the *nouveau roman,* for example) and not with that Balzacian pseudo-literature of the twentieth century, which no-body — in academic criticism at least — would even dream of defending. And if it should be necessary to seek a resemblance with the world, let this be a resemblance with what is real — that is, the universe of dreams, sexual fantasies, and nocturnal anxieties simulta-neously confronted and produced by our unconscious — and not with the factitious world of familiarity, the world of so-called conscious life, which is no more than the insipid, soothing product of our censors (ethics, reason, respect for the establishment).

The cinema screen is by no means the world, and it is even less a window open onto it; it is merely the place where filmic forms and substances confront one another, just as a painter's canvas is a space in which pictorial forms and substances come face to face. And it is also the place where our narrative faculty is questioned by, and through, these forms and substances. Film is not an image of the world; like every work of art, it is, in a hesitant, an unreasonable, and a moving way, a questioning of the world. Similarly, the image of an actor on the screen constitutes neither a character of flesh and blood nor even the image of such a character; it is simply one of the functions involved in the totality of the film — a function that calls into question (or even throws into crisis) the very notion of character.

The camera is another one of these functions — the one that indicates the point of view, that is, the source of the images. In this way, it constitutes a narrative presence — or rather one of the narrative presences in the film, because the characters and the editing itself can also fulfill this role *at the same time.* And the camera cannot be any more neutral than they can. All that it can do (yet this is a great deal) is play with the idea of neutrality: It is one of the poles at which objectivity and subjectivity collide. It is undoubtedly the primary place where this collision occurs. One could almost say that the camera, through its very functioning, denounces the snare of realism. It allows it to materialize, yet also exposes its two-faced character. For, on the one hand, it gives us a representation of the real world that leaves us with a strong sense of objectivity, while, on the other hand, it cannot help but direct its glance toward a chosen stretch of space and then, from the continuous fabric of the world, cut out a circumscribed fragment. The camera does not unveil reality; it *imagines* it. Selecting camera position and placing the frame are already two operations of the imagination.[7]

Then comes montage, which exposes all over again the illusion of realism: Fragments and shots cut out of the continuum, endowed with a specific point of view, are now rearranged to form a new — entirely new — composition, revealing still more flagrantly the intervention of the creative spirit. The subjective objectivity of the camera (which is also capable of panoramic sweeps and dollies of varying complexity) combines with montage cuts to facilitate the juxtaposition of more or less distant moments in diegetic time as well as more or less distant shots taken from different angles. And this combination creates surprising effects and paradoxical, multidimensional, moving spaces that — like the spaces of our dreams — endlessly swerve, change course, and disappear.

Since the days of Freud, we have believed that what takes place in our dreams is infinitely more interesting (because it's richer, less prearranged, more capable of revealing our relations with reality) than the gestures and words, the thoughts and settings, that constitute the reassuring fabric of our socialized life (the one that realism deals with). Thus, cinema — so long as it can be yanked from its cushy yoke of realism, be it of the bourgeois or of the socialist variety — will emerge as a privileged instrument for understanding contemporary man and no doubt for shaping the man of the future as well.

Notes

1. This document, entitled in French "Manifeste contrepoint sonore," first appeared in English in *Close Up* (London) in October 1928, based on a German translation. The first translation from Russian into English was by Jay Leyda in Sergei Eisenstein, *Film Form* (New York: Harcourt Brace, 1949), pp. 257–59. — TRANS.

2. In the original, Robbe-Grillet used the term *volonté réductrice*. Reductionism must be understood as the practice of reducing (or circumscribing, or limiting) behavior, actions, or events, or the interpretations of behavior, actions, or events, so as to make them conform to the ideological (overt or covert) premises of a certain dogma (world view, etc.). As a synonym of procrustianism (involving thus both "cutting" and "stretching"), this variety of reductionism has been around for a long time. I have translated *volonté réductrice* as will-to-reduction following the model of the will-to-power, hoping that some of the lingering resonance of the older expression will carry the translation along. — TRANS.

3. *Trame reconciliée* is here translated as "reconciled and compromised story line" because the English cognate lacks the stronger connotations of its French equivalent. A reconciled story is one whose elements have been reconciled with the prescriptive norms of the establishment and, therefore, one whose integrity as art has been compromised. — TRANS.

4. *Heimlich* means, literally, "homelike"; *unheimlich* means "unhomelike." They can be translated as "familiar" and "unfamiliar." *Unheimlich* carries the connotations of "strange" and "uncanny." Robbe-Grillet's point is that reality is *not* familiar to us but instead is "*étranger*," translated here as "foreign and strange." — ED.

5. The same cannot be said of a static picture. A photograph (a document, a snapshot souvenir, etc.) is perceived as the record of an event that happened in a more or less distant past.

6. A brief reminder concerning this important notion of *diegesis* [the Greek word for narration — TRANS.]: As elaborated by Etienne Souriau around 1920, film time is the duration and chronology of the images unfolding on the screen whereas diegetic time is the duration and chronology of the allegedly real events that the film represents. Of course, this notion loses much of its relevance in a modern work like *Last Year at Marienbad,* where the existence of a diegesis exterior to the film is strongly contested. We shall come back to this point.

7. In the original, *l'imaginaire*. — TRANS.

Alexander Kluge, 1932–   4

Though less well known in the United States than other members of the new generation of German filmmakers, such as Werner Herzog and Rainer Werner Fassbinder, Alexander Kluge has gained considerable renown in Europe. His stories and films have reached a broad, popular audience, and his incisive critical essays on art and society are recognized as important signposts of current tendencies in the new German Left. An important collection of his short stories, *Lebensläufe* (1962), was translated into English by L. Vennewitz as *Attendance List for a Funeral* and was published in the United States in 1966, but Kluge's films have not yet received commercial distribution in this country. A good deal has, however, been written about his film work in journals of German studies, particularly about *Abschied von gestern* (*Yesterday Girl*, 1966) and *Gelegenheitsarbeit einer Sklavin* (*Part-Time Work of a Domestic Slave*, 1973). His most recent films are *Die Patriotin* (*The Patriot*, 1979) and *Die Macht der Gefühle* (*The Power of Emotion*, 1983).

Kluge has placed himself clearly in the lineage of an important German intellectual tradition, that of the Frankfurt School of critical theory. Associated with broad critiques of mass media and of institutional support for art and culture, Frankfurt critics such as Theodor Adorno, Walter Benjamin, and Max Horkheimer exerted enormous influence on the generation of critics and artists that succeeded them. Perhaps the most important notion developed by the Frankfurt critics, for Kluge, was that of the "public sphere" (*Offentlichkeit*). Initially, the term referred to the sphere of institutions and activities that, opposed to private life, organizes the diverse needs and qualities of individuals into a social, or collective, form. At its extreme, the term implies that this organization of needs is crucially determined by those who hold power and that, consequently, the implicit values of the process are highly ideological. Often writing in collaboration with sociologist-philosopher Oskar Negt, Kluge refines the concept of public sphere to suggest that the social form into which needs are organized is "not necessarily in the interest of those whom it purports to represent."[1] When individuals realize that their needs are not being served, they may begin to create, in art or social practice, an "oppositional public sphere," which refers, according to Kluge, to "a type of public sphere which is changing and expanding, increasing the possibilities for a public articulation of experience."[2] By virtue of their potential to express and to embody an oppositional public sphere, films can transform social structures and increase the audience's awareness of their relation to those structures.

To appreciate the thrust of Kluge's notion of public sphere, we need to understand what he means by the "private ownership of experience." Whereas dominant ideology will always attempt to maintain the control of those in power by leading individual subjects to believe that the structures of power are part of the nature of things, the intersubjective experience of everyday life actually remains immune to this brainwashing process, particularly if art and critical theory carry out a campaign to enlighten individuals about their own oppositional potential. As is clear, then, the theory of an oppositional public sphere represents a significant revision of classical Marxism. Rather than seeing the workplace and the residual conflict between labor and capital as the crucial points around which to organize against bourgeois power, proponents of this view target the more amorphous structures of everyday experience and, secondarily, the structures of mass media, the control of which, they feel, can be more easily wrested from the hands of the ruling class than the control of, say, factories. Thus, an important item on the agenda of the new Frankfurt School critics, as was the case for their mentors, is the analysis of the means of mass media production and reception, with a view toward liberating them for a more democratic use.

Kluge elaborates some of the implications of his theory in the following essay, but one must refer to his German texts, only parts of which have been translated into English, for a fuller explanation. His first important volume to appear on this subject was *Öffentlichkeit und*

Erfahrung (Public sphere and experience, 1972), written in collaboration with Oskar Negt. This work, like his more recent *Geschichte und Eigensinn* (History and obstinacy, 1981), also written in collaboration with Negt, develops the concept of public sphere to embrace a notion of history that is compatible with the interests of individual subjectivity. Kluge's essays on film, literature, and other arts appear in the published script of *Die Patriotin* (The patriot, 1979), parts of which were translated by T. Y. Levin and M. Hansen in *New German Critique*.[3] Kluge's appraisal of the New German Cinema appears in a volume coauthored with Klaus Eder, *Ulmer Dramaturgien: Reibungsverluste* (Ulm dramatic theory: Friction losses, 1980).

Crucial to Kluge's understanding of the inviolability of human experience is the idea of fantasy. What interests Kluge is the degree to which fantasy is susceptible to social control. On the one hand, because of its ordinarily private nature, fantasy lies outside both state control and the public sphere. In Kluge's words, it "escapes domestication." On the other hand, however, there are certain types or elements of fantasy that, Kluge says, are "made to conform." This social regulation of fantasy, or "fantasy under domination," leads to the most extreme forms of alienation. Kluge suggests that the public sphere should grant fantasy "the status of a communal medium."[4] In this way, that which is normally relegated to the area of wishful thinking might, through communal interaction, become articulated as a clear utopian vision. And like other neo-Marxists, Kluge believes that utopian propositions hold important possibilities for future forms of social organization because, disregarding "real obstacles," they offer "perspectives different from those inherent in things as they are."

In his film practice, Kluge has aligned himself with Eisenstein and the montage tradition. In *The Patriot,* he takes Brecht's discussion of a photograph of the Krupps factory, a war ammunitions plant, one step further. Brecht had said that the photograph "yields practically nothing" about the institution, that "the genuine reality has slipped into the functional," because the photo fails to tell us anything about the human relationships and relations of power implicit in the existence of the factory.[5] Kluge points out that more can be learned about the factory if two photographs are studied. Because of the relationship that develops between two shots, "information is hidden in the cut which would not be contained in the shot itself. This means that montage has as its

object something qualitatively quite different from raw material."[6] But
montage cannot be used exclusively, Kluge adds; to do so would mean
neglecting the photographic principle that makes montage possible —
"the immediate, identificational representation in which the object of
which I speak is also present in the image." Montage is the means by
which the filmmaker takes these self-contained images and posits a
relationship among them. Once spectators can distinguish between
"two radical poles," two justaposed images, then they "can decode
everything else." Like the sailor who uses the sextant to calculate
relative distances and thus to determine his position at sea, the filmmaker uses montage to take measurements among objects and people.
Montage "is the art of creating proportions."[7]

Kluge insists on the integral meaning of the individual shot,
independent from the constructed whole, and this distinguishes his
work from that of Eisenstein. Critics have suggested, on this account,
that Kluge's compositions should instead be called "collages." Collage
is different from montage; it "collects or sticks its fragments together
in a way that does not entirely overcome their fragmentation. It seeks
to recover fragments as *fragments*,"[8] whereas montage imputes an
overarching relation to the joined fragments. Miriam Hansen counters
that neither the Eisenstein model nor the collage principle is satisfactory to describe Kluge's practice. Encouraging the spectator's own
discourse to "insert itself into the film" in the "empty space between
shots," Kluge develops a montage of overlaid discourses:

> Whereas a concept of montage based on representation, even though
> it be dialectical, still predetermines the position of the spectator in
> its overall design, a concept of montage as discourse allows the
> spectator to choose his or her own distance or involvement; the
> continuous overlayering and unmaking of one discourse by another
> provides both an excess and an indeterminacy of meaning in which
> the spectator's own experience can crystallize.[9]

Kluge has expressed a hostile attitude toward the mimetic tradition in cinema. Echoing the words of Robbe-Grillet's "For a New
Cinema," he complains that the subordination of sound to exclusively
representational uses has led to a narrowness of expression. He
prefers to "literarize" the cinema, that is, to insert literary elements
into his films in order to withhold some of the cinema's power of

visual concreteness. Hence, we find his films, like those of Godard, filled with illustrations from children's books and popular magazines, still photos, film footage that has been refilmed, and printed intertitles. It is as though he feels the strong visual appeal of cinema must be neutralized or somehow restrained before it can be used to its full potential. Kluge's practice thus recalls the principles of Brecht, who first applied the term "literarization" to the theater. "Literarizing," said Brecht, "entails punctuating 'representation' with 'formulation.' "[10] By their use of elements from other media and art forms, Kluge's films gather a dialectical strength. Illusionistic representation is interrupted, short-circuited, by the intervention of "foreign" matter, which subsequently, through collage, modifies the major narrative in a significant manner.

The most common type of intrusive collage element is the intertitle, which Kluge has used in a manner reminiscent of Godard's film practice. In *Part-Time Work of a Domestic Slave,* for example, he clearly states the theme of family life with an intertitle near the beginning of the film that reads: "One would like to embrace all of society and yet one remains in the safe stage of the family."[11] In the same scene, he elaborates on the comforts of the nuclear family by cutting in old-fashioned pictures that we associate with early reading primers and that bear such titles as "From the Children's Room," "All Eyes Are on You," and "It Is Good to Rest After Work." This powerful sequence, composed basically as a collage, permits Kluge to represent the family as both the primary social unit of safety and comfort and an outmoded institution that promotes false consciousness.

It is in these terms that Kluge can be said to have an "antagonistic" attitude toward realism: In his films, events are depicted not in an effort to have them conform to some preordained notion of what is real but rather to induce in the spectator a questioning attitude.

Kluge's cinematic enterprise is closely tied to a new conception of history. Basing his work on the conviction that individuals are not wholly determined by history but rather generate their own histories, he develops a narrative strategy by which history is seen as a "phantasmagoric construct of reality."[12] *Yesterday Girl* is a film that interrogates the relationship between individuals and the history that is foisted upon them. The protagonist, Anita G., is a prototypically deracinated individual who crosses from East to West Germany and is asked over and over again to explain her background, her history. As a Jew born during Adolf Hitler's rise to power, her being "on the run" is presented as her inevitable condition. She becomes, in Kluge's words, a "seismograph" of the discrepancies that exist between the official version of the recent past and people's actual words, gestures, and attitudes. Figures of authority, such as a female probation officer and a university professor, provide advice for Anita in a professional rhetoric of which she — and the spectator — can make no sense.

Anita G. first appears in a short story that bears her name.[13] In that story, Kluge goes into detail about her vagrancy. Always on the run because of unpaid bills or a jumped probation sentence, Anita G. roams from one end of Germany to another. She tries to find a man who will protect her, but each time she discovers a suitable lover the law catches up with her and she is forced to flee. Section titles such as "Need for protection," "Hostile Nature," and "Persecution, protegé, two alternatives" clearly thematize the diverse elements of Anita's dilemma. The story ends with Anita giving birth to a child in jail, where she has gone to seek refuge. The child is then taken to a state institution, and Anita has a nervous breakdown, which is brought under control with penicillin. This final detail sheds light on the inefficacy of the state penal and medical institutions, suggesting that Anita's condition is no more psychological than a virus and that there is perhaps an equivalent virus running through the veins of the state apparatus.

Kluge's questioning of traditional views of the state and contemporary history is taken even further in his film *The Patriot* through the principal character, Gabi Teichert, a history teacher committed to discovering ways of communicating history as it really was. The title of the film is ironic because, early in her quest, Gabi discovers that she will have difficulty rendering German history in a patriotic way. Instead, she interviews people and attends important political events, such as the Social Democratic party convention, in order to inquire into "all the dead of the empire." However, this enterprise does not remain pure necrology; Gabi soon begins to direct her attention less to the dead and more to those parts of memory that have been erased by official versions of history. In telling her story, Kluge suggests another novel usage for cinematic practice: as a "construction site." Cinema becomes the site for a reconstitution of the possibilities of memory (as in Resnais's *Hiroshima mon amour*) rather than the mausoleum of embalmed images that Bazin once described it as. This reconstitution would be, if not of the memory of the repressed material itself, that of the memory of the discourse of repression.

An American author whose work bears interesting parallels with that of Kluge is Walter Abish. In his *How German Is It?* (1979), Abish recounts a story of contemporary Germany in which the characters fail to recognize the signs of lingering Nazism around them. In a crucial scene, work crews digging up a street to do pipeline repairs uncover a huge mass burial pit. The perpetuation of the signs of the Third Reich is made gradually more evident as the story unfolds, with nothing more telling than a scene in which one of the main characters ominously raises his right arm in the famous "Sieg Heil" salute as he undergoes a hypnotic cure. As in Kluge's *Attendance List for a Funeral,* where the main point is that the Germans' retention of the past is determined exclusively by motives of private gain and individual reputation, Abish's text graphically demonstrates that even the most thoroughly repressed material will resurface.

Kluge and Abish share the narrative technique of setting up a situation in which a moral or political lesson can be neatly demonstrated. Far from allegory or *Tendenzliteratur* (a work aimed at following a particular ideological line), this method produces in the reader or spectator sudden, often comic, shocks of recognition. For instance, Kluge demonstrates the prejudicial nature of the notion of "newsworthiness" in a scene in *Part-Time Work of a Domestic Slave* when Roswitha, the heroine, goes with her friend Sylvia to a newspaper office in an effort to convince the editors to print a story about dangerous auto accidents and the lack of proper safety precautions. The editors make it clear that page one of their paper is reserved for political items. After objecting that "this is a political item!" Roswitha concludes that what is political depends on what interests the newspaper represents. "Do you seriously think," she asks the editors, "the fact that Goppel may possibly resign in 1974 is more important than the fact that five thousand children will die in the next five years?" [14]

The film ends with an even more pointed and pithy instance of the object lesson. As a result of Roswitha's political activities, her husband has lost his job. Roswitha is forced to sell sausages out in front of the factory where her husband used to work. She wraps the sausages in political leaflets. A security officer, peering through binoculars, recognizes Roswitha from her previous activities. "Sausages aren't dangerous in themselves," he declares. "But there's something behind this. This business must have some meaning. But what?"[15] In this way he sums up, unwittingly, the situation of the worker and the film viewer: Just as the sausages are cloaked in a message that may enlighten the people who buy them, so the entire process of buying and selling is mystified by a system — at once economic and psychological — of commodity fetishism.

Kluge's work may appear more "idea"-oriented than that of any other contributor to this volume. If his writing is more "political" than that of most filmmakers and writers, it is because he considers both writing and filmmaking to be institutions that can be understood only in a particular social and historical context. If his filmmaking seems less "pure" than most others', it is because he insists on the material heterogeneity of cinema. Never reluctant to introduce seemingly extraneous matter into the film text, be it from literature or from a popular magazine, Kluge welcomes the opportunity of subverting the ordinary relations between sound elements and visual elements. Most important, Kluge views film production and reception as part of the broad public sphere that constitutes today's culture. Cinema plays a crucial role in mediating between the interests of a bourgeois power structure and the needs of individuals. As such, it puts the very notion of production in a new light. According to Kluge:

> The concept of production not only includes the manufacturing of the film but also its exhibition and appropriation by the imagination of the spectator. One might even reverse this argument: It is the spectator who actually produces the film, as the film on screen sets in motion the film in the mind of the spectator.[16]

Notes

1. Miriam Hansen, "Cooperative Auteur Cinema and Oppositional Public Sphere: Alexander Kluge's Contribution to *Germany in Autumn*," *New German Critique* 24–25 (Fall/Winter 1981–82):39.

2. Alexander Kluge, "On Film and the Public Sphere," *New German Critique* 24–25 (Fall/Winter 1981–82):211.

3. "On Film and the Public Sphere" appeared in the special double issue of *New German Critique* on New German Cinema ([Fall/Winter 1981–82]:206–20).

4. Kluge, "On Film and the Public Sphere," p. 215.

5. Brecht's discussion of the Krupps factory appears in *Der Dreigroschenprozess, Gesammelte Werke* (Frankfurt: Suhrkamp, 1967), vol. 18, p. 161. It was discussed and translated in part by Ben Brewster, "Brecht and the Film Industry," *Screen* 16, no. 4 (Winter 1975–76):16–33.

6. Kluge, "On Film and the Public Sphere," p. 219.

7. Ibid., pp. 219–20.

8. Brian Henderson quoted in Miriam Hansen, "Alexander Kluge: Crossings Between Film, Literature, Critical Theory," in S. Bauschinger, S. L. Cocalis, and H. A. Lea, eds., *Film und Literatur: Literarische Texte und der neue deutsche Film* (Bern: Francke Verlag, 1984), p. 172.

9. Ibid., p. 182.

10. *Brecht on Theater,* edited and translated by J. Willett (New York: Hill & Wang, 1964), p. 43.

11. Jan Dawson, *Alexander Kluge and* The Occasional Work of a Female Slave [translation, with variant title, of screenplay of *Gelegenheitsarbeit einer Sklavin* plus interview with Kluge] (New York: Zoetrope, 1977), p. 187. Subsequent references to the screenplay are to this edition.

12. Miriam Hansen, "The Stubborn Discourse: History and Story-Telling in the Films of Alexander Kluge," *Persistence of Vision* 2, no. 4 (1985):22.

13. In *Attendance List for a Funeral* (New York: McGraw-Hill, 1966).

14. Dawson, *Alexander Kluge and* The Occasional Work of a Female Slave, p. 17.

15. Ibid., p. 24.

16. Kluge quoted in Hansen, "Cooperative Auteur Cinema," p. 39.

Alexander Kluge

Word and Film

I.

Experts and publicists have proposed a whole series of views on film and language. These views resemble and contradict each other.[1] Statements chosen at random, corresponding to various conceptions of film, have one thing in common: they proceed from a fixed notion of film as well as an established, or presumably established, notion of language. The issue at hand, however, requires going beyond such general definitions. As trivial as it may sound, words can interact with film in a hundred different ways. Add to this the diversity of conceptions of film. For every one of these conceptions, for every kind of literary expression, the issue presents itself differently and demands a different answer. Walter Hagemann argues that film does not raise any new questions, "because it does not speak a new language; rather it conveys the old language through a new medium. This is the real reason for the backlash which the language of film suffered with the advent of sound."[2] We have to examine how the old language relates to the old film, how new forms of language available today relate to new concepts of film, and how the interplay of word and film may produce new, nonliterary forms of language. Given the essay format, we can only outline a set of problems, we cannot offer any solutions. The following speculations, therefore, are merely intended as examples.

This essay, coauthored with Edgar Reitz and Wilfried Reinke, was originally published as "Wort und Film," in *Sprache im technischen Zeitalter*, no. 13 (1965), pp. 1015–30; this version, translated by Miriam Hansen, is reprinted from *October*, vol. 46, pp. 179–98 with the permission of the Massachusetts Institute of Technology. The authors are teachers at the Hochschule für Gestaltung at Ulm, where Kluge and Reitz founded the Film Department in 1965.

II.

In the cultural history of the cinema, the transition to sound marks a radical break. In the beginning of the silent era, films often consisted of lengthy shots of theatrically staged scenes. This method proved problematic when making the transitions from one scene to the next. The principle of montage was the answer to this problem of transition, which could not have been solved otherwise. Montage, in turn, set free a whole range of forms of filmic expression. Without montage, neither the German, nor the Russian, nor the French cinema of the 1920s would have been conceivable. With the introduction of sound, however, film — or rather, commercial film — reverted to the naturalism towards which it had aspired in its early stages. Thus, the addition of sound actually entailed an impoverishment rather than the extraordinary opportunity that it could have been and should be today; this is why Chaplin, in his first sound films, used sound so sparingly, if at all.

As Walter Benjamin has shown, film works on the principle of attention without concentration; the viewer is distracted. This disposition permits film images to move along by association, which involves temporal gaps between shots as well as leaps of logic. The introduction of sound, then, makes it possible to create polyphonic effects which before could only have been deployed successively. François Truffaut, for instance, uses verbal effects like adjectives in conjunction with particular images; other films utilize various registers of sound and thus achieve an epic[3] multiplicity of layers. The current movement in filmmaking, which can be observed on an international level, points toward an emancipation of film sound, in particular of verbal language. These films make it difficult to determine whether speech is subordinated to action, image to speech, or action to theme, or vice versa. The films as they are elude this kind of hierarchical definition.

Why are such innovations so hard to accomplish in Germany? Why does the emancipation of film encounter such powerful obstacles? A major reason for this is the intellectual indifference of German film productions — they just have not contained an idea in years. Apart from the particular conditions in Germany, however, two other reasons have been important. (1) The pressures of naturalism: Allegedly, audiences who are interested in nothing but "sitting and staring" do not wish to be disturbed by language they have not heard a hundred times before in the media and everyday life. (2) The demand for coherence and superficial continuity makes every film conform to the model of the novella. "Pure entertainment and what it implies," as Adorno and Horkheimer say, "the relaxed abandoning of the self to diverse associations and happy nonsense, is cut short by what is currently marketed as entertainment; it is impeded by the surrogate of a coherent meaning by means of which the culture industry insists on ennobling its products, while actually misusing them admittedly as a pretext for the presentation of stars."[4] This procedure is typical of conventional commercial films, but it can also be found in films produced with artistic intentions. Cinema is hampered in this regard by modelling itself on the genre of the novella, which prevents cinema from developing its epic possibilities. Only in the epic ranges of film, however, could language fully unfold. As far as the construction of plots is concerned, even silent film, with its limited registers, could do better than the multi-level sound film.

III.

Let us compare film and literature as modes of expression, choosing two examples at random. Is film capable of condensation? Can film attain the same expressive effects as highly differentiated language? Can film be precise? Helmut Heissenbüttel recently quoted the following sentences from Barbey d'Aurevilly's *The She-Devils* [1874]: "and to all this fury she replied like the female of the species [*Frauenzimmer*], who no longer has any reason to care, who knows the man she lives with down to his bones, and who knows that at the bottom of this pigsty of a common household lies eternal warfare. She was not as coarse as he, but more atrocious, more insulting, and more cruel in her coldness than he was in his anger."[5] With prose of such a high degree of figuration, film cannot compete.

Film cannot form metaphoric concepts [*Oberbegriffe*] (pigsty of a common household, fits of fury) or clichés (the female of the species); it is not capable of antithetical discourse on such a level of abstraction; it can never condense in such a manner; finally, film does not have the means to imitate the internal movement of language — which is what distinguishes this text — unless the filmmaker decides to quote the text. It might be interesting to imagine ways in which the event described could be rendered in filmic terms. This would probably require a short film of about twenty minutes, which could be broken down into the following sequences:

— study of the argument between husband and wife;
— study of irritated, reactive behavior of this woman and of women in general;
— study of marital habits;
— study of the habit of loving someone "down to the bones";
— the helplessness of both in the course of a long marriage, largely on the part of the husband;
— the history of the bourgeois marriage over the past two hundred years;
— the condition of eternal warfare;
— the biological superiority of the woman, her coldness;
— visual analysis of the conflict by means of a montage sequence which alternates, over an extended period of time, between the facial expression of the woman and that of the man, thus conveying the disproportionate and asynchronic nature of their struggle.

This filmic treatment would attempt, with great effort, to destroy the superficial sense of precision which film conveys on account of its excessive visual presence [*Anschauung*]; likewise, one would have to recover the degree of abstraction inherent in language by accumulating details. Only then would a film be capable of achieving any degree of conceptual precision.

As is well known, language has an advantage over film, owing to several thousand years of tradition. Modern Western languages derive from the differentiated languages of antiquity, which in turn are influenced by more archaic languages. If the cinema were to cultivate the narrative forms necessary to cope with the Barbey text over a longer period of history, at a later date a whole range of filmic metaphors would be available to filmmakers, allowing them to achieve the same economy of narration as is now available in the figurative and conceptual ranges of language. Even today we can discern developments in this direction. Louis Malle, for instance, alludes to individual films by Chaplin and thus evokes the aura of Chaplin's oeuvre as a whole. Another instance would be the conventions of a genre like the western, which can be quoted and repeated with figurative brevity. Most of the more recent westerns are animated by allusions to the old clichés of western narratives. The stagecoach, the entry into the saloon, the beginning of the showdown, the new sheriff, the almost masochistic position of the drunk judge, the iconography of the western hero, and the code of honor that binds all participants — through all these elements the accumulated aura of the genre is present in each individual western. This opens up a space for ambiguity, polyphony, and variation, which, as is well known, has often made the western a vehicle for political, social, and psychoanalytic messages; it might just as well encourage poetic modes of expression. Only when the cinema will have sufficiently enlarged its tradition of figuration will it be able to develop abstractions and differentiations comparable to those of literature. Because it already includes language anyway, film would actually have the capacity to articulate meanings that elude the grasp of verbal expression. Contemporary cinema, however, is not prepared for this project, since neither film production nor the spectator has as yet realized film's verbal and visual possibilities. The cinema, as we see it at this point, is not merely in the hands of the film authors (just as literature is not the product of writers alone), but is a form of expression which depends as much upon the receptivity of a social formation as on the imagination of its authors. A truly sophisticated film language requires a high level of filmic imagination on the part of spectators, exhibitors, and distributors alike.

Such a project, however, meets with almost total opposition from the cultural establishment, which regards the contamination of human minds by filmic images as a disastrous development. Instead, there is a tendency to impose upon the cinema the aesthetic ideals of the classical arts (which, in this context, could be said to include still photography). This creates a kind of visual "culture" which, in effect, robs film of its specific means of expression. The misleading ideal of the priority of image over word derives from a contemplative, purist position whose proponents dismiss filmic expression or content as merely secondary, a position that ultimately results in formalism. A cinema split between, on the one hand, the formalism of experimental film (whose experiments do not seek any new experience but rather aim to perpetuate a metaphysical "state of transition") and, on the other, the superficial naturalism of narrative film will never be able to compete with the great tradition of literary language.

Would a twenty-minute adaptation of the two sentences by Barbey have a substantially different, or even more complex, meaning than those two sentences? The film would have to use language, over and above the image track. Language in this case would not be literature, but an integrated part of the film. Compared to the literary source, the film would probably fall short of the precision achieved there; in terms of visual detail, however, it would be superior to the written text. At first sight, this would produce an effect similar to that which would have been produced if Marcel Proust had used the Barbey text to satisfy his own narrative proclivities for fifty to three hundred pages. The film would still remain on the side of visual presence. Yet the analytic capability of the camera might afford additional perspectives on the subject matter which would go beyond subjective experience. Thus we would have an accumulation of subjective and objective, of literary, auditory, and visual moments which would preserve a certain tension in relation to each other. This tension would make itself felt, among other places, in the gaps which montage created between the disparate elements of filmic expression. In layering expressive forms in such a manner, the film would succeed in concentrating its subject matter in the spaces between the forms of expression. For the material condensation of expression does not happen in the film itself but in the spectator's head, in the gaps between the elements of filmic expression. This kind of film does not posit a passive viewer "who just wants to sit and stare." Obviously such a conception of cinema remains a utopian project, given the limited ambitions of both film producers and audiences today; in the future, however, cinema could surpass even the tradition of literature, at least in certain aspects. The combination of verbal, auditory, and visual forms and their integration through montage enable film to strive for a greater degree of complexity than any of these forms in isolation. At the same time, the multiplication of materials harbors all the dangers of the *Gesamtkunstwerk* [total work of art].[6]

The relatively greater precision available to literary language is not merely a blessing. Centuries of tradition have endowed language with such polish and refinement that it has become immune to large areas of reality. Every expression, according to Kant, oscillates between concept [*Begriff*] and sensuous perception [*Anschauung*]. "Perception without concept is blind; concept without perception remains empty." Throughout most of its metaphors and expressions, language has settled into a compromise between these two poles; it is neither concrete nor really abstract. Film, by contrast, combines the radical concreteness of its materials with the conceptual possibilities of montage; thus it offers a form of expression which is as capable of a dialectical relationship between concept and perception as is verbal language without, however, stabilizing this relationship, as language is bound to do. This opens up particular opportunities for the insertion of literary language into film, especially because it might help rid that language of some of its literary constraints.

Let us raise the question from the reverse angle. Is film capable of controlling its degree of precision? Can film refract or deconstruct [*auflösen*] a given expression? How can it maintain a sufficient degree of indeterminacy? Does film have the option of remaining imprecise? Literary language can easily do so by using a conventional expression as a stylistic device. "When the secretary opened the door, a young lady, pretty as a picture and dressed to tease, entered the room" — such a phrase could not be reproduced in filmic terms. Film does not grant the variety of impressions that words like *pretty as a picture* and *dressed to tease* or *young lady* may provoke in the imagination of different readers; the image always refers to an individual instance. This could be counteracted somewhat by devices such as an extreme long shot or close-up, both of which introduce a high degree of indeterminacy. Likewise, iconic information can be reduced by means of shallow focus, high contrast, shots of extreme brevity or duration, transgressions of chronological order, multiple exposure, negation of the image track through sound or written text. All these, and other devices that one might use to achieve the effect of indeterminacy, are devices that interfere with reality and that question the apparent concreteness of iconic information. If a film were to give its viewers conceptual instructions as they are implied in phrases like *dressed to tease,* for instance, or *pretty as a picture,* it would have to resort to concrete clichés — which is what Hollywood films tend to do. We conclude, therefore, that film, insofar as it uses its resources legitimately, cannot convey any really precise mental images.

We cannot ignore the fact that producers of commercial films, like those of dime novels, have no intention whatsoever of disturbing the massive circulation of their products by anything that resembles precise description. The empty shells of literary commonplaces, such as abound in bad novels, are ideally suited for deploying narrative clichés. In the course of its history, conservative narrative cinema has succeeded in amalgamating the prefabricated forms of imagination with prefabricated vernacular language, so that people have come to expect this amalgam from any narrative film. If the pretty young lady above actually were to appear in a film, this event would be read in a way similar to its literary equivalent. Nonetheless, commercial cinema has to keep reestablishing the basis of these conventions. While literary commonplaces may have a certain degree of legitimacy, since they appeal to something in the reader's imagination which is not yet totally absorbed by cliché, and while such commonplaces may even be stylistically necessary, as for instance in Madame de Lafayette's *Princess of Clève* or in Brecht's plays, film inevitably distorts reality when it typifies. For film allows inference from the concrete only in the direction of a cliché; yet it is incapable of creating a general image of concrete multiplicity. The question remains whether or not individual films can avoid this dilemma through particular uses of language, for instance by speaking about things on the sound track which will not appear on the image track.

IV.

There are no rules for combining word and image in film. We can roughly distinguish between modes of dialogue, modes of commentary, and more independent combinations of word and image.

Dialogue

Narrative cinema promotes the fictitious ideal of realistic dialogue. This type of dialogue is supposed to accompany the image track in a "natural" manner. Dialogue is motivated by narrative action, or all too often substitutes for action. Such is the case not only in commercial films, but also in films that simply adopt stage conventions to the screen, for example, *Twelve Angry Men* [1957; directed by Sidney Lumet, based on a play by Reginald Rose], *Les jeux sont faits* [1947; directed by Jean Delannoy, based on a play by Sartre], *The Time of Your Life* [1948; directed by H. C. Potter, based on a play by William

Saroyan]. In either case, both language and the image track are subject to the regime of narrative. Such a concept of dialogue hinges on the belief that narrative events relate to each other as an organic whole, that drama is still possible. Take a film like *Password: Heron* [*Kennwort: Reiher,* Rudolf Jugert, 1964], recently awarded the Federal Film Prize; consider, for instance, the moment at which the characters note, via dialogue, that they "have been waiting here for hours." Immediately following the accidental killing of a patriot, a man emerges from a completely different chain of dramatic events and happens to identify the dead "comrade," whom he had not seen in twenty years, and thus the enigma gets resolved. The entanglement comes about, in the first place, because the hero stumbles into the very center of the French Resistance, led by an old man who, on the basis of a parallel chain of events dating back to World War I, is bound to misunderstand the hero. If measured against a strictly realistic standard, such dramaturgy (unlike that of Ibsen, who first invented this kind of dramaturgical incest) would collapse. At the same time, such films are defined by a grotesque effort to make the illusion appear realistic. Realism in this sense extends only to the detail; the film as a whole remains in the realm of fiction. It is a realism without enlightenment, a realism intended to cover up the fact that once more we have been cheated out of reality.

It has become apparent that, as a rule of thumb, dialogue is not a suitable means for advancing action. Moreover, dialogue is a specialized branch of film production, which is to say that the texts are written by specialists as mere supplements to the image track. As we see in the work of Antonioni, however, the function of dialogue can just as well be taken over by the image track, while spoken dialogue is carried along like a shell or fossil. Spoken dialogue in this case does not tell us anything about the actual inner movements of the film; dialogue loses its function as dialogue. "We have replaced dialogue with the communiqué," as Camus says. One might add that, precisely because it no longer serves any narrative purpose, dialogue is now available as a medium of reflection. When the prostitutes in Jean-Luc Godard's *Vivre sa vie* [1962] quote Montaigne, when Zazie and the other characters in Louis Malle's film *Zazie dans le métro* [1960] spout argot, their speech no longer has anything to do with Ionesco or Samuel Beckett; on the contrary, moments like these, when dialogue is actually not needed, allow for the development of specifically cinematic forms of expression. Godard and other film authors realize this opportunity when they apply to dialogue the same principles of montage as to the image track.

Voice-Over Commentary

Voice-over commentary is usually reserved for documentary film. It has the reputation of being "uncinematic," not only because it seems to be tied to a particular subject matter, but also because it assumes a certain autonomy in coordinating text and image and because it is often merely superimposed over live sound. There seems to be a general injunction against using voice-over in a way that would merely duplicate the events on the image track. This injunction presumes that commentary and a sequence of images are identical if they refer to one and the same thing; as a rule, however, this is not the case. A documentary on industrial work processes, for instance, shows a worker taking a scoop of liquid metal from one container and pouring it into another; voice-over: "The worker removes a small amount of liquid alloy for testing purposes to ensure a consistent quality in the final product." Or, in another film, the voice-over explains: "The extract can be obtained from the abdominal cavity of the dead mouse without difficulty"; the image shows a dead animal laid out on a red surface and rubber-gloved hands manipulating a syringe in its belly.[7] In both instances, the image would remain illegible without the voice-over, and it would take a considerable amount of demonstration to produce the same meaning.

Voice-over commentary is not limited to documentary film; it may also be used in fictional genres — as, indeed, it has been — with interesting effects. Narrative events tend to come across in different ways depending on whether they are enacted on the image track or narrated by a voice-over. A double-track description may stylize an event and produce a mutual distancing effect [*Verfremdungseffekt*], as it calls attention to the material difference of verbal and visual expression. The voice-over in this case may be identifiable as that of a particular character within the diegesis — and thus associated with a particular narrative function — or the voice could be altogether foreign to the narrative.

A special case in this context is the insertion of written titles. This practice has a tradition of its own dating back to the silent era. Whereas at that time written titles were the only way of confronting image and language, their special effect today is one of muteness. The result is an overlay of filmic events with the inner voice of the reading spectator — the spectator has to assume a more active role. The language of written titles, which does not assume any particular voice and thus cannot really be attached to characters within the diegesis, is even further removed from the filmic events than any conceivable form of voice-over. This greater distance, however, gives it an affinity with literary language. The increased participation of the spectator, in turn, creates a peculiar identification of the meaning of this language with the visually concretized events of the film (a recent impressive example in this respect is Godard's *Vivre sa vie*). Written language may enter a film in a variety of shapes and combinations: e.g., text superimposed upon moving images, inserts of written text, or text superimposed upon background images [*Stehkader*]. Writing may even push images aside completely; whole passages of film could consist of writing; written and spoken texts could be interwoven in many different ways.

Language at Liberty

Under this rubric, we are dealing with language that, detached from narrative events, accompanies and colors the image track, language that is not motivated by any subjective or objective point of view as is the case with dialogue or commentary. Examples of such use of language can be found in *Hiroshima mon amour* [1959] by Marguerite Duras and Alain Resnais, in *The Parallel Street* [*Parallelstrasse*, 1961] by Ferdinand Khittl, in *Moderato cantabile* by Peter Brook [1960; text by Duras], and in other films. Its mode may be recitation, poetic mediation, or "nonsense language," as in *Zazie*. In the cinema, words may be used more freely than in their usual syntactic or grammatical configurations. Film permits the disruption of the linear sequence of scenes, as well as of individual shots. In the field of literature, an author like Hans G. Helms tries to liberate language from the conventions of grammar and existing vocabulary. Nonetheless, his writing depends upon elements of literary language. If he abandoned even those tenuous semantic links, he would lose the last means of conveying expression, an objective to which even a writer like Helms is still committed. We could imagine, however, an experimental film (albeit one of extreme artistic intensity) which forcefully utilizes the oscillation between literary, visual, and auditory elements as well as the gaps between these elements; such a film might succeed in producing clusters of expression which are not required to yield meaning down to the last detail, which can be understood without having to be prefabricated or historically reconstructed. In a world in which everyone else conforms to rational reason, someone at least could be unreasonable. Since the totalizing quest for meaning has itself become irrational, literary language should be shifted to areas in which it is not totally subjected to the imperative of meaning, as it is in its proper field. Language in film may be blind.

V.

We have been speaking of possibilities; let us now focus on actual instances and develop some criteria for the combination of language and film.

(1) Michelangelo Antonioni, *L'Avventura* (1959), scene 3.

Text:

SANDRO: Would you like me in profile?
SANDRO: What is it? Is something wrong with me?
SANDRO: But your friend is waiting for you downstairs.
ANNA: She'll wait.

Image:

Sandro's apartment: a small room with white stucco walls, crowded with books and draftsman's materials. He moves across the room quickly, straightening his things.

He puts a towel in the bathroom. Anna runs up the stairs leading to the room and they embrace as she reaches the top. They part, and she stares at him intently. Walking to the center of the room, she turns around to stare at him again; then she turns away, drops her bag on a table, and goes to the balcony window. Sandro advances uncertainly to the center of the room and Anna stares again, appraising him with her eyes, judging.

Sandro faces her, somewhat baffled by her silence and the intensity of her regard.

He puts his suitcase down and strikes a pose of mock nobility, turning sideways.

Anna circles him slowly and silently, then begins to unbutton her dress, looking back at him to see his reaction.

She walks toward the bedroom; he follows.

Anna enters the bedroom, and through the grillwork of the bedstead, we see her remove her dress. Sandro walks in and, finding her in her slip, takes her in his arms and kisses her.

Anna presses herself up against him with such a violent passion that Sandro is somewhat dismayed. But only for an instant. Soon they are feverishly kissing each other, and it is almost with a sense of sheer animal pleasure that Sandro abandons himself.[8]

Commentary: What actually goes on between the two characters takes place on the image track. Detached from the image track, the text would not make sense. It does not consist of ordinary, "natural" speech, but a highly stylized form of language. This is even more evident at other points in the script. The difference between the inner movement of the filmic image and the movement of the dialogue paradoxically makes us aware of the sound of language. This device can also be found in films by Roman Polanski and Louis Malle.

(2) Alain Resnais, Marguerite Duras, *Hiroshima mon amour (1959)*.

Image and text: (*The streets of Hiroshima, more streets. Bridges. covered lanes. Streets. Suburbs. Railroad tracks. Suburbs. Universal banality.*)

SHE: . . . I meet you.
       I remember you.
       Who are you?
       You kill me.
       You feel good to me.
       How could I have known that this city was made to the size of
          love?
       How could I have known that you were made to the size of my
          body?
       I like you. How great. I like you.
       What slowness all of a sudden.
       What softness.

> More than you can know.
> You kill me.
> You feel good to me.
> You kill me.
> You feel good to me.
> I've got the time.
> Please.
> Devour me.
> Deform me, make me ugly.
> Why not you?
> Why not you in this city and in this night so much like the
>   others you can't tell the difference?
> Please . . .

(Very abruptly the woman's face appears, filled with tenderness, turned toward the man's.)

SHE: It's extraordinary how beautiful your skin is.

(He sighs.)
> You . . .

(His face appears after the woman's. He bursts out into an ecstatic laughter that has nothing to do with their words.)[9]

Commentary: Here we have a pure instance of parallelism between image and literary text. The image track does not settle on any particular scene; instead, moving shots of bridges and streets dissolve into each other and form a kind of impressionist tableau. This tableau effect also emanates from the sound track. The visual texture colors the language; the spoken text modifies the meaning of the image track. Both resonate with associations of Hiroshima/Nevers — love, death, and so on. The method of composition is basically the same as in music by Richard Wagner or Richard Strauss. The film here taps emotional connotations which exist in the social imaginary, in the spectator's head, rather than in the film itself. Without this point of reference, images and words would disintegrate, as would the Duras text, with its abrupt changes of mood. The immersion of language in image, the emergence of language from image, the mutual pursuit of verbal and visual texts, figures of parallelism and collision, polyphony — all these word/image constellations can be found in this work and in Resnais's other films as well. Even if one resents the pathos of the texts, one has to acknowledge Resnais's originality.

(3) Ferdinand Khittl, *The Parallel Street* (1961).

Image track:

A title card with the number 305. Documentary footage of Tahiti, an island in the Pacific: shots of a fishing expedition, of a girl named Roarai, of whaling, of a seaplane starting and landing in the laguna between a coral reef and the beach. Then a series of shots from the burial site "at the big rock" near the capital of Madagaskar, Tananarive: the ceremony of Famadhina, the so-called turning of the dead. A body that has been dead for three years is disinterred and given a new shroud, a "lamba." The corpse remains laid out for twenty-four hours, surrounded by dancing and celebrations; then it is returned to the burial chamber.

Sound track:

"The plane is due at eight. If you have ever been in love, you know that the plane can come at any time. That it always comes at eight. The farewell without meaning recalls the spot behind the ear. The arc below the knee. To arrive only to say good-bye. Having never before thought of the warmth of this hair.

"Everyone listens to the dying odor of the old fish. The airplane comes at eight. Try not to think of it: the heart has already given up. A forgotten caress — your skin. A boat without wings, its sails smelling of hibiscus flowers. *Ia ora na* — welcome."[10]

Commentary: The text in this case confronts a rather stark, naive image track. The author of the images and the writer are two different individuals who evidently did not succeed in integrating their respective intentions. The image track diverts attention to some degree from the bombastic quality of the text; but as a result, image and text move along in a rather disconnected manner. The effect at first is one of surprise, owing to the juxtaposition of unrelated elements; also, the fixed speed of the film tends to impair our literary judgment in a way that does not hold in the case of reading a written text. Such surprise tactics, however, will not produce a cinematic integration of word and image. The words spill over the margins of the image. A film does not acquire a poetic quality through words alone. Nonetheless, *The Parallel Street* enjoyed a considerable success at various festivals, in particular with the leading French reviewers at Cannes in 1964. This once again confirms the impression that if one arbitrarily accumulates interesting ingredients and adds some sort of text, one ends up with an arbitrary product that may still reap success, since "he who gives generously, offers something to everyone."

(4) Orson Welles, *Citizen Kane* (1941): a sequence from the "News on the March" section.

Text and image:

Its humble beginnings, in this ramshackle building, a dying daily.	Street. Truck passing to left exits, showing old Inquirer Building in background — three colored men standing at left by window — one skates across to right . . .
Kane's empire, in its glory, held dominion over thirty-seven newspapers, two syndicates, a radio network, an empire upon an empire.	Picture of map of U.S. Circles widening out on map.
The first of grocery stores . . .	Building. Camera shooting across street to Kane grocery store — convertible car passing in foreground.
. . . paper mills . . .	Mill. Huge roll of paper moving up to foreground.
. . . apartment buildings . . .	Street. Camera shooting up over trees to row of apartments at right background.

. . . factories . . .	Factory. Camera shooting over smokestacks of a factory, steam pouring out of them.
. . . forests . . .	Lake. Man in foreground — tree crashing into lake below in background.
. . . ocean liners.	Ocean. Camera shooting down to liner moving to foreground below.[11]

Commentary: This is an example of voice-over used in a fictional context. Of course, *Citizen Kane* also uses dialogue that differs little from conventional dramatic dialogue and obviously is not crucial to the textual and stylistic principles of the film. The voice-over commentary in this sequence more or less describes what we see on the image track. One could say that the image illustrates the text just as the text illustrates the image. When the voice-over speaks of "forests," the image track uses the rhetorical device of *pars pro toto* and shows a tree. When the text concerns the perspective of a whole continent through a long shot so extreme as to suggest that the continent could not be captured in a single image, the voice-over implies this extensity by way of enumeration. When connotations of "humble" and "ramshackle" dominate the commentary, three black people can be seen in one of the lower windows of the building. The mutual energizing of text and image is rather schematic, but at the same time incredibly robust. *Citizen Kane* is the kind of film in which neither sound nor image track, in itself, has much artistic distinction, although together they constitute a work of art.

It would be interesting to explore further examples of the interaction of word and film, especially in the large realm of commercial film. The current use of language in film is likely to come across as highly dilettante. Often an especially badly written text serves to underscore the common remark, "the camera work was excellent." On the map of the arts, film has always been placed next to photography. As a thorough inquiry into the history of cinematic forms would probably show, film has a much greater affinity with literature than with photography.

VI.

Cinema depends upon language not only within each film but also through all the stages of preparation and planning. Without highly differentiated skills of articulation, no filmmaker can approach the realization of his ideas. Author, cinematographer, and producer need to communicate with each other, a task for which the prevailing jargon of the industry is crudely inadequate. The unnecessary hierarchy that determines the production process of special features is just one aspect of this lack of verbal differentiation; another is the "speechlessness" which characterizes the studio sound of the ordinary commercial film. The organizational structure of film production in Germany only aggravates these problems; but these problems are not intrinsic to filmmaking, nor is the prevailing organization of production unalterable. According to a well-known nineteenth-century German thinker and political economist, all thought is mediated by language. Unlike the classical arts (and even television, which actually employs a considerable number of intellectuals), cinema has to compensate for a lack of tradition. Therefore, cinema is in a situation different from that of the classical arts, whose very purpose is to escape tradition. German cinema would benefit greatly from intellectual centers, which would have to be established independently from the commercial centers of production so as to exert influence upon the latter. Such intellectual centers, however, should above all foster an awareness of the immense lead that literary language still has over the expressive means of the mass media.

Cinema today stands at the crossroads of an important development. On the one hand, we can already envision a complexity of expression that film could achieve and the kind of intellectual institution that would encourage such complexity; on the other hand, we can just as well imagine an institutionalization of filmmaking that would merely canonize the inferior products of the status quo and make film into a specialized branch of the mass media, thus perpetuating the current ratio of ten percent specials to ninety percent regular commercial features. Such films cheat not only the loyal patrons in whose name they pretend to be made, but also those who produce them, not to mention those who expect to see a work of art. It would be better if academies designed to teach that kind of filmmaking did not exist at all. The worst that could happen to film would be to be banished to its own domain.

Notes

1. Authors quoted in the original German version of this text are Walter Hagemann, *Der Film, Wesen und Gestalt*, Heidelberg, 1952; Curt Hanno Gutbrod, *Von der Filmidee zum Drehbuch: Handbuch für Autoren*, Wilhelmshaven, 1954; Béla Balázs, *Der Film: Werden und Wesen einer neuen Kunst*, Vienna, 1961; N. A. Lebedew, *Literatur und Film*, Leipzig, 1954; Fedor Stepun, *Theater und Film*, Munich, 1953; Feldmann, Goergen, Keilhacker, Peters, *Beiträge zur Filmforschung*, Emsdetten, 1961; and Rudolf Arnheim, *Film als Kunst*, Berlin, 1932. — TRANS.

2. Hagemann, *Der Film, Wesen und Gestalt*, pp. 46ff.

3. In addition to its conventional meaning, the term *epic* here invokes the particular connotations of Brecht's concept of epic theater. — TRANS.

4. Max Horkheimer and Theodor W. Adorno, *Dialectic of Enlightenment*, Amsterdam, Querido, 1947, p. 169; translated from the German original.

5. Jules Amédée Barbey d'Aurevilly, "A un dîner d'athées," in *Les diaboliques: les six premières*, Paris, Editions Garnier Frères, 1963, p. 288; translated from both the original and the German version cited in the text.

6. Implied here is a critique of the *Gesamtkunstwerk* as developed in the context of the Frankfurt School. This critique focuses on the ideological trajectory linking Wagner's aesthetics with the total mobilization of effect in both the capitalist culture industry and fascist mass spectacles; cf. Walter Benjamin's epilogue to "The Work of Art in the Age of Mechanical Reproduction" in *Illuminations*, New York, Shocken, 1969; Theodor W. Adorno, *In Search of Wagner* (1937–38), London, New Left Books, 1981, and the chapter on the culture industry in *Dialectic of Enlightenment*, New York, Seabury, 1972. — TRANS.

7. These examples are taken at random from a medical and an industrial documentary. They may sound idiotic, but they highlight the interaction between commentary and images which go beyond mere illustration.

8. Michelangelo Antonioni, *L'Avventura*, New York; Grove; 1969, pp. 15–16; and *Screenplays of Michelangelo Antonioni*, New York, Orion Press, 1963, pp. 99–100.

9. Marguerite Duras and Alain Resnais, *Hiroshima mon amour*, New York, Grove, 1961, pp. 24–25. Translation slightly emended. — ED.

10. Ferdinand Khittl, *Parallelstrasse*, script in *Spectaculum: Texte moderner Filme*, Frankfurt, Suhrkamp, 1961, pp. 346–47.

11. Pauline Kael et al., *The Citizen Kane Book*, New York, Bantam, 1974, pp. 317–18.

Ronald Sukenick, 1932–   5

 onald Sukenick is part of a significant movement that might be called "underground writing." Like the underground filmmakers, these writers eschew commercial distribution, preferring to publish their works at small presses. Their fiction is considered too risky by trade publishers because of the kinds of experiments with language and form they indulge in. The substance of these works, again like their cinematic counterparts, tends to challenge the tacitly accepted tenets of the conventional novel. And to the extent that such tenets are jettisoned, these novelists are relegated to the margin. Sukenick was one of the first to recognize the dilemma faced by American experimental writers: The major publishing houses' monopoly of the market meant a concomitant monopoly on the form and content of novels published. His founding (with Jonathan Baumbach) of the Fiction Collective was aimed at helping to remedy that situation.

A connoisseur of the experimental in literature, Sukenick published a critical work entitled *Wallace Stevens: Musing the Obscure* in 1967. It is significant that his literary publishing career began with a work on Wallace Stevens, one of our greatest modern poets, who was significantly influenced by Mallarmé and the French symbolists. In Sukenick's fiction, we also find an affinity for the kinds of experiments with language and form found in the writings of those late nineteenth-century poets.

Like Mallarmé, he seems attracted to the idea of a book about nothing. His novel *Out* (1973) literally dies out by means of a typographical system according to which the lines in each chapter are grouped into sections, with chapter 1 composed of nine-line groupings, chapter 2 of eight-line groupings, chapter 3 of seven-line groupings, and so on. The last chapter is made up of single lines of increasing fragmentation, with the last page reading:

this way this way this way this way this way this way this

way out this

way out [1]

Out is a paradigm of the contemporary reflexive novel, laying bare its own machinery at every turn. No sooner do we get to know the characters of the first chapter, Rex, Velma, and Carl, and the circumstances that link them, than we move into a totally different set of events in the next chapter, with Harrold, Trixie, and Jojo. The diminishing number of lines imparts an aleatory feel to certain chapters, as when Harrold phones Information at the start of chapter 8 and asks for "Eight." The next line of the chapter reads "Eight, the voice responds, you're it they hang up Harrold replaces the receiver."[2] Dialogue and action flow together without the usual punctuation cues. Description is almost entirely absent, except when it serves to set the stage for some kind of mystical experience (the book abounds with revelations and frequently takes on an oracular tone):

. . . white seabird wings sweep-

ing sky endures to night stars boat rocks like a cradle way

out R's emptiness floods with flow of S's mind sky dark sea

wash salt smell wave spray ebbs into vacancy around him . . . [3]

As in many modern novels, such as those of Robbe-Grillet, Baumbach, and Stoltzfus, what holds the book together is repetition: Characters in nearly every scene are carrying sticks of dynamite, drivers pick up suspicious-looking hitchhikers, people of all ilks are constantly on the verge of suicide or some other rash act. The characters themselves are held together only by the general notion of the anti-hero. No central protagonist carries on a quest for any coveted object; men and women relate to one another with no more passion than that of the present moment; groups do not seem to represent significant social or political tendencies that we know from our actual world. Sukenick is interested

instead in the consciousness of "marginal" members of society —
those who, though not actually outcasts, lead tawdry lives with only
narrow glimpses of imagination.

His first novel, *Up* (1968), recounts the adventures of, among
others, one Strop Banally, "boy genius of the communications industry." It includes its own review,[4] a party to celebrate the end of the
novel,[5] and unconventional intertitles that read like newspaper head-
lines: "TEEN PUNKS TERRORIZE STRAPHANGERS" and "RED OR DEAD."
The main character is, surprisingly, Ronald Sukenick. By giving his
own name to the protagonist, Sukenick flies in the face of the tradition
according to which the fictional character is clearly separate from the
writer. In *Up*, we are forced to postulate a writer named Sukenick and
a character named Sukenick. The book is not an autobiography; a cross
between the works of Laurence Sterne and Franz Kafka, it includes a
characterization of a person who reflects directly the author's major
preoccupations.

The funniest scenes involve Ronnie and Nancy, a young woman
he lusts after during his last year in high school. Early in the novel, he
tells us that he has seduced her, only to qualify the statement later as
a lie, a case of "adolescent braggadocio."[6] Ronnie finally gets the
opportunity he has been waiting for with Nancy when she invites him
to her apartment. Here, however, he discovers that his beloved has
posed for a number of pornographic publications, including *Prisoner
of Lust* and *Confessions of a Nude Model*. Yet despite this revelation
— or perhaps because of it — Ronnie achieves bliss in Nancy's arms.

Sukenick's prose in this novel vacillates between straight report-
age and fragmentary sense perceptions. His use of fragmentation
brings to mind the cut-up experiments of William Burroughs and Brion
Gysin.

> screen fade skeletal barbed wire corpses hand impaled on electric
> fence stiffen naked in snow robbed of canvas inmate pajamas lie
> denuded in charnel stockpiles . . .[7]

Unlike the stream of consciousness experiments of Joyce and other
early modernists, this unpunctuated prose does not purport to be the
inner thoughts of a character or even the reworked machinations of
some individual consciousness. Instead, it is a carefully composed
collage of impressions, largely nouns, that accumulate into global

images. In *Up,* the global scene is that of a Nazi concentration camp. The fragmented prose serves to defamiliarize the scene, to evoke the camp in a way that prevents the reader from fusing the description with some stereotype of concentration camp crimes. Secondarily, by its lack of grammatical patterns of order and subordination, the writing emphasizes the most gruesome aspects of the mass murders: the tenderness of the whole bodies before they are exterminated, the tangibility of the skin against the snow, the dehumanization of the operation ("charnel stockpiles"). Sukenick has continued, in works that include *The Death of the Novel and Other Stories* (1969), *98.6* (1975), and *Long Talking Bad Condition Blues* (1979), to experiment with outer-limit experiences and characters who are drawn to the out-of-the-ordinary aspects of everyday life. More precisely, he orchestrates the relations among people and circumstances that in a way gives the reader the feeling of uncanniness, or what Freud called *das Unheimlich* (see chapter 3, note 4). As in Baumbach's work, scenes that are initially played "realistically" are subsequently replayed as fantasy. Figures and backgrounds seem less important in themselves than in the interplay they give rise to, or to their potential for inducing déjà vu in the reader. Sukenick aspires to write what one of his characters in *Out* describes: "a book like a cloud that changes as it goes."

Sukenick, well known among other experimenters in fiction, is the founding editor of *The American Book Review,* a monthly review devoted largely to small-press fiction and poetry and to controversial issues affecting American writers and intellectuals. Out of his work with this review came an important critical study, *In Form: Digressions on the Act of Fiction (1985).*

One of the most surprising attitudes he reveals in this critical work is an aversion to the term "experimental." According to Sukenick, all contemporary fiction is "exploratory"; the term "experimental" simply tends to privilege one type of exploration over another. He is tired of the worn-out oppositions between experimental and conventional and between commercial and noncommercial. Fiction writers today, Sukenick claims, begin by questioning the medium itself. In this way, their work remains anterior to all the genres and subgenres of the novel. Rather than endlessly puzzling over what the novel is, we, in our criticism of fiction, "should make a progressive effort to defamiliarize the novel, to de-define fiction, as fiction simultaneously creates and decreates itself."[8]

In these terms, Sukenick's own fiction takes on a metalinguistic quality — that is, as it forges new forms it challenges certain dogmas about the novel as genre. The unpunctuated flow of discourse reaches an apogee in *Long Talking Bad Condition Blues*. The units of this novel result not from chapter breaks but from alternations in spacing. The first section of the novel, made up of evenly spaced, unpunctuated prose describing Carl Drecker and some of his preoccupations, is followed by a section of prose that has large spaces between each group of words:

> then one day it was spring and everything seemed to
> resolve into emerging units   one emerging unit was
> Veronica and Drecker the dentist who started appearing
> very frequently   he started appearing very frequently
> at The Same Thing their new hangout but why . . .[9]

Subsequent sections are spaced as columns on the left side of the page. These three major space patterns become the principle organizing factors in the novel. *Up* alternates between descriptive prose and the fragmentary mode of sensory consciousness. *Out* dwindles away according to a random principle of a decrease in number of lines per page with each succeeding chapter.

A chief characteristic of Sukenick's new novel form, then, is the elevation of spacing and punctuation to the level of global form. In this way, he has created a new mode by which atmosphere and setting become secondary to the patterns created by typography. These patterns, rather than character traits or repeated actions, become the leitmotivs of another kind of fiction.

How, then, do these innovations in literature relate to the cinematic form that Sukenick claims in his essay was so inspiring to him as a developing writer? Sukenick seems to be extremely sensitive to the way movies shape our ways of thinking. In particular, he considers cinema to have educated us about the potentialities of storytelling. It is not so much that movies tell stories in a wholly new way but rather that they "reinstitute story as a way of thinking." For Sukenick, art is not important as a conveyor of truths; nor is it important for its composition of objects or situations. He is interested in process, especially the process of human consciousness as it begins to invent. Thus, the affective projection encouraged by film, radio, and television becomes a dynamic model for a reader-engaged fiction. Far from stultifying the imagination, as some media critics have argued, these popular forms have liberated new ways of perceiving, which, as Sukenick has said elsewhere, is the aim of art: "All art deconditions us so we may respond more fully to experience."[10]

Notes

1. Ronald Sukenick, *Out* (New York: New York University Press, 1967), p. 294.

2. Ibid., p. 28.

3. Ibid., pp. 291–92.

4. Ronald Sukenick, *Up* (New York: Dial Press, 1968), pp. 38–41.

5. Ibid., pp. 323–28.

6. Ibid., p. 170.

7. Ibid., p. 147.

8. *In Form: Digressions on the Act of Fiction* (Carbondale: Southern Illinois University Press, 1985), p. 48.

9. Ronald Sukenick, *Long Talking Bad Condition Blues* (New York: Fiction Collective Two, 1979), p. 12.

10. Quoted in Jerome Klinkowitz, "A Persuasive Account: Working It Out With Ronald Sukenick," *North American Review* 258, no. 2 (Summer 1973):51.

Ronald Sukenick

Film Digression

Going to the movies. Down Graves End Avenue — now MacDonald — under the El past Malamud's delicatessen, location of *The Assistant,* to the Culver Theater Saturday afternoon with the kids. In the boondocks of Brooklyn, the early forties. Every Saturday a ritual in the flickering darkness. Initiation, via electronic ghosts, gigantic shadows, to reality. Because for us, moving from traditional immigrant cultures into an America in process of redefining itself, reality was always elsewhere, and the Culver Theater, cheap, smelly, floor covered with Cracker Jacks, was the authoritative elsewhere for eight-year-olds, spitting us out onto Graves End Avenue after three hours with irresistible pre-fab attitudes, ways to behave, things to want. There was no way to resist. My father always complains about movie prices because he can remember when they cost a nickel, and how he used to help Norma Talmadge with her homework so she could go hang around the Biograph Studio, my mother how her family forbade her to go for a screen test on grounds it was disreputable. But we, the kids, were surrounded, no resistance. Every Saturday we were pulverized and remolded. I still recall that feeling of mental granulation after seeing a double feature. I feel it even now watching TV. The stupefaction of the mind adjusting to the energy and rhythms of the spreading electrosphere. We were the first generation not only dipped in the electronic bath, but left to swim, or sink, in the ambient technology of wave forms. There was, of course, radio. Soap operas, comedy shows, war news, "The Lone Ranger" and Dodgers games. But the radio you could shut off, change the station. Once you entered the Culver, you were in an environment over which you had no control. A little like the Theatre, but the Theatre was Broadway. There were at least ten years between

Reprinted from Ronald Sukenick, *In Form: Digressions on the Act of Fiction* (Carbondale: Southern Illinois University Press, 1985), pp. 83–98, by permission of the publisher.

my first movie and my first Broadway show. Movies were on Broadway, too, but they were also at the Culver and almost anywhere else you happened to be: recorded wave patterns, movable environments.

What did that mean, growing up in the electrosphere? It meant, for one thing, that we were surrounded by stories. Of course, there were books, mostly comic books, image and word. I learned how to read with comic books. But they were stories told through images, the words were mostly dialogue. A lot like the movies, except the movies moved. That was the thing about movies and the radio, they kept moving past your mind like the scenery from a car, except you couldn't go back. They were irreversible and they had their own speed that you had to accommodate to, stories which in that way were a lot like life. And because of that quality, information in the electrosphere was a lot like stories, the anecdotal newsreels, *The March of Time,* current events as "developing stories," history as narrative, not retrospective narrative, not omniscient narrative, but history on the basis of incomplete developing information, the latest bulletins. History in process, as process. The war news on the radio in ongoing installments. This is not like reading *Pride and Prejudice,* or even Hemingway. The old novel, with its implications of depths and perfections, everything captured and understood once and for all, in a static and tightly woven texture for eternity. In the electrosphere there is no eternity. There is only infinity, everything always changing forever. There is no perfect, ultimate statement of anything, because there is no ultimate and no perfection. If it's not right the first time say it again, that might be a little closer, or one thing added to the next might get you there, but if you go back and revise, by the time you're done everything will have moved past you. You'll get a perfect statement of something that's already beside the point, the point being to keep up with the speed of your mind, which is most approximated by the speed of electricity. Growing up in the electrosphere, you learn how to deal with speed, the speed at which information comes in at you, the speed of assimilating it, developing new integrations with it. This is what the movies teach you, to stay on the surface, to stay with the images and sounds as they move through your mind, to process strange streams of information and unfamiliar environments quickly into meaningful integrations, too much happening too quickly to be handled by discursive thought. Later, within the developing story, there may be time for a playback or two, for what is traditionally known as "thought." Meanwhile, I'm too busy thinking to have time for thought. Thought is the province of the university, which is totally dedicated to playback, while outside the academy walls we're improvising on the basis of the ongoing, the arbitrary, the unforeseeable, which demands our constant invention.

A lot is made of the way movies have affected fiction via its techniques — montage, quick cuts, short scenes. But I'm talking about movies reinstituting story as a way of thinking. The electrosphere has taught us, has required us, to narrate ourselves as we go along. We imagine ourselves as if we were on film or radio or TV because we have to imagine ourselves in terms of the way information comes in at us, and that image of ourselves in the media gives authority to our experience, makes it real, while at the same time the need for that reflection induces a kind of schizophrenia that in turn increases our need for media reflection to make our experience real. All media induces schizophrenia, increasing the need for feedback, in order to determine where between self and reflection the reality lies. Reflection leads to self-consciousness leads to reflection as thought. How can writing deal with this new, electrospheric narrative situation? And, in fact, why do we need writing to do it? Three techniques: collage, improvisation, and arbitrary form. Collage, of course, in the sense of montage, film not only uses but is the model for. But collage also in the sense the painters use it, the sense of Rauschenberg's use of the word "assemblage": a way of importing foreign material into the text, in whatever medium it may be. This film can do only with difficulty, while writing can use anything that can be coded in language or still image, through photograph, design, or quotation. Improvisation requires a supple medium — music, painting, or language. The more abstract the medium, the easier to improvise, while movies are the most concrete and, in a sense, the most cumbersome of the media. And the only arbitrary limitations that movies easily avail themselves of are the technological ones, while writing can impose any limitation it can invent in its self-consciousness. Henry Miller fast, improvisatory writing; Joyce collage; Raymond Roussel arbitrary form.

With these three techniques, perhaps, narrative writing can encounter the flow of the mind encountering the flood of experience in the electrosphere. In improvisation, the mind's language solos like speech without sound, like an ongoing sentence that forgets how it

began, the mind's internal monologue which, even as it falsifies the
past, invents the future. I'm not advocating writing like speaking —
Céline, Miller — but rather that speaking is like thinking. So writing
as the written extension of all that mental jazz, recording the mind's
ongoing music, like taping a saxophone solo. And collage is to get the
stuff into it, the kitchen sink, the disparate, miscellaneous, random
materials of experience, beyond the ongoing mental categories of
what's acceptable, especially those of art and literature. And arbitrary
form to constantly try to break down those categories, to force thought
beyond what it already thinks, meaning beyond what is meant, to
de-fab the pre-fab, mediating meditation into the unpremeditated. Thus
narrative writing moving us into a fuller consciousness beyond the
restrictive, if acute, diagrams of discursive thought, beyond its obsessive replay, with invention, fiction, being a sort of normal consequence
of that ongoing solo that progressively questions the fact of the past in
order to improvise the possibilities of the future, a dialogue there
between the possible and the impossible to reclaim the impossible.
Writing then as a movement into fuller consciousness, but writing also
in its functions of memory and prophecy, word on page still unsur-
passed in the technology of information retrieval, utterly different from
the ephemeral improvisations of speaking and thinking. Writing as the
most supple and powerful replay technology, and there its supreme
advantage as the most self-conscious of forms, paradoxically more
self-conscious even than thought in the mind.

My own experience writing films persuades me that ideally they
shouldn't be written. Films are not the writer's medium, anyway.
They're the director's medium or even, when you think of packaging,
the producer's medium. Francis Ford Coppola has constructed a system of filmmaking that could eventually do away with the written
script. It involves faster retrieval of more information about recorded
sounds and images, so that composition of the film can become a
process of ongoing improvisation and revision, as in writing. And, in
fact, that is basically how a script is written and rewritten, but over a
long period of time, and timelag is what Coppola's system avoids,
making filmmaking that much more the director's medium. Composition, recording, and editing are all almost simultaneous, so the making
of the film gets very close to the process of thinking about it by the
director, an extension of his thought process. Thus in terms of creative

process, filmmaking begins to approach the suppleness of writing. In theory this should allow for the creation of more various and original work, less limited by the technology of the medium. From my point of view as a writer, this is a relief, in a way. Films are involved with images and ideas; initially they have little to do with writing or language. I think what we are going to see, in fact, is a process in which the various media will essentialize themselves on the basis of technology. One sign of this is that within the various media the genres are beginning to break down and the forms are beginning to combine and essentialize what a particular medium can technologically do best. So, for example, the written media — poetry, fiction, nonfiction, journalism — have over the last ten or fifteen years begun to combine in various new and interesting integrations, aiming, I would guess, toward forms more appropriate to an essentialized writing technology. Its possibilities are not therefore narrowed, but expanded with the help of new technological developments like tape-recording, xeroxing, print-variable and computerized typewriters, word processing, photo-offset and computerized printing. Genre is traditional, medium is technological. We live in a technological, not a traditional, culture. So we will soon have, apparently, movies without scripts, so that the visual becomes visual and the written, written, a kind of separating out of the media via the centrifugal energy of technological evolution and the intellectual revolution that is both its cause and effect. The breakdown of genre will be accompanied by an increasing definition of media, and we may end up with a series of more and more highly defined media which will themselves become principles of composition in the sense that the genres have been.

I see a tendency for the media to become increasingly abstract so that they become more direct extensions of thinking. Language may polarize increasingly into writing and speaking, for example, with speech language facilitated more and more by the tape recorder, by language spoken over the media, and by the relatively new tendency to read poetry out loud instead of assuming its real location is on the page. Written language may have less and less to do with speech and more and more to do with the rhythms of the mind itself. Writing so polarized may become increasingly concrete, more word on page, more written. But this process of concretion should also allow for more abstraction. The more concrete, the more a thing-in-itself the symbol,

the more abstract information it can carry. When the meaning of a
symbol is reduced to "degree zero," that is, when it has only formal
meaning, it is most powerful as a carrier of information. A digital
computer is more powerful than an analogical computer because it
stores information in terms of a yes/no code, as opposed to an imitative
code. A yes-or-no indication is more simple and carries less meaning
in itself than an analogical indication, and so it can carry more information. The computer chip may become the model for abstracting and
reproducing information, and perhaps creating and communicating
directly through the computer will be the ultimate medium, into which
one might feed data that can be fed back in a variety of narrative forms,
written, visual, oral, all of them at once, or in some form that bypasses
the senses altogether, feeding directly into the brain, having the embodiment, say, of something like a waking dream. In any case,
Coppola's system works with computerized signals and, in fact, bypasses direct, sensuous, analogical recording, going instead to signals
on tape. This is something like the way music is now being recorded,
with digital signals instead of analogical imitation of the sound. In both
cases the principle holds: because the system is more abstract, it can
record more information in a more manipulable way. The more abstract
the recording of information, the more concrete the reproduction, the
more sensuous, finally. Increased abstraction means the ability to store
more information in a more retrievable form so that reproduction can
be more detailed, precise, and clear. At the same time, as I have said,
Coppola's system makes his medium more like a direct extension of
thinking, because it allows quicker feedback on more information. He
doesn't have to wait months for the editing to see what the film is going
to look like, for example. He can see what the film looks like right
away and edit as he goes along. What was, in traditional filmmaking,
a record of the thinking of the scriptwriter, modified by the thinking
of the actors and director, and, later, the editor, becomes now a form
of narrative thinking for the director. He is recording his own thinking
almost directly, the way a writer does, the thinking that is involved in
composition. As the painting is a recording of the artist's performance,
and writing of the writer's performance in composition, so now, as
Coppola is aware, the film — more than a recording of an action —
becomes the recording of the director's performance in composition.
So the location of interest in the film must shift and essentialize. It

becomes less an imitation of an action in the world and more a mode of visual narrative thinking. Its situation, then, is not unlike that of the contemporary novel. Yet it is less like writing and more itself, as film, as it ideally should be, bypassing writing because there is no longer a need for a script. On the other hand, writing, in the contemporary narrative, more and more bypasses simulation of image, also known traditionally as description. Writing need no longer try to make the reader see, but instead deals in concrete bits of information which the reader may translate into a wide variety of reference: The sky is blue, the baby died. While the language of film becomes more and more visual, depending less on language cues. All of this is interesting not only in terms of where these arts are going but in trying to arrive at what their natures are, considering their technology.

But we are not going back to silent film. What is the relation of film and language, image and word? To what extent can we leave language behind and communicate through images? Images, still or moving, can sometimes communicate more information more easily and quickly than language. Take road signs, for example, where information is coded as image, as opposed to saying on a sign that there might be a locomotive coming around the curve, look out. But the concreteness and immediacy of the image is also its limitation. Images are too specific to compose a flexible mode of communication. A picture of a locomotive remains, as referent, a picture of a locomotive. Context might expand its reference some, or even a given tradition, but finally it is too cumbersome as a signifier. Image can be used in various ways to modify meaning in a written text. But though it may be true that a picture is worth a thousand words, a thousand words can be recombined in thousands of ways to denote thousands of meanings, while the denotation of the picture can remain only the denotation of the picture. Unless the context can be changed. And there may lie the clue to the use of language in film. Even a sparing use of language, as with a single-word caption at the bottom of a cartoon, for example, can give the contextual information necessary to shift contexts, to multiply meanings, to make film a far more complex and supple medium.

This points to the use of the sound track, in general, of course, through sounds and music as well as language, and it seems to imply that film is a much more language-dependent art than writing is image-dependent, or even that film can exist only as a rather limited and stunted medium without the use of words. Talk about the "language" of film may imply a state to which it aspires but at which it can never arrive, unlike theater, which does not deal in images, or painting, which deals only in images. Perhaps one of the models for film should be comic books (note the recent *Superman*), a medium that also proceeds frame by frame, the difference being that, while comic books deal with written language, film deals with spoken language: written language and image versus spoken language and image. In comic books the equivalent of the sound track would be the words written in the balloons, but there is no equivalent in film of the narrative material in the captions. This suggests that in order to exploit the maximum potential of film, the use of subtitles should be reinstituted, along with the sound track. That side of language which proceeds through the graphics of writing would seem a natural complement to a visual art, especially since writing is one of the most pervasive objects in our culture. This, of course, has been recognized by the many painters who, since the cubists or, to speak of another stage of development, since Robert Indiana, have been using written language as part of their subject.

Written language in film could serve multiple purposes — in the form of subtitles, for example — not only to enrich the meaning of the continuum of images, but also to remind the audience of the artifice of the medium, and thus, in a Brechtian sense, to break the usually hypnotic relation between medium and viewer that amounts to a form of mind control, as opposed to that liberation and expansion of consciousness which seems to me characteristic of contemporary art at its best. For this purpose, in fact, why limit the use of written language in films to subtitles? Why not lay the language on the frame in whatever position it seems most appropriate? On a vertical column along one side, say, as in Japanese painting, or scattered through the frame, randomly, or in graphic design that might itself enhance visual significance. Furthermore, the contrast between writing on the frame and writing in the frame, that is to say, photographs of writing, might set up an interesting dialectic among the levels at which we engage in discourse, especially in terms of the authority of the various levels. For example, a subtitle on a photograph would have more authority than a photograph of a subtitle. Why? And might this not lead us to the conclusion that the authority of the frame is finally technological rather than ideological, a state of affairs which, once conscious, we might then wish to subvert? Political and ideological consequences of the technology of the moving image are not negligible. Given their capability for inducing near hypnosis, film and television are undoubtedly the most powerful techniques in the mass technology of mind control. Assuming we want to deprogram ourselves, it is important to remember that maximum consciousness means minimum control. Theoretically, and for similar purposes, we might also make use, on the surface of the film and the frame, of the graphic techniques used by such film painters as Brakhage. At the level of sound track, voice-overs could be used to create another stratum of meaning, as opposed to that projected by the images and the speech continuous with the images; that is, voice-overs could create a discontinuity between language and image.

What should images sound like, what should words look like? These are the questions we have been asking, and they make sense only with film which, even essentialized, remains a composite form. More attention, in a general way, however, should be focused on what words look like. We're talking about writing. Writing is by definition a graphic entity, and is very different from speech, which is purely sonic. In an essentialized form of writing, words should no more have a sound than images should. Speech rhythms are interesting in writing only because they are closer to the rhythms of the mind than textual syntax usually is. The point of an essentialized writing is to be abstract enough to bypass speech and get directly into an extension of the process of thinking. Tape-recording is a case in point. Tape-recording is interesting because it breaks free more easily from the rules and categories of written language into a more flexible language, which, however, remains mere talk until you get it on the page. Talk is talk, no matter what kind of talk; we're all used to it. To its rhythms, to its suppleness, to its communicative immediacy, and to the negligible value we attribute to it, justly, in comparison with writing or thinking — just talk. Only on the page does electronically recorded speech of any kind acquire the power of writing. On the page, where, first of all, it gains a revolutionary thrust opposed to official syntax, where its superficiality — that is to say the way recording keeps language to its surface in the same way that film does because of its movement — does not allow us to dwell, to sink into the culture's prefabricated profundities. Only on the page does that surface quality become significant, a way of saying that however much the word may resound with associative and etymological resonances, it is still fundamentally a mark on a page, an image on a surface, a visually concrete manifestation whose power of abstraction comes from the fact that it is a real object, in the same sense that a computer chip is a real object.

Thus, one of the jobs of the essential writer is to clear words of their associative and etymological meanings in the same way you might erase information from a computer chip, erasing meaning until you arrive at essential form, essential structure on a larger scale, which then becomes available for the creation of new meaning. This accounts for the otherwise inexplicable power of Gertrude Stein's nonsense, for example, or the efficacity of Burroughs's cut-up method. Burroughs says,

> The study of hieroglyphic language shows us that the word is an image . . . the written word as an image. However, there is an important difference between a hieroglyphic and a syllabic language. If I hold up a sign with the word "rose" written on it, and you read that sign, you will be forced to repeat the word "rose" to yourself. If I show you a picture of a rose, you do not have to repeat the word. You can register the image in silence. A syllabic language forces you to verbalize in auditory patterns. A hieroglyphic language does not.[1]

The word has to be severed from its relations with the auditory world. We are no longer a culture of mouth readers. We no longer have the time to shape the words with our lips as we read. Can we afford a language whose power is so attenuated? Speed-reading won't do the trick. But the very phenomenon of speed-reading — its popularity and its effect on you when you read — is instructive.

In speed-reading, you pick out the major features of the message and try to ignore the details. The details are there at another level if you wish to go back or if you wish to slow down at a certain point. Why not score written language so that this kind of reading becomes not an imposition on a writing meant to be read in another way but a way of maximizing the power of language and showing us how to read, giving us cues for reading, in the most effective way? Why, for example, have print moving from left to right, left to right, in a solid block down to the end of the page? Why not break up the page so that the important features are written, let's say, in isolation or in larger type or both, so that the details are there in blocks of smaller print if you wish to read them. Why stick with grammatical syntax, when fragments or run-on might be more effective? Why not use a picture or a graphic image when it might communicate better, that is to say, faster and more? Why not reinstitute calligraphy as the most flexible of written forms which now, as reproducible as print through xerography and offset, could become a mass medium?

Writers should do everything they can to release words from their normal contexts and associations, to make them available for creative use. In so doing we will rediscover the magic of language in a demystified and practical form. The word treated as literal thing creates new configurations which we then notice or create in the world, the way mathematicians create equations on the basis of pure formal elegance which are then found to describe previously unknown phenomena in the world. Or, like a cubist portrait that its subject comes to resemble. (Gertrude Stein: "It doesn't look like me." Picasso: "It will.") Collage, assemblage, montage are techniques that allow words and images to be brought into new contexts and new combinations, in which old meanings are lost and new ones are created. Montage is basic to the vocabulary of film and assemblage important to that of painting. Collage has obviously been basic to the vocabulary of creative language throughout the twentieth century, to the point where now we might even begin to think of it not so much as a dated technique but a principle basic to our language, and therefore available for further development. The collaging of all sorts of graphic signs, images, photographs, along with words, in a more fluid and dynamic language integration seems a distinct possibility. And if electronics discovers a technique, might it not also be possible to incorporate the moving image?

The technology of the page is still more powerful than any other for communicative and creative purposes in language, including that of the computer, because of the page's "retrieval system," scanning, paging, availability visually of information through simple eye movement on any page in any order. What about an electronic scroll that might heighten some of these characteristics, one that could store more information in much less space, much more cheaply than book production, whose expense is becoming a barrier to its utility? What about a scroll whose configuration could be changed at need for purposes, for example, of examining a macro-section projected onto a large broadsheet or, at the other pole, could be broken down into fiche for detailed examination of another kind, fiche that could contain segments of information of any size, from paragraph to sentence to word to syllable? Suppose we could arrive at the electronic equivalent of a page with its concrete material advantages and still under the control of the eye and the hand moving in any direction at any speed at the will of the reader, either in successive stills or in controllable motion, depending on the pace and purpose desired? Here film and television are both the models and the means of investigation. What about an improved version of written words, finally, one that breaks away from the sonic base of syllabification, on the one hand, but does not move into the cumbersome concretions of hieroglyphs, on the other — a new calligraphy, a line, say, that curves and telescopes and accordions on the basis of a frequency system, music without sound, Mallarmé's musician of silence bypassing the senses as much as possible to address the mind more directly? "Reading creates a solitary, tacit concert played in the mind, which grasps its meaning through the slightest vibration . . . poetry close to the idea is music par excellence" [Mallarmé].

Here we stop talking about any one of the media as a separate entity and start invoking, as we have, painting, film, television, and music, as well as written and spoken language; we grope, as many artists now do, toward a fundamental change in language itself, growing out of and creating a fundamental change in the culture, which, from this point of view at least, makes talking about film in isolation seem trivial, if not impossible.

Note

1. William Burroughs, *Le Job, entretiens avec Daniel Odier* (Paris: Belfond, 1979), pp. 85–86. Quoted in Marc Dachy, *Des Energies transformatrices du langage* (Paris: FNAGP, 1980), no pagination. Translation by Sukenick. Reprinted as *The Job* (New York: Grove, 1970), p. 51.

Part 2

Writing Film Into a System

Jorge Luis Borges, 1899–1986   6

uring his lifetime, Jorge Luis Borges was the best-known Latin American writer. He was the first writer to achieve in the twentieth century an international status to rival that of the major mod ernists. Although his writing can be related to a number of important literary traditions, he is credited with having defined, like Kafka, a new kind of fiction writing that reflects a special aspect of modern existence. Though the reader might be surprised at first to consider film among his influences, Borges joined others of his generation in welcoming the new art with an unusually perceptive, highly witty criticism.

He wrote his first story at age seven and had his first work published in 1923 — a volume of poetry entitled *Fervor de Buenos Aires*. During this early period, Borges was very active in the literary movements of the time, the number of which reflected, to some extent, the avid activity of writers and artists in Europe. His *Manifesto ultraísta*, for example, written in 1921, was a response to and an embrace of the Spanish Ultraísta movement. During this same period, he helped found the reviews *Nosotros* and *Proa* and collaborated on the review *Martín Fierro*.

His first short stories, which would establish him as a major writer, appeared in 1941 in *El Jardín de senderos que se bifurcan* (The garden of forking paths). At this time, his collaborations with Adolfo Bioy Casares, a lifelong friend, began. Together, and sometimes with the help of other Argentine writers, including Victoria and Silvina Ocampo, they brought out anthologies of fantastic literature, of Argentine poetry, and, under the pseudonym of H. Bustos Domecq (constructed with the names of the maternal grandfathers of each), a collection of original detective stories.

One is tempted to say that, before Borges, Argentine literature —
and, more generally, Latin American literature — was perceived as just
one more of the Third World literatures. With his first collection, and
with the publication of *Ficciones* in 1944, Borges became the premier
Latin writer. Following the translation of his early works in Europe
(the first French translation of his work was in 1939), he soon became
known as a master of a new form of the short story that he had virtually
invented. As he owes little to classic modernism, the European literary
establishment was hard pressed to categorize Borges. Nevertheless, by
the 1950s, the writings of major Europeans, such as Michel Foucault
and Roland Barthes, began to include references to and quotations of
his work.

Throughout this period, Borges also translated key works by
European writers into Spanish, further solidifying his position on the
cutting edge of European literature. He spoke English fluently almost
from birth because of the influence of his English paternal grand-
mother, and he was given private English lessons from an early age.
When he was nine years old, he translated a children's story by Oscar
Wilde, "The Happy Prince." Owing to extensive travel with his parents
all over Europe, he became equally familiar with French, German, and
Italian. Among his numerous translations of important works are
Virginia Woolf's *A Room of One's Own* (1936) and *Orlando* (1937),
Kafka's "The Metamorphosis" (1943), and Walt Whitman's *Leaves of
Grass* (1969).

After a number of professional reversals as the result of his
opposition to the Peronist regime in Argentina, Borges was named
director of the Biblioteca Nacional in 1955. From this point on, the
figure of the library, which was already strong in his writing, would
occupy a central place in many of his stories. For example, he began
"The Library of Babel" (1941) with a bold premise: "The universe
(which others call the Library) is composed of an indefinite, perhaps
an infinite, number of hexagonal galleries. . . ."[1] Similar to the opening
of Kafka's "The Metamorphosis" (in which Gregor Samsa wakes up
one morning transformed into a gigantic insect), the sentence
demonstrates Borges's gift for combining improbability with a quasi-
scientific exactitude. In it, one sees an indication of the kind of
intellectual game that later became Borges's hallmark, the precise,
slightly understated diction that commands all of his prose and the

modest creation of an alternative world that, long before the heydey of science fiction, sent minds reeling in metaphysical vertigo.

So great is the imprint of Western philosophy on his writing that readers sometimes forget that Borges's early loves included gaucho literature and tangos. Indeed, even though he is justly revered as an international master, one finds, with a little prompting perhaps from Borges himself, the traces of gaucho motifs in much of his early writing. Gaucho literature, a bit like our westerns, was based on the experiences of cowboys and *rancheros* of the Argentine plains. It celebrated hard-working individuals who, through diligence and self-sufficiency, managed to prevail against a hostile nature. Similar in spirit was the tango lyric, which valorized the struggles of those urban lowlifes (criminals and prostitutes) who, born into hardship, managed to hold their own.

More important than its theme was the form of Borges's major writing. For him, the short story was not simply the ideal form for his ideas, it was the *only* form. When asked why he had never written a novel, he responded without hesitating that he never had any ideas that could not be adequately conveyed in a short story. Taking into consideration the sly wit of this comment, one must see in Borges's exclusive use of the short story genre an implicit critique of the twentieth-century penchant for long novels heavy with description and circumstantial detail. A disciple of Edgar Allan Poe and Guy de Maupassant, Borges stressed economy and terseness in composition. In his stories, consequently, one searches in vain for the merely decorative touch or for a detail that does not somehow contribute to the total effect.

The stories of *Ficciones* are exemplary in this respect. In each one, Borges starts with a strong, albeit improbable, premise and constructs a tight narrative that manages usually to leave the reader in the dark, or at least puzzled, about the story's ultimate philosophical or symbolic implications. "Pierre Menard, Author of Don Quixote," for example, posits an effete French symbolist poet who assumes the nigh impossible task of writing Miguel de Cervantes's great work of the seventeenth century — not copying or *re*writing it, but actually writing the masterpiece as though it were his own creation. "The Garden of Forking Paths" presents us with a sinologist who has discovered a book that includes all possible versions of the future, including not only the paths taken but also those not taken. "Funes, the Memorious" is about a man whose memory is so complete that he cannot think of anything without recalling its every detail. "Tlön, Uqbar, Orbis Tertius" tells of an alternate universe constructed by a secret sect who have managed to introduce references to their universe into the *Encyclopaedia Britannica*.

As is clear, then, an important ingredient in Borges's short stories is the strong situation that they begin with. In addition, the close, almost microscopic attention with which his narrators handle telling details is quite remarkable. Borges was no opponent of a slightly metaphysical vocabulary, and his sentences are imbued with a civility that borders on excessive refinement. Offering a solution in "The Library of Babel" to the ancient conflict between those who consider the Library to be limited and those who consider it limitless, the narrator states:

> I dare insinuate the following solution to this ancient problem: *The Library is limitless and periodic.* If an eternal voyager were to traverse it in any direction, he would find, after many centuries, that the same volumes are repeated in the same disorder (which, repeated, would constitute an order: Order itself). My solitude rejoices in this elegant hope.[2]

Among the many influences on Borges's writing, which he himself is the first to enumerate, are the works of Poe, G. K. Chesterton, and Robert Louis Stevenson. Whereas Poe is highly regarded with considerable consistency in most quarters, Chesterton and Stevenson are, at least in the United States, regarded as quite minor literary figures. In their work, nevertheless, Borges found certain models of action and diction that contributed to his unique style. It is in Poe, however, that one recognizes the idiosyncratic, perhaps mad, narrator that Borges exploited with particular success. Even more important, Poe seems to have represented for Borges the origins of the fantastic, such as it is practiced in the modern period. Conventions of the fantastic mode, such as the detective, the missing piece of crucial evidence, and the positioning of the reader on a fence of uncertainty about the reality of what has been narrated, became key strategies for his own compositions.

Borges's relation to philosophy is equally important. What might at first pass for random name-dropping in his writings turns out to be a rather systematic allusiveness to the pillars of modern idealism. Beginning with the *Historia de la eternidad* (History of eternity, 1936), Borges built a body of essays that rivals his body of fictions. With his tongue always slightly implanted in his cheek, he addressed issues that, to the minds of more illustrious thinkers, might appear nearly insurmountable. Examples include "New Refutation of Time" (1946) in *Other Inquisitions* and *Historia universal de la infamia*, (1935; translated as *A Universal History of Infamy*, 1972). As one reads his essays, it becomes evident that the distance between them and his works of fiction is very small. Borges entertains ideas and poses questions in both forms with an equal combination of wit and perspicacity.

During the late 1930s and early 1940s, Borges was a film critic for the Argentine periodical *Sur*. As a master of the cleverly made plot, he had respect for that staple of North American production, the fiction film. In the essay that follows, in fact, you will notice the care with which he examines the structure, consistency, and believability of certain classics of U.S. cinema, such as *Morocco, Hallelujah, The Informer,* and *The Green Pastures*. Beyond their stories, however, Borges was interested in the films' combination of continuity and discontinuity. Theories of montage had been elaborated and put into practice by Eisenstein and others during the preceding decade. It seems quite natural that Borges, who was so sensitive to the effects of continuity in literature, would pay close attention to the principle of continuity and discontinuity in cinema. Beyond its basic technical mechanisms, film was also, for Borges and his entire generation, a kind of ideal of representation. In it they saw the potential remake of reality itself. Indeed, it is this idea of a machine that literally reduplicates reality that his friend Bioy Casares used as the basis of *The Invention of Morel* (1940), for which Borges wrote the introduction.

He was so drawn to the narrative possibilities of cinema that he wrote two screenplays. (The general argument of one of them, *Les Autres* [The others, 1974], is included in his essay in this volume.) *Invasión* (1969) tells of a futuristic takeover of Buenos Aires by a mysterious race of aliens. Its kinship to classic models of the fantastic is evident. *Les Autres* (written in French because the film is presented as an homage to Paris) was a collaboration with Bioy Casares. Its relation to the fantastic tradition is more subtle. A man whose son commits suicide is so preoccupied by his son's death that he investigates the suicide in every possible way: He becomes a series of people (hence, the title of the film) in an effort to get to know all of his son's friends and to learn all he can about the circumstances surrounding his son's death. The surprise ending places in doubt the finality of death as well as the relation between death and life.

Notice that the very suggestion Borges makes in his essay about Victor Fleming's *Dr. Jekyll and Mr. Hyde* (1941), that is, that the characters would be improved if, rather than having one actor assume both roles, there were two actors assuming the same role, can be seen as the seed of the plot of *Les Autres*. The hero, Spinoza, makes a kind of benevolent Jekyll/Hyde in that he must continually change identity in order to investigate the past.

In Borges's fiction, we find a classic purity of diction along with an extraordinary play of the imaginary, such that comparisons to cinematic discourse may seem beside the point. Unlike his compatriot Manuel Puig, Borges did not graft onto his plots either the content or the narrative feel of the movies. His generation revered the cinema for what it could do and for its resuscitation of certain moribund narrative traditions. We find in his work more the respect for a medium of another order than the enthusiasm of a convert. Rather than imitating the cinema in his fiction, he disciplined his writing into an instrument of precision and imaginative speculation that could rival anyone's camera.

Notes

1. Jorges Luis Borges, *Ficciones,* trans. A. Kerrigan et al. (New York: Grove Press, 1962), p. 79.
2. Ibid., pp. 87–88.

Jorge Luis Borges

The Future of a Fiction

Allegory Inside and Outside Cinema

It is commonly observed that allegories are tolerable in direct
proportion to their inconsistency and vagueness, which does not signify an apology for inconsistency and vagueness but, rather, a proof
— a sign, at least — that the genre of allegory is a mistake. "The genre
of allegory," I said, not the components or suggestions of allegory. (The
best and most famous allegory, *The Pilgrim's Progress from This World
to That Which Is to Come*, by the Puritan visionary John Bunyan, must
be read as a novel, not as a prophecy; but if we eliminate all the
symbolic justifications, the book will be absurd.)

The measure of allegory in *The Petrified Forest* (Archie Mayo,
1936) is perhaps exemplary: light enough so as not to invalidate the
drama's reality, substantial enough so as not to invalidate the drama's
improbabilities. On the other hand, two or three weaknesses or ped-
antries in the dialogue continue to annoy me: a confused theological
theory of neuroses, the summary (totally and minutely inaccurate) of
a poem by T. S. Eliot, the forced allusions to Villon, Mark Twain, and
Billy the Kid, contrived to make the audience feel erudite in recogniz-
ing those names.

Once the allegorical motive is dismissed or relegated to a secondary level, the plot of *The Petrified Forest* — the magical influence of
approaching death on a random group of men and women — seems
admirable to me. In this film, death works like hypnosis or alcohol: it
brings the recesses of the soul into the light of day. These characters
are extraordinarily distinct: the smiling, anecdotal grandfather, who
sees everything as a performance and greets the desolation and bullets

From Edgardo Cozarinsky, *Borges in/and/on Film*, translated by Ronald Christ and Gloria
Waldman, with additional material translated by Keith Cohen. Copyright by Lumen Books (New
York), 1988. Copyright of English translation by Ronald Christ, 1988. Orig. *Borges en/y/sobre
cine* (Madrid: Fundamentos, 1981).

as a happy return to the turbulent normalcy of his youth; the weary
gunman Mantee, as resigned to killing (and making others kill) as the
rest are to dying; the imposing and absolutely vain banker with his
diplomat's air of a great man of our conservative party; the young
Gabrielle, who is given to attributing her romantic turn of mind to her
French blood and her qualities as good *ménagère* to her Yankee origins;
the poet, who advises her to reverse the terms of that attribution, which
is so American — and so mythical.

Theology and Ideology Reconciled

Let us imagine a translation of the Bible to the time and space —
conventional — of Gaucho literature. (It is impossible that someone
has not already yielded to the temptation of trying this.) In such a
reduction, the Devil is Mandinga, God is Daddy Dios, Abel is a rancher
murdered by the farmer Cain, Pontius Pilate is the Commanding
Officer, the Virgin Mary interrupts her hymn to the Holy Trinity in
order to respond "Conceived without sin!" to the "Hail Mary, full of
grace!" of a dusty, early-rising Angel, who has not gotten off his
wolf-gray horse. It is pointless to reveal other touches no less predict-
able and cumbersome: my readers can already get a foretaste of the
special horror of this wild, biblical hodgepodge. I want them to imagine
it, and to detest it, so that then I may declare: That, precisely, is what
The Green Pastures (W. Keighley and M. Connelly, 1936) is not.

To deny that identity is not to pretend that the bituminous Dead
Sea — and Paradise — differ less from Louisiana and Georgia than
from the Province of Buenos Aires. My thesis is different. I think that
to appropriate the men of scripture or the men of Eduardo Gutiérrez[1]
bothers us for the simple reason that it is an arbitrary procedure.
(Which, let it be said in parentheses, is the annoying original sin of our
creole *Faust* — its joining of the sixteenth century to the nineteenth,
of Saxony to Bragado, is totally haphazard.)[2] Not so Connelly's *The
Green Pastures*. The author states that *"The Green Pastures* is an
attempt to present certain aspects of a living religion in the terms of its
believers. The religion is that of thousands of Negroes in the deep
South. With terrific spiritual hunger and the greatest humility, these
untutored black Christians — many of whom cannot even read the
book that is the treasure house of their faith — have adapted the

contents of the Bible to the consistencies of their everyday lives."[3] The numerous anachronisms (and anatropisms) that the adjustment gives rise to certainly do not exhaust the film's charm. We are amused when God saves the 10¢ cigar, which the Archangel has just offered him, "for later"; we are amused when rheumatic pains warn Noah of the approaching flood; we are amused when God, walking through the fields, asks some flowers how they are, and they answer him in chorus, with a piping, childlike voice: "We O.K., Lawd."

People will tell me that the foregoing is ingenuous. I reply: Yes, just as ingenuous as that "Lord God walking in the garden in the cool of the day" (Genesis, 3:8). Do I dare add that I prefer the idea of a human God, an awkward God, a God capable of repenting, to the idea proposed by the theologians of a happily verbal monster, made up of three inextricable Persons and nineteen attributes? — to the idea of a God who, as H. G. Wells said, cannot act because he is all-powerful and eternal, cannot think because he is omniscient, cannot move because he is ubiquitous and is already everywhere?

Betraying the Fantastic, or
Dr. Jekyll and Mr. Hyde *Transformed*

For the third time, Hollywood has defamed Robert Louis Stevenson. In Argentina, this defamation (1941) is called *El hombre y la bestia* (The man and the beast): It has been perpetrated by Victor Fleming,[4] who repeats with unfortunate faithfulness the aesthetic and moral errors of the version — the perversion — by Mamoulian. I shall begin with the latter, the moral errors.

In Stevenson's 1886 novel, *Dr. Jekyll and Mr. Hyde,* Dr. Jekyll is morally double in the way all men are double, while his hypostasis — Edward Hyde — is fiendish without respite and without alloy; in the 1941 film, Dr. Jekyll is a young pathologist who practices chastity while his hypostasis — Hyde — is a profligate with traces of the sadist and the acrobat. For the philosophers in Hollywood, Good is the courtship of the chaste and wealthy Miss Lana Turner; Evil (which similarly concerned David Hume and the heresiarchs of Alexandria), illegal cohabitation with Fröken Ingrid Bergman or Miriam Hopkins. It is futile to note that Stevenson is completely innocent of this limitation or deformation of the problem. In the book's last chapter, he states the vices of Jekyll: sensuality and hypocrisy; in one of the *Ethical Studies* — from the year 1888 — he tries to list "all the displays of the truly diabolic" and proposes the following: "envy, malice, the mean lie, the mean silence, the calumnious truth, the backbiter, the petty tyrant, the peevish poisoner of family life."[5] (I would affirm that ethics do not include sexual matters so long as they are not contaminated by treason, greed, or vanity.)

The structure of the film is even more rudimentary than its theology. In the book, the identity of Jekyll and Hyde is a surprise: the author saves it for the end of the ninth chapter. The allegorical tale pretends to be a detective story; no reader guesses that Hyde and Jekyll are the same person. The very title of the book makes us postulate them as two. There is nothing easier than transferring this device to the screen. Let us imagine any detective mystery: two actors well known to the public figure in the plot (George Raft and Spencer Tracy, let's say); they may use analogous words, they may refer to events that presuppose a common past. When the mystery remains unsolved, one of them swallows the magic drug and changes into the other. (Of course the successful execution of this plan would allow for two or three phonetic adjustments: the changing of the protagonists' names.) More civilized than I, Victor Fleming avoids all surprise and mystery: in the early scenes of the film, Spencer Tracy fearlessly drinks the versatile potion and transforms himself into Spencer Tracy with a different wig and Negroid features.

Going beyond Stevenson's dualist parable and getting closer to the *Parliament of the Birds,* which Farid al-din Attar composed in the twelfth century A.D.,[6] we may imagine a pantheist film, whose numerous characters finally resolve into One, who is everlasting.

Homage to Paris in the Fantastic Mode[7]

The following is the synopsis of the original scenario for *Les Autres* (The others), which borrows freely from stock elements of the classic fantastic story.

The son of a Paris bookseller commits suicide. His father, a man of fifty-odd years, who thought he understood his son, now feels that he never really knew him at all and tries to seek him in those who were his friends.

Earlier there had been a costume ball, a film that was to be made, a sham duel, and a poker game that turned out to really be a duel. Then, all at once, death. And afterwards, as the bookseller progresses in his quest, more and more unforeseeable events begin to crop up.

There's a man who's surprised to be who he is, a magician who calls himself Artaxerxes, a woman whom the son had loved, and a forsaken gambler. There's the film that was going to be made but isn't, the woman who cannot forget the other side of the ocean, and there's an apparition in a procession of horseback riders. There's a man who flings money into the fire and beats the woman; there's the bookseller, who rediscovers love with this woman, and this woman who betrays him with another man who resembles the dead son. And there's a crime in an observatory and a final revelation: After the son's death, the bookseller went from being one man to being another, then to being still others. He had no control over these changes — something was happening to him that he could not understand, something that took hold of him completely. He was the man who was surprised to be who he was, the magician who appeared and disappeared, the ruffian who snatched the money from the gambler and thrashed him, the stranger who, for one night, stole the woman from him. He ceased being one man and became many. Now he can be everybody, and he no longer knows who he is.

These, then, are the fictional elements of a film (directed by H. Santiago, 1974), whose plot was conceived in French, composed in French, and, in a way, given by France to three Argentines for whom Paris is their second home. Just as *Invasión* is Buenos Aires,[8] I wanted *Les Autres* to be the film I owed to Paris. (So that I might have the opportunity of "treating" Paris: of giving a particular view of Paris in sights and in sounds.) It is a perfectly classic plot, organized no doubt around the half–Anglo Saxon, half-Oriental traditions of the fantastic — with one exception: the "final explanation" of the mysterious entanglement — which clears the whole thing up — belongs itself to the realm of the fantastic.

The plot is, therefore, traditional. It starts off with quotidian occurrences not without a certain romantic quality about them, then gets caught up in an ever-deepening mystery, and finally plunges into

the imaginary (which is perhaps not so imaginary after all). This plot
is all the more disturbing as its progress is Cartesian.

Thus, with its extremely rigorous development, the plot was so
constructed that a bet could be upheld:

> Not to attempt to muddle the story and then to reproduce this
> muddlement on the screen, but to take an opposite course of action:
> to confront the story as a "natural object" (like a face or a street or
> a sound) and to handle it with cinematographic tools, so as to turn it
> into cinematographic material.
> Set the art in motion, but let the story progress by itself.

Therefore, no "psychology": rather, a sequence of acts and gestures — character-signs overlapping one another in an ineluctable
unfolding of events. And dialogue that makes no pretense of being
realistic, that has been almost always kept at the functional, quotidian
level, so that its compact construction might clinch the subtle mis-
matching to which all the other elements of the film contribute.

The locations of the events were chosen according to their varying
degree of applicability to our "sequence of acts and gestures." Places,
colors of Paris that fill the screen, as if they had set themselves up
around the protagonists in order to create a different yet specific space.

The film's multiple and complex acoustical space is essential to its
overall structure. Continuing where we left off in *Invasión*, we have
used sounds from every possible source, thus modifying the image and,
at the same time, placing our story in the very realm of the fantastic
from which it sprang.

In conclusion: rather than talking about "a metaphor of mythoma-
nia," "a study of schizophrenia" — or else "the fugitive self," "the
search for the Whole," or other vast pronouncements — let us say that
Les Autres is a very simple tale of love and death as related to identity.

Notes

Unless otherwise indicated, these notes are provided by the translators, Gloria Waldman
and Ronald Christ.

1.   Eduardo Gutiérrez (1853–90) was an Argentine author of numerous gauchesque
     novels in the serial or *folletín* manner.

2. He is referring to *Fausto,* a gauchesque poem published in 1870 by the Argentine poet Estanislao de Campo (1834–80). In pointedly picturesque language, the poem gives the impression of one of the gauchos who has attended a performance of Charles François Gounod's *Faust.*

3. Marc Connelly, *The Green Pastures* (New York: Farrar and Rinehart, 1929), p. 55. Borges's translation conforms substantially to the opening paragraph of the "Author's Note," quoted here.

4. Victor Fleming's 1941 film *Dr. Jekyll and Mr. Hyde* was released under the Spanish title *El hombre y la bestia.* Rouben Mamoulian's version of *Dr. Jekyll and Mr. Hyde* dates from 1932. — ED.

5. Borges's translation conforms to Stevenson's original, which is quoted here from "A Christmas Sermon," *Ethical Studies,* in *Collected Poetical Works* (London: W. Heinemann, 1924), vol. 26, p. 71.

6. Borges refers to this work several times in his writings, including the entry under "El Simurg" in *The Book of Imaginary Beings,* translated by Norman Thomas di Giovanni in collaboration with Borges (New York: Dutton, 1969). The myth tells of a group of birds that set out to find the Simurg, the king of the birds. Finally, thirty of them reach their destination, only to realize that they are the Simurg and that the Simurg is each and all of them. Edward FitzGerald translated parts of the poem as *The Bird-parliament: A bird's eye view of Faria-Uddin Attar's Bird-parliament.* First published in *Letters and Literary Remains of Edward FitzGerald,* edited by William Aldis Wright (New York: Macmillan, 1894), vol. 2, pp. 433–82. Orig. edition, 1889.

7. This section was written in collaboration with Adolfo Bioy Casares and Hugo Santiago. — ED.

8. *Invasión* (Hugo Santiago, 1969, based on a scenario and an idea on which Borges, Bioy Casares, and the director collaborated) is set in a futuristic, dystopic Buenos Aires. According to Borges, it is "the story of a city — imaginary or real — besieged by powerful enemies and defended by a few men, who may not be heroes. They fight until the end, without ever suspecting that their battle is endless" (*Borges in/and/on Film,* trans. Ronald Christ and Gloria Waldman [New York: Lumen Books, 1988], p. 72). — ED.

Pier Paolo Pasolini, 1922–1975   7

O ne of the best-known Italian filmmakers of the modern period, Pier Paolo Pasolini produced an extensive body of literary as well as film work before his tragic death in 1975. He was one of the younger postwar filmmakers who were to make their mark not only on Italian cinema but on European and world cinema as well during the two decades following World War II. Unlike De Sica, Zavattini, and Rossellini, however, whose influence stemmed from the rediscovery of the documentary potentials of cinema (so-called neorealism), Pasolini was drawn to the lyric possibilities of film form; many of his greatest films contain a personal vision that goes beyond a story, a theme, or a central character.

If the influence of neorealism remained in force in Italy during most of the 1950s, a new direction was signaled at the end of the decade by the appearance of Antonioni's *L'Avventura* (1959) and Fellini's *La dolce vita* (1960). These innovative works by filmmakers who had come of age and produced their first efforts under the aegis of neorealism seemed to owe more in spirit and style to the French New Wave than to their Italian forebears. The films were aimless and diffuse in plot structure, the characterization was inconclusive, and the predominant themes centered on anguish, absurdity, and unrequited love in a style that reminded contemporary viewers of existentialism.

It was in the context of this new oppositional movement that Pasolini's first film, *Accattone* (1961), was made. He had been actively involved in the film world since 1954. Among his early works were the filmscript for the masterpiece *Le Notti di Cabiria* (*Nights of Cabiria,* 1957), directed by Fellini, and the filmscript for his own novel, *Una Vita violenta* (*A Violent Life,* 1958), directed by Brunello

Heusch and Paolo Rondi, 1962, and *La Commare secca* (The grim reaper), directed by Bernardo Bertolucci, 1962. His reputation was largely restricted to Italy until 1964, when he directed *Il Vangelo Secondo Matteo* (*The Gospel According to St. Matthew*). Using camera set-ups that were shocking in their plainness and a sound track composed of a hodgepodge of music associated with the Passion, ranging from J. S. Bach's *St. Matthew Passion* to Odetta singing "I Feel Like a Motherless Child," Pasolini retold the most familiar story in the Western world with a rawness and ideological boldness that laid bare his neorealist roots. Following this film, he directed a series of adaptations, first of Greek classics, *Edipo Re* (*Oedipus Rex*, 1967) and *Medea* (1969), and then of serial storytelling masterpieces, *Il Decamerone* (*The Decameron*, 1971), *I racconti di Canterbury* (*Canterbury Tales*, 1972), and *Il fiore delle mille e una notte* (*The Arabian Nights*, 1974).

Even before he entered the world of cinema, Pasolini had established himself in Italy as an important poet. He wrote his first book of poems, *Poesie a Casarsa* (1942), in his native Friulan dialect, an Italian of rough sonorities that he often went back to and never tired of evoking. Hailed by Alberto Moravia as "*the* major Italian poet of the second half of this century," Pasolini celebrated the downtrodden, nameless proletarians and peasants of Italy in his literary work. Moravia viewed Pasolini's poetry against the backdrop of postwar Italy, noting his lament for his dishonored homeland, the predominant theme of his poetry, and his nostalgia for "rural culture": "Pasolini found himself living in a disastrous period for Italy, i.e., at the moment of a catastrophe without parallel, after military defeat, with two foreign armies fighting each other on its soil."[1] The setting of many of his poems is urban Rome, where he spent most of his adult life:

> That breathless run
> between narrow construction sites,
> the burnt-out banks by the Tiburtina . . .
> Those lines of workers, unemployed, thieves
> getting off, still greasy with gray sweat
> from beds where they slept head-to-foot
> with their grandchildren in small dirty bedrooms,
> dusty as wagons, grimy and gay . . .
> Those city outskirts cut up in lots, all alike,

> parched by the too-hot sun
> among abandoned quarries,
> broken embankments, hovels, sweatshops . . .[2]

He wrote some of his most celebrated poems in the form of Dante's tercet, such as "The Ashes of Gramsci" (1954), a poem that created a furor when published. Though formally restrained and dignified, it combined an extremely personal eulogy of Antonio Gramsci (the Italian socialist and one of the founders of the Italian Communist Party, who died in prison, where he was serving a twenty-year sentence) with a very elliptical commentary on contemporary Italy. Identifying intensely with Gramsci, whose grave fails to commemorate his greatness, Pasolini decries, on the one hand, Gramsci's relative obscurity ("There you lie, banished, listed with severe / non-Catholic elegance, among the foreign / dead") and, on the other hand, his own inability to support Gramsci wholeheartedly:

> Yet without your rigor, I survive because
>
> I do not choose. I live in the non-will
> of the dead postwar years: loving
> the world I hate, scorning it, lost
>
> in its wretchedness — in an obscure scandal
> of consciousness . . .[3]

Pasolini's prose is even more evidently committed to the dispossessed and politically powerless. In three of his works that have been translated into English, *The Ragazzi* (1968, orig. 1955), *A Violent Life* (1968, orig. 1959), and *Roman Nights and Other Stories* (1986, orig. 1965), the central figures are working-class or lumpen proletarian boys, whose furtive fun and seemingly necessary petty thievery become the strands that hold together very moving chronicles of the Italian working poor during a period of increasing class stratification.

Beyond his solid literary reputation, Pasolini became known to many as an enfant terrible of Italian religion and politics. An ardent Catholic attracted to contemporary interpretations of Christ as principally the savior of the lower classes, he complicated his theological views by a loyal adherence to Italian communism. Although in the political turmoil of Italy in the 1950s most intellectuals were attracted to communism, Pasolini's liberal and radical views were not consistent with what many Westerners would consider a conventional leftist program. His views on abortion, for example, brought him closer to the Catholics: "I am traumatized by the legalization of abortion because I consider it, as do many others, a legalization of homicide."[4] And his political views became widely known and much publicized when, following the events of May 1968 in France, he was invited to address the students at Vincennes. Rather than praising their efforts to reform the French university system, he chastised them as privileged children of the bourgeoisie, pointing out that workers' children would never have the leisure time to indulge in "student revolution."

If these contradictions were not enough, Pasolini's sexual orientation further complicated his relations with the Communists, who expelled him from the Party in 1950 because of a charge against him of corrupting minors. Though absolved by the court of appeals in 1952, Pasolini continued a rough journey with his fellow Communists until 1956, when, with the Soviet invasion of Hungary, Italian leftists began to defect from the Party. But for the Party loyalists, Pasolini's homosexuality was unacceptable on a number of grounds. First, Pasolini was openly gay. Second, he had not denied the earlier accusations of sexual improprieties committed with three sixteen-year-olds; rather, he defended his right to commit those acts. Finally, the Party held that Pasolini's sexual inclinations, nourished by reading the works of "bourgeois and decadent" writers, were tantamount to a kind of "intellectual deviationism" that ultimately allied him with the bourgeoisie.[5]

Pasolini, however, had never loved the Communists ("They are inflexible, they are gloomy / in their judgment of you: those who wear / hairshirts can't forgive," he declared in one poem);[6] and so, in open defiance of their censorious attitude, Pasolini publicly stated: "I am and will remain a Communist." Well in advance of political and cultural trends, then, Pasolini was an advocate of gay rights by 1950, after being a revisionist Catholic and a committed Communist throughout the period that many ideologues would characterize as antireligious and apolitical.

The best way to gain an appreciation for Pasolini's unique intermixture of politics, religion, and sexuality is to trace the development of these themes in his films. For, even though his aesthetics and politics differed fundamentally from the neorealists', he agreed with their contention that film, like a *roman à thèse,* could be used to advance an argument. As early as 1964 he had borrowed the cinema verité style of the realists and New Wave directors to conduct an inquiry into love and sexuality: *Comizi d' amore* (Assembly of love). The object of the film, a sort of modern-day *Symposium,* was to offer a public view of the widespread confusion and misapprehensions surrounding love and loving relationships. To this end, Pasolini went through the streets and ethnic neighborhoods of Rome conducting an opinion poll on the subject. Not surprisingly, Italians appeared frightened by open discussion of such things — particularly as recorded on film — and seemed hostile to anything they didn't understand.

The point of the film, which had no commercial success whatsoever, was to use the medium as a forum for the discussion of issues relevant to the society as a whole. With *Teorema* (1968), Pasolini attempted the same thing, except this time he did so through fiction. A handsome young man appears out of nowhere and ingratiates himself into a typical bourgeois Italian family. By the end of the film, everyone in the family — father, son, and housemaid included — has become infatuated with this stranger, to the point of being willing to give up everything in order to be with him. Through this parable, Pasolini launched a critique of middle-class morality and contemporary materialism. The beauty of the project is in the simplicity of the premise; just as its title indicates, the film proceeds like the working out of a theorem. Yet the story is such that it suggests at least two different interpretations. On the one hand, it is a commentary on the relativism of personal property and material goods when desire is placed in the balance. The father, for example, a wealthy industrialist, in a breathtaking back-traveling shot, undresses in the middle of Torino's busy train station and proceeds literally to walk away from his consumerist life. On the other hand, the story also suggests a Christographic reading: the antimaterialist force of a new Messiah born in an era of rampant acquisitiveness. So great is the spiritual force of the Lord, according to this interpretation, that each person's previous life becomes irrelevant, worthless, repugnant.

If intellectual theorizing is the dominant mode of *Teorema,* it is pure storytelling that predominates in the three-film sequence beginning with *The Decameron.* The key narrative link among these three films — each involves multiple storytellers whose narrative activity is prompted by a communal event — is so strong that one is obliged to account for Pasolini's attraction to this genre. After all, isn't film the medium least likely to succeed in adapting literary works in which the act of narrating is so pronounced? If we compare these works to *The Gospel According to St. Matthew,* we notice that they, unlike *The Gospel,* do not involve the use of a familiar story in order to critique the ideology of its most widespread interpretation. Pasolini admitted that a purpose of *The Gospel* was to get Italians to "read the Gospel for the first time." He used the film, in other words, as a means of disseminating the Bible. And there is no doubt that a fundamental message of Pasolini's *Gospel* is the universality of Christianity: hence the African and African-American music and the use of nonprofessional actors. The film, according to its filmmaker, reveals his "religious view of the world" and not any particular view of Christianity. The religion adumbrated in the film, he claims, is "a mutilated religion because it hasn't got any of the external characteristics of religion."[7]

In contrast with the strong tendentiousness of the *Gospel,* the power of the storytelling masterpieces might be said to lie in their structure. It is surprising, therefore, to see the extent to which Pasolini has reorganized the works of the masters. In the case of *The Decameron,* rather than replaying the circumstances that give rise to the ten days of storytelling (the great plague of Florence in the fourteenth century), Pasolini plunges right into one of the funniest stories: Andreucci da Perugia, tricked by an opportunistic woman, falls into a cesspool and, repelling by his odor all who approach, ends up impersonating a dead man in order to obtain a valuable ruby. What becomes immediately apparent is Pasolini's preference for imbricated narration over serial narration. Accordingly, several of the stories in *The Decameron* and other films are told as second-degree narratives within the main story. In *The Arabian Nights,* for example, a character interrupts the action of his story in order to tell a tale about an Ethiopian princess, who in turn tells a story about a woman who is forced to hide her son in an underground cave on a remote island. The effect of this story-within-a-story-within-a-story is to de-emphasize the dramatic development of any one of the tales and to valorize the pleasure of storytelling in and of itself.

The Canterbury Tales, like the other serial narratives, puts more emphasis on the raucous action of the tales than on the colorful storytellers. Pasolini's selection of images in all of these films reflects his political proclivities: Stories predominate that deal with peasants and other lower-class characters. The point does not seem to be to valorize the working classes as such but rather, precisely in the manner that Giovanni Boccaccio and Geoffrey Chaucer brought the bawdiness and irreverance of the culture of the common people into aristocratic culture, to introduce into a bourgeois culture an appreciation for the simple absurdities of everyday life.

It is in this sense that Pasolini's decision to make a whole series of such films takes on meaning. It is as though the lower classes of the past, as memorialized in the tales of Chaucer, Boccaccio, and *The Arabian Nights,* were in jeopardy of being forgotten or merely covered over by layer after layer of ruling-class culture. The direct storytelling mode of these serials, moreover, could be considered in danger of disappearing as well, given the modern preference for inconclusive stories about personal anguish. Pasolini praised with reservation the new cinema of his day, which he called "the cinema of poetry" in a famous essay by the same title. For him, the works by such directors as Antonioni, Godard, and Resnais return to us the possibility of lyrical elevation in an age of capitalist leveling. Not since the era of Charles Baudelaire, Pasolini argued, has the bourgeois subject been treated so thoroughly, so unabashedly, with open, empathetic scrutiny.[8]

It is in "The Cinema of Poetry" that Pasolini introduces the concept of the "*im-segno,*" which he elaborated on in later writings. Formulated at a time when film semiotics was in its heyday, the idea runs counter to the principles articulated by leaders in the field, such as Umberto Eco and Christian Metz. According to the latter, the film image is regulated according to certain codes that we are more familiar with in literature and in painting. The film image, in these terms, gains its meaning principally from its arrangement within a sequence. Pasolini argued that, on the contrary, the film image comes into a film already bearing a certain cultural baggage. There is no such thing, in his view, as a neutral image. Hence, he refers to the film image as the *im-segno,* or image-sign. Like the morpheme in linguistics, it enters into combination with other image-signs on the basis of denotative and connotative values. Thus, for Pasolini, the film image is not a neutral building block but rather a culturally determined sign whose sequentialization depends to some extent upon that cultural determination.

The implications of this theory are interesting. If cinema uses the already-coded images of the real world, then we are inevitably confronted with the question of how the real world is itself encoded. Pasolini addresses this question in one of the essays collected here, "The Code of Codes," where he argues that reality is a language; rather than being impervious to systematization, as the semioticians had argued, reality's objects and images can be catalogued according to certain laws and rules. The result is that all the cultural codes (literature, cinema, linguistics) are subordinated to this "code of codes," which is responsible for transforming "nature into cultural phenomena." "All life," consequently, is transformed "into speech."

It is tempting to see in Pasolini's idea of a code of codes an overvaluation of the material of cinema, the images of the real world. No other film theoretician of the contemporary period has argued with such insistence for the primacy of nature in the cinematic process. Not since Eisenstein's essays on "non-indifferent nature" has anyone else come forth with a view that has the potential of turning filmmaking into something more akin to science than to art. For if nature discloses so many codes and rules of organization, it might be up to the filmmaker to make sense of them and classify them for the untutored viewer. Many have regarded Pasolini's theory as the product of a naive polemicist. But perhaps as cinema develops alongside science we shall discover that his views were not far from the mark.

Pier Paolo Pasolini had the potential for creating a highly personal, unique body of cinematic work. Even though his life was cut short, his work forms a monument to the most literate impulses of film narrative. His works are a triumph of an original aesthetics in an age of imitators and modishness.

Notes

1. Alberto Moravia, foreword to Pier Paolo Pasolini, *Roman Poems,* trans. L. Ferlinghetti and F. Valente (San Francisco: City Lights Books, 1986), p. 3.

2. Pier Paolo Pasolini, "Memories of Misery," in *Roman Poems,* p. 25.

3. Pier Paolo Pasolini, "The Ashes of Gramsci," in *Poems,* trans. N. MacAfee (New York: Vintage, 1982), p. 11.

4. "Coitus, Abortion, Power's False Tolerance, the Conformism of Progressives," trans. J. Schiesari, in B. Allen, ed., *Pier Paolo Pasolini: The Poetics of Heresy* (Saratoga, CA: Anmi Libri, 1982), p. 116.

5. Enzo Siciliano, *Pasolini: A Biography,* trans. J. Shepley (New York: Vintage, 1982), p. 136.

6. From "La Religione del mio tempo" (The religion of my time), *Le Poesie* (Milan: Garzanti, 1975), pp. 233–34; quoted in Siciliano, *Pasolini,* p. 212.

7. Cited in Oswald Stack, *Pasolini on Pasolini* (Bloomington: Indiana University Press, 1969), pp. 77, 79.

8. Pier Paolo Pasolini, "The Cinema of Poetry," in *Heretical Empiricism,* trans. B. Lawton and L. K. Barnett (Bloomington: Indiana University Press, 1988; article originally appeared in 1965).

Pier Paolo Pasolini

Aspects of a Semiology of Cinema

The Screenplay as a "Structure That Wants to Be Another Structure"

The concrete element in the relationship between film and literature is the screenplay. I am not concerned, however, with observing
the mediating function of the screenplay and the critical elaboration of
the literary work which it undertakes, "figuratively integrating it" with
the equally critical perspective of the cinematographic work which it
presupposes.

In this note, what interests me about the screenplay is the moment
in which it *can be considered an autonomous "technique, a work
complete and finished in itself.* Let us consider the case of a writer's
script which is not taken from a novel or — for one reason or another
— translated into a film.

This case offers us an autonomous script that can represent an
actual choice of the author very well: the choice of a narrative technique.

What is the standard of evaluation for such a work? If one considers it to belong completely to "writing" — that is, nothing more than
the product of a "type of writing" whose fundamental element is that
of writing through the technique of the screenplay — then it must be
judged in the usual way in which literary products are judged, and
precisely as a new literary "genre," with its particular prosody and its
own metrics, etc., etc.

But in so doing, one would perform an erroneous and arbitrary
critical operation. If there isn't the *continuous allusion to a developing*

Reprinted from Pier Paolo Pasolini, *Heretical Empiricism,* translated by Louise Barnett and Ben
Lawton (Bloomington: Indiana University Press, 1988), pp. 187–96, 199–212, 261–63, 264–66,
and 276–83.

cinematographic work, it is no longer a technique, and its appearance as screenplay is purely a pretext (a situation which has yet to occur). If, therefore, an author decides to adopt the "technique" of the screenplay as autonomous work, he must accept at the same time the allusion to a "potential" cinematographic work, without which the technique he had adopted is fictitious — and thus falls directly into the traditional forms of literary writings.

If instead he accepts the allusion to a "potential" visualizable cinematographic work as substantive element, as structure of his "work in the form of a screenplay," then it can be said that his work is both typical (it has aspects that are truly similar to all actual, functional screenplays) and autonomous at the same time.

Such a moment exists in all screenplays (of high-quality films): that is, all screenplays have a moment in which they are autonomous "techniques," *whose primary structural element is the integrating reference to a potential cinematographic work.*

[. . .]

The foremost characteristic of the "sign" of the technique of the screenplay *is that of alluding to meaning through two different paths, [which are] simultaneous and converging.* That is: the sign of the screenplay refers to the meaning according to the normal path of all written languages, and in particular of literary jargons, but, *at the same time, it hints at that same meaning, forwarding the addressee to another sign, that of the potential film.* Each time our brain, confronted by a sign of the screenplay, simultaneously travels these two paths — one rapid and normal, and the other long and special — in order to understand its meaning.

In other words: The author of a screenplay asks his addressee for a particular collaboration: namely, that of lending to the text a "visual" completeness which it does not have, but at which it hints. The reader is an accomplice immediately — in the presence of the immediately intuited characteristics of the screenplay in the operation which is requested of him — and his representational imagination enters into a creative phase mechanically much higher and more intense than when he reads a novel.

The technique of screenwriting is predicated above all on this collaboration of the reader: And it is understood that its perfection consists in fulfilling this function [of collaboration] perfectly. Its form, its style, are perfect and complete when they have included and integrated these necessities into themselves. The impression of coarseness and of incompleteness is thus apparent. This coarseness and this incompleteness are stylistic elements.

At this point a conflict takes place among the various aspects under which a "sign" is presented. The sign is at the same time oral [phoneme], written [grapheme], and visual [kineme]. Through an incalculable series of conditioned reflexes of our mysterious cybernetics, we always have simultaneously present these different aspects of the linguistic "sign," which is therefore one and three. If we belong to the class which holds culture captive, and therefore we at least know how to read, the "graphemes" appear immediately to us simply as "signs," infinitely enriched by the simultaneous presence of their "phonemes" and their "kinemes."

There are certain "writings" already in the tradition which require of the reader an operation similar to the one which we have described above: for example, the writings of symbolist poetry. When we read a poem by Mallarmé or by Ungaretti, in the presence of the "graphemes" that are at that moment in front of our eyes — the lin-signs[1] — we do not limit ourselves to a pure and simple reading; the text requires us to cooperate by "pretending" to hear those graphemes acoustically. In other words, it sends us back to the phonemes, which are simultaneously present in our mind even if we are not reading aloud. A verse of Mallarmé or of Ungaretti attains its meaning only through a semantic expansion, or an exquisite barbaric coercion of the individual meanings which is obtained through the supposed musicality of the word or of the nexus of the words. That is, giving denotations *not through a particular expressivity of the sign but through a prevarication of its phoneme.*[2] While we read, we thus integrate in this manner the aberrant meaning of the special vocabulary of the poet, following two paths, the normal *sign-meaning* and the abnormal *sign–sign-as-phoneme–meaning.*

The same thing occurs in screenplay-texts (let's go ahead and invent this new expression!). Here, too, the reader integrates the incomplete meaning of the writing of the screenplay, following two paths, the normal *sign-meaning,* and the abnormal *sign–sign-as-kineme–meaning.*

The word of the screenplay-text is thus characterized by the ex-

pressive accentuation of one of the three moments through which it is constituted, the kineme.

Naturally the "kinemes" are primordial images, visual monads [which are] nonexistent in reality, or virtually so. The image is born of the coordinations of the kinemes.

This is the point: This coordination of "kinemes" is not a literary technique. It is another *langue,* predicated on a system of "kinemes" or of "im-signs,"[3] on which the film metalanguage is established by analogy to written or spoken metalanguages. [The film metalanguage] has always been discussed (at least in Italy) as a "language" analogous to the written-spoken one (literature, theater, etc.), and the visual component is also seen by analogy to the figurative arts. Any study of film is therefore vitiated by the genesis in a linguistic model which film has in the mind of whoever analyzes or studies it. The "film element" — a definition that has had only a superficial acceptance in Italy — is not capable of hypothesizing the possibilities of film as *another language,* with its own autonomous and particular structures: the "film element" tends to postulate film as another specific technique, predicated by analogy on the written-spoken language, that is, on what is for us language as such (but not for semiotics, which is indifferent in the presence of the most varied, scandalous, and hypothetical sign-systems).

Therefore, while the "kineme" in written-spoken languages is one of the elements of the sign — and, above all, the one least taken into consideration, given that we are used to perceiving the word as written-spoken, that is, above all, as phoneme and grapheme — in film languages the kineme is the sign par excellence: one must instead speak of the im-sign (that is, accordingly, the "kineme," which, separated from the other two aspects of the word, has become an autonomous, self-sufficient sign).

What is this fundamental visual monad which we define as the im-sign, and what are the "coordinations of im-signs" from which the image is born? Here, too, we have always reasoned instinctively, keeping in mind a sort of literary model — that is, making a continuous and unconscious analogy between film and expressive written languages. We have, that is, identified the im-sign with the word by analogy, and we have built upon this premise a sort of surreptitious grammar, vaguely, accidentally, and in some way sensuously analogous to that of written-spoken languages. In other words, we have in mind a very vague idea of the im-sign that we generally identify with the word. But the word is a noun, a verb, an interjection, or an interrogative. There are languages in which nouns predominate, others in which verbs predominate. In our common Western languages, language consists of a balance of definitions (substantives) and of actions (verbs), etc., etc. What are nouns, verbs, conjunctions, interjections in cinematographic language? And, above all, is it necessary that *they exist* in obedience to our law of analogy and custom? If cinema is *another language,* cannot this unknown language be predicated on laws that have nothing to do with the linguistic laws to which we have become accustomed?

What is the im-sign physically? A frame? A given number of frames? A pluricellular length of frames? A meaningful sequence of frames that has a certain duration? This still remains to be decided. And it will not be until we have the data to write a grammar of cinema. To say, for example, that the im-sign or the monad of cinematographic language is a "syntaxeme," that is, a coordinated whole of frames, is still arbitrary. In the same way it is arbitrary to say, for example, that cinema is a totally "verbal" language; that is, that in cinema there are no nouns, conjunctions, interjections, unless they are one with verbs. And that therefore the nucleus of film, the im-sign, is a group of images in movement, whose duration is indeterminable, shapeless, and magmatic. A "magmatic" grammar by definition, therefore, to be described through unusual paragraphs and chapters in the written-spoken grammars.

What is not arbitrary is to say instead that cinema is predicated on a "system of signs" which is different from the written-spoken one; that is, that cinema is another language.

But it is not another language in the sense that Bantu is different from Italian, for example — to juxtapose two languages which are placed in juxtaposition only with difficulty. And this does make sense, if *the translation also* implies an operation analogous to what we have seen for the screenplay-text (and for certain forms of writing such as symbolist poetry): It requires, in other words, a special collaboration on the part of the reader, and its signs have two channels of reference to the meaning. It has to do with the moment of literal translation with the text on the facing page. If on one page we see the Bantu text and on the other the Italian text, the signs of the Italian text that we perceive execute that double carom that only extremely refined thinking machines such as our brains can follow. In other words, they convey the meaning *directly* (the sign "palm tree" that indicates the palm tree) and *indirectly,* sending us back to the Bantu sign that indicates the same palm tree in a different psychophysical or cultural world. The reader, naturally, does not understand the Bantu sign, which for him is a dead letter; however, he perceives at least that the meaning conveyed by the sign "palm tree" must be integrated, modified. . . . How? Perhaps, without knowing how, by that mysterious Bantu sign. In any case, the feeling that it must be modified in some way does modify it. The operation of collaboration between the translator and the reader is thus double: *sign-meaning, and sign-sign of another (primitive) language-meaning.*

The example of a primitive language approximates what we want to say about film: that primitive language in fact also has structures immensely different from ours, belonging, let us suppose, to the world of "untamed thought." However, the "untamed thought" is in us, and there is a fundamentally identical structure in our languages and in primitive ones: Both are constituted of lin-signs and are therefore reciprocally compatible. The two respective grammars have analogous designs. (So while we are used to suspending our grammatical habits because of the structures of another language, even the most compromising and difficult, we are not instead capable of suspending our cinematographic habits. This situation will not change until a scientific grammar of cinema is written, as a potential grammar of a "system of im-signs" on which film is based.)

Now, we were saying that the "sign" of the screenplay follows a double road (*sign-meaning; sign–film-sign–meaning*). It is essential to repeat that the sign of literary metalanguages also follows the same path, bringing forth images in the collaborating mind of the reader: The grapheme now accentuates its own being as phoneme, now its being as kineme, according to the musical or pictorial quality of the writing. But we have said that in the case of the screenplay-text, the characteristic technique is a special and canonical request for collaboration from the reader *to see the kineme in the grapheme, above all, and thus to think in images, reconstructing in his own head the film to which the screenplay alludes as a potential work.*

We must now complete this initial observation, pointing out that the kineme thus accentuated and functionalized, as we were saying, is not a mere, albeit dilated, element of the sign, but is the sign of another linguistic system. The sign of the screenplay therefore not only expresses *"a will of the form to become another" above and beyond the form; that is, it captures "the form in movement"* — a movement that finishes freely and in various manners in the fantasy of the writer and in the cooperating and friendly fantasy of the reader, the two coinciding freely and in different ways. All of this happens normally in the context of writing, and it presupposes only nominally another language (in which form finds fulfillment). It is, in other words, an issue which establishes a rapport between metalanguages and their reciprocal forms.

What is most important to observe is that the word of the screenplay *is thus, contemporaneously, the sign of two different structures,* inasmuch as the meaning that it denotes is double: *And it belongs to two languages characterized by different structures.*

If, in formulating a definition in the necessarily limited field of writing, the sign of the screenplay-text is presented as the sign that denotes a "form in movement," a "form endowed with the will to become another form," in formulating the definition in the wider and more objective field of language, the sign of the screenplay-text is presented as the sign that expresses *meanings of a "structure in movement," that is, of "a structure endowed with the will to become another structure."*

This being the situation, what is the typical structure of the metalanguage of the screenplay? It is a "diachronic structure" by definition, or better still, to use that expression that generates a crisis for structuralism (particularly if understood conventionally, as by certain Italian groups), an expression used by Murdock, an actual "process." But a specific process, in that it is not a question of an evolution, of a passage from a phase A to a phase B, but of a pure and simple "dynamism," of a "tension" which moves, without departing or arriving, from a stylistic structure — that of narrative — to another stylistic structure — that of cinema — and, more deeply, from one linguistic system to another.

The screenplay-text's structure, which is "dynamic" but without functionality, and outside the laws of evolution, lends itself perfectly as object for a clash between the by now traditional concept of "structure" and the critical concept of "process." [. . .]

In conclusion, in cinema we unquestionably have systems or structures, with all the characteristics of every system and of every structure: A patient stylistic examination, such as that of an ethnologist among the Australian tribes, would reconstruct the permanent and solid data of those systems, both as schools (the international "cinema of poetry," as a kind of exquisite gothic) and as actual individual systems.

It is possible to do the same thing through a long and careful analysis of the "usages and customs" of screenplays: Here, too, as we all know intuitively or by experience not transformed into scientific research, a series of characteristics in tight rapport among themselves, endowed with a constant continuity, would constitute a "structure" typical of screenplays. We have seen, above, its "dynamic" characteristic, which, it seems to me, is a blatant case of a "diachronic structure," etc., etc. (with the "chronotope" of which Segre speaks as the essential internal element).[4]

The interest which this case offers is the concrete and demonstrable "will" of the author: which seems to me to contradict the assertion of Lévi-Strauss: "One cannot at one and the same time rigorously define a phase A and a phase B (which would be possible only from the outside and in structural terms) and empirically reanimate the passage from one to the other (which would be the only intelligible way of understanding it)."

In fact, in the presence of the "dynamic structure" of a screenplay, *of its will to be a form which moves toward another form,* we can very well define phase A with rigor from the outside and in structural terms (for example, the literary structure of the screenplay) and phase B (the cinematographic structure). But at the same time *we can empirically reanimate the passage from one to the other because the "structure of the screenplay" consists precisely in this: "passage from the literary stage to the cinematographic stage."*

If Lévi-Strauss were wrong in this case and Gurvitch and American sociology, Murdock, Vogt, were right, then we would have to accept the contention of the latter and adopt as our own their necessity to stress more the "process" than the "structure."

Reading, in fact, neither more nor less than reading a screenplay, means empirically reanimating the passage from a structure A to a structure B.

(1965)

The Written Language of Reality

"It doesn't matter," Socrates used to say, "however, first of all we must be careful that an unpleasant event doesn't befall us."
"Which one?" I ask.
And he answered, "To become misologists; that is, that an aversion and antipathy to all discussion rises in us. In the same way in which another becomes a misanthrope and develops an aversion and an antipathy for his fellow men. *Oh! Truly there is no greater calamity than this antipathy for all discussion."*

— Plato, *Phaedrus*

I. A linguistic preamble: The minimal unit of expression and double articulation

[. . .] The thesis put forth in these pages is that there is an actual audiovisual *"langue"* of cinema and that one can consequently describe or sketch out its grammar (which, as far as I am concerned, is certainly not normative!). But it is an essay by Christian Metz, "Film: *Langue* or *langage?"* (*Communications* no. 4), which compels me to review, to rethink, and to refuse many points of my thesis . . .[5]

The disagreement between Metz and myself appears to be deep but perhaps not incurable: Perhaps reconciliation is possible on the common ground offered by the concept of "discourse" furnished by Buyssens, *Les langages et le discours,* which I find cited by Metz but which I have yet to read firsthand.[6] Perhaps the "substance" he speaks of has something in common with the "language of action, or reality itself" to which I alluded above, and which is therefore given as "something linguistic" which is not, however, either *"langue"* or *"parole."* And Metz himself, commenting on this hypothesis by Buyssens, exclaims: "Langue, discourse, parole: a complete program!" Furthermore, Metz, in order to abandon his rigid definition of cinema as simple "art language," could make the effort to consider cinema as an enormous deposit of "written language" composed primarily of texts of narrative, poetry, and documentary essays. Should we perhaps resign ourselves immediately to not hypothesizing a possible *"langue"* predicated on this archaeological material only because it is made up of simple "art language" texts?

And so my rough grammatical outline is born, as a result of a crisis, and negatively, from the reading of Christian Metz, who, in defining cinema as *linguaggio* and not *lingua,* believes it possible to describe it semiotically, and not to make a grammar of it.[7]

The points of Metz's theory that I would like to discuss seem to me to be the following:

1) Metz dismantles the preceding linguistic theories concerning cinema without identifying the fact that they were primarily and in part unconsciously stylistic theories: that their code was not linguistic but prosodic. And that, in any case, many aspects of film communication are, given the particular circumstances in which cinema was born (let us reiterate, in fact, that cinema is only a "written" language), of prosodicostylistic derivation. (Moreover, this also happens often for linguistic conventions: Many expressions enter into the code, losing their initial expressiveness, etc., etc., and thus becoming conventional processes.)

2) Metz speaks of an "impression of reality" as a characteristic of film communication. I would say that it is a question not of an "impression of reality," but of "reality" itself — as we shall see better further on.

3) Metz has recourse to Martinet, with considerable justification, to demonstrate that cinema cannot be a language. In fact, Martinet says that there cannot be a language where the phenomenon of "double articulation" does not occur.[8] But I have two objections to make to this: first and foremost, that (as I said in the preamble) it is necessary to expand and perhaps revolutionize our notion of language, and *perhaps also to be ready to accept the scandalous existence of a language without a double articulation;* second, that it is not true, after all, that this second articulation does not exist in cinema. A form of second articulation also exists in cinema, and this, I believe, is the most relevant point of my paper.

But here is what I mean when I state that cinema, too, has a "second articulation."

It is not true that the smallest unit in cinema is the image, when by image we mean that "view" which is the shot, or, in other words, what one sees looking through the lens. All of us, Metz and I included, have always believed this. Instead: *The various real objects that compose a shot are the smallest unit of film language.*

I believe that there cannot be a shot composed of a single object, because there is no object in Nature composed only of itself and which cannot be further subdivided or broken down, or which, at the least, does not present different "manifestations" of itself.

No matter how detailed the shot, it is always composed of various objects or forms or acts of reality.

If I frame a close-up of a speaking man, and behind I perceive some books, a blackboard, a piece of a map, etc., I cannot say that such a shot is the smallest unit of my film discourse: because if I exclude one or the other of the real objects in the shot, I change the frame as signifier.

Now, if I wish, I can certainly change the shot. I cannot, however, change the objects which compose it, because they are objects of reality. I can *exclude them* or *include them,* that is all. But, whether I exclude or include them, I have an absolutely special and conditioning relationship with them. Scandalous from a linguistic point of view. Because, in the language that I am using with the shot of this "speaking man" — the language of film — reality, in its real and special objects and manifestations, remains, *is itself an instance of that language.*

To presume to express ourselves cinematographically without using objects, forms, acts of reality, including and incorporating them in our language, would be as absurd and inconceivable as presuming to express ourselves linguistically without using consonants and vowels, that is phonemes (the components of the second articulation).

The moneme "teacher" cannot be considered apart from the *t e a c h* and, in other words, all the phonemes which compose it: in the same way in which my shot of the teacher cannot be considered apart from the face of the teacher, the blackboard, the books, the piece of map, etc., which compose it.

We can define all the objects, forms, or enduring acts of reality to be found in the film image with the word "kinemes," precisely by analogy with "phonemes."

The phonemes in a language are few, approximately twenty, more or less, in the principal European languages. They are obligatory; we do not have other choices: At best we can try to learn some phonemes which are alien to us and which sound barbaric to our ears — the pharyngeal fricatives, the glottids, the clicks, etc., but we would not be expanding our options by much.

The kinemes have this same characteristic of obligatoriness: we can only choose from among the kinemes that exist, that is, the objects, forms, and acts of reality that we perceive with our senses.

As opposed to the phonemes, which are few, however, the kinemes are infinite, or at least innumerable. But this is not a qualitatively relevant difference. In fact, in the same way in which words or monemes are made up of phonemes, and this composition constitutes the double articulation of language, so the monemes of cinema — the shots — are composed of kinemes. The possibility of composition is equally varied for phonemes and kinemes (it should be noted that the compositional possibilities of linguistic monemes could be infinitely greater than they actually are).

The foremost characteristic of the phonemes is their untranslatability, that is, their brutality and natural indifference. An object of reality, as cinema, is also per se untranslatable, that is, a brute piece of reality. We are dealing with a different type of untranslatability, certainly less categorical. And this is, perhaps, the weak or questionable aspect to my theory. All things considered, however, it also seems to me that if the kinemes, the ultimate elements of the language of cinema, those which correspond to phonemes in language, have characteristics which are — per se — different from those of phonemes, the double articulation is thus assured in the language of cinema. (If there were a need for this.)

I must still add, however:

The language of cinema forms a "visual continuum" or "chain of images": In other words, it is linear, as is every language, which implies a succession of monemes and kinemes — which necessarily evolves in time. For the monemes, or shots, the demonstration is obvious. For the kinemes — or objects and forms of reality — of which the monemes, or shots, are composed, it is necessary to observe: It is true that they *apparently appear all together to our sight* and, in essence, to our senses, *and not in succession;* but there is nevertheless a succession of perception. We perceive them physically at the same time, but there is no doubt that a cybernetic graph of our perception would indicate a curve of succession. In the moneme that I took as an example, the shot of the close-up of the teacher, in reality we pick out successively the kinemes of the face, then that of the blackboard, then that of the books, then that of the map (or in a different order): It is, in sum, an addition of real details that indicate to us that the man is a teacher.

We know, furthermore, that beyond guaranteeing the economy of language the "double articulation" also guarantees its stability. But cinema doesn't need such a process of collective stabilization in showing an object, because it uses the object itself as part of the signifier: Thus the "value of the signified" is definitively assured!

We also know — still following in Martinet's footsteps — that every language has its own particular articulation, and that consequently "the words in one language do not have exact equivalents in another." But does this perhaps contradict the notion of a film language? No, not at all; because film is an international or universal language, the same for anyone who uses it. Therefore it is physically impossible to compare the language of cinema with another language of cinema.

Still paraphrasing Martinet, who represents the final and defining moment of Saussurean linguistics, we could conclude these first notes with the following definition of the language of cinema: "The language of cinema is an instrument of communication according to which we analyze human experience — in an *identical* manner in the different communities — in units which reproduce the semantic content and endow the monemes (or shots) with *audiovisual* expression; the audiovisual expression, in turn, is articulated in distinct, successive units, the *kinemes* or objects, forms, and acts of reality, which remain *reproduced* in the linguistic system — which are discrete, unlimited, and the same for all men regardless of their nationality."

From this it follows (still paraphrasing Martinet) that: (1) the language of cinema is an instrument of communication which has a double articulation and is endowed with a manifestation consisting in the audiovisual reproduction of reality; (2) the language of cinema is one and universal, and there is therefore no justification for comparisons with other languages: Its arbitrariness and conventionality concern only itself.

II. The grammar of the language of cinema

Before sketching the outline of my grammar of the language of cinema, I must, however, reiterate what I said above in piecemeal fashion or implicitly, enunciating it in more definitive and violent terms.

It is well known that what we call language, in general, is composed of oral language and written language. They are two different matters: The first is natural and, I would say, existential. Its means of communication is the mouth and its means of perception the ear: The channel is thus mouth-ear. As opposed to written language, oral language brings us without historical discontinuity to our origins, when such oral language was nothing more than a "cry," or a language of biological necessities, or, better still, of conditioned reflexes. There is a permanent aspect of oral language which remains unchanging. Oral language is thus a "static continuum," like nature, outside, that is, of historical evolution. There is an aspect of our oral communication that is therefore purely natural.

Written language is a convention that fixates this oral language and substitutes the graphic eye–reproduction channel for the mouth-ear channel.

Well, "cinema," too, can lay claim to a dichotomy which is strangely, and perhaps some will say insanely, analogous to this one.

To make myself understood I must [assert] . . . that there is first of all a *language of action* (which we can define as semiological by analogy with expressions such as "language of style," "language of flowers," etc., etc). . . .

It seems to me that the first language of men is their actions. The written-spoken language is nothing more than an integration and a means of such action. Even the moment of greatest detachment of language from such human action — that is, the purely expressive aspect of language, poetry — is in turn nothing more than another form of action: If, in the instant in which the reader listens to it or reads it, in other words, perceives it, he frees it again from linguistic conventions and re-creates it as the dynamic of feelings, of affections, of passions, of ideas; he reduces it to an audiovisual entity, that is, the reproduction of reality, of action — and so the circle is closed.

What is necessary, therefore, is the semiology of the language of action or, in simplest terms, of reality. That is, to expand the horizons of semiology and of linguistics to such an extent as to lose our heads at the very thought or to smile with irony, as is proper for specialists to do. But I have said from the beginning that this linguistic research on cinema matters to me, more than in itself, for the philosophical implications which it demands (perhaps even if I see them not as philosopher, but as poet, impatient to get to his own work . . .).

In reality, we make cinema by living, that is, by existing, practically, that is, by acting. *All of life in the entirety of its actions is a natural, living film; in this sense, it is the linguistic equivalent of oral language in its natural and biological aspect.*

By living, therefore, we represent ourselves, and we observe the representation of others. The reality of the human world is nothing more than this double representation in which we are both actors and spectators: a gigantic happening, if you will.

And in the same way in which we think linguistically — within ourselves, in silence, with what might be defined as a shorthand composed of rough, extremely rapid and also extremely expressive, albeit inarticulate, words — in the same way we also have the possibility, within us, to sketch out a cinematographic monologue; the processes of dreams and memory, both involuntary and, above all, voluntary, are the primordial outlines of a film language, understood as conventional representations of reality. When we remember, we project in our heads small, interrupted, contorted or lucid sequences of a film.

Now these archetypes of reproduction of the language of action or, in the simplest of terms, of reality (which is always action) have found concrete form in a common mechanical medium, the cinematographic. *It is, therefore, nothing more than the "written" manifestation of a natural, total language, which is the acting of reality.* In other words, the possible "language of action," for lack of a better definition, has found a means of mechanical reproduction *similar to the convention of written language as compared to oral language.*

I don't know if there is something monstrous, irrationalistic, and pragmatic in my references to a "total language of action," of which written-spoken languages are no more than an integration, in that they are an instrumental symbol of it; and of which film language would instead be the written or reproduced equivalent, which would respect its totality, it is true, but also its ontological mystery, its natural undifferentiation, etc. — a sort of reproductive memory without interpretation. . . .

III. Fishing in Reality: the grammatical modes of cinematic language

The foundation and determination of the grammar of cinema lie in the fact that the minimal units of the language of cinema are objects, forms, and actions of reality which have been reproduced and have become a stable, fundamental element of the signifier.

This persistence, through the mechanical reproduction of reality in the language of cinema, instead of becoming merely symbolic — as in written-spoken language — gives this language a completely special constitution.

Written-spoken language is neither a reproduction nor a nomenclature; however, without horrifying the linguists, I believe one can say that in its morphological, grammatical, and syntactical modes it is, so to speak, *parallel* to the reality that it expresses. In other words, the grammatical chain of signifiers is parallel to the series of signifieds. Its linearity is the linearity through which we perceive reality itself.

A graph of the grammatical modes of written-spoken language could thus be *a horizontal line* parallel to the line of reality — a world to be signified, or more simply, with a daring neologism, a *Significando* (a word with which it would always be right to humbly indicate Reality).

Instead, the graph of the grammatical modes of film language could be *a vertical line:* a line, that is, that *fishes* in the Significando, continuously takes it upon itself, incorporating it in itself through its immanence in the mechanical audiovisual reproduction.

What does the grammar of the language of cinema *fish* from reality? If fishes its smallest units, the units of the second articulation: the objects, the forms, the acts of reality which we have called "kinemes." After having fished them, it keeps them in itself, encapsulating them in its units of first articulation, the monemes — that is, the shots.

In this vertical axis which fishes in reality, that is, in this grammar of the language of cinema, we can distinguish the following four modes: (1) Modes of orthography or reproduction; (2) Modes of creating substantives; (3) Modes of qualification; (4) Modes of verbalization or syntax.

These four phases of the grammar of film are successive, obviously, only in a theoretical construct.

1. Modes of Reproduction (or Orthography). They consist of that series of techniques — which are acquired during one's apprenticeship — that are suitable to reproduce reality: the knowledge of the camera, of the process of shooting, of the problems of lighting, etc. and furthermore, practice in the composition of the raw material of film. (In this context I wish to recall that the analogy between cinema and the figurative arts has always been a questionable concept. The composition of the world in terms of presences and absences, etc., in front of the camera has some analogy with painting only in the sense that both film and painting "reproduce" reality with means proper to each. And this reproduction of reality gives to film — and perhaps also to painting — the characteristic of that abnormal and special language which is *solely a written language,* "the written language of action." There are therefore certain elements — let us call them compositional — that are in the matrix of both cinema and painting; it is with these that cinema is concerned — only indirectly, therefore, and as a result of a stylistic decision of the author, through the previous experience of painting.) In addition to the norms of cinematographic reproduction, the norms of sound reproduction are also part of the orthographic mode, because the reproduction of reality, indispensable to obtaining the units of second articulation, is an audiovisual reproduction. (Therefore I absolutely reject the notion that the true cinema is the silent cinema. It may be the true form of the art film, and in any case it belongs to the stylistic history of cinema, and I am not surprised that abandoning silent films caused so much pain to authors. It was, in fact, a meter of sorts, of extremely limiting prosody and, precisely as such, it was extremely imaginative. Silent film can thus still be the stylistic "choice" of the author who loves a strong and obsessive selectivity of prosodic options.)

2. Modes of Creating Substantives. I have called this aspect of grammar the creation of substantives, by analogy with the "substantives" of language. In reality the name is not correct, and it would be necessary to invent another. Shots or monemes can represent objects, forms, or acts of reality — that is, mobile or immobile reality, reality detailed or generalized, etc. — however, *the shot has the unchanging characteristic of creating a moneme with the units of second articulation.* This moneme is in itself and at the same time a noun, an adjective, or a verb — according to our usage. As we shall see, however, its qualities as adjective or verb affect the moneme only in a second phase; its first phase is that of being simply a moneme, that is, in the simplest of terms, a word which, because of its special nature — given that it is composed of objects — is primarily a substantive.

I believe that in the "modes of creating substantives" one must distinguish two phases:

1) The limitation of the second unit of articulation, that is, of the kinemes. This means that the person who speaks in terms of cinema must always choose from the unlimited objects, forms, and actions of reality according to what he wants to say. In short, he must first of all try to make *a closed list* from the list of kinemes. This will never be possible, and therefore only a relative closure, or a tendency toward closure, will be achieved. From this predictably derives an "open list" of the units of first articulation or film monemes (shots); these can therefore be infinite. But the precautionary or potential limitation of the kinemes will cause what we might call the "infinity of signs" of film words to find a limit precisely in the units of second articulation that constitute them — a limitation that produces, then, both an open list of monemes and their tendency to a less particular and transitory form of monosemia. Example: I want to describe a school. I immediately set a limit to the infinite things in reality, a choice of those things in the context of the academic environment. The shot of the teacher in front of a blackboard, a map, etc., is a moneme which is presented as tendentially monosemic: a teacher. While, in short, the "nature " of phonemes is *in us,* a subjective fact of the speaking individual — that is, of his body — the "nature" of kinemes is in the reality outside of us, in the social and physical world. It conserves those characteristics of this reality that cannot be eliminated. By this I mean that if cinema, as lexicon, that is, as a series of monemes (and semantemes and morphemes), is an individual and universal language, still as lexicon it is differentiated ethnically and historically. I will not find a burnoose among the kineme-objects of the Western world. I will instead find it in the Orient. Hence the substitution of national language differences, with some ethnohistorical variants.

2) The establishment of an always changeable series of nouns, contour lines, in their moment of the pure and simple shot, understood as a set of kinemes, and not considered in terms of their values of quality, duration, opposition, and rhythm. The shot, as a set of kinemes pure and simple, is thus a word which has the character of a noun, is not qualified, nor is it placed in relation to the rest of the discourse through syntactical (or editing) ties.

Thus understood, the substantive shot or moneme *corresponds to what is called in written-spoken languages the relative clause.* Each shot, in short, represents "something which is": a teacher *who* teaches, students *who* listen, horses *that* run; a boy *who* smiles; a woman *who* looks, etc., etc., or simply an object *which* is there. This series of relative clauses formed by a single moneme is the so-called "material" of the film. Such relative clause monemes, as lexical collection, are ideally fixed; if the camera catches them in movement they must be considered to be as numerous as are the theoretical shots of which the camera movement is composed.

Finally, it should be understood that there is no coincidence between "moneme" and shot; very often a shot is a sequence, however minimal, in which two or more monemes or relative clauses are *accumulated.*

The first form of syntax — that is, technically, of editing — thus may be found within the shot, through the *accumulation* of relative clauses.

3. Modes of Qualification. Various phases (not chronological, naturally) can also be distinguished in modes of qualification. As the word states, the means of qualification serve to qualify the substantives gathered in the manner described above, and are therefore different.

1) Profilmic qualification. This is used primarily in narrative (that is, nondocumentary) films. It consists of pure and simple exploitation, or the transformation of the reality to be reproduced. Or in the "makeup" of objects and persons. In the example already used, if the teacher is too young while he should be elderly, he is made up with white hair, etc. If the shot does not strike the director as being sufficiently expressive — to be that noun–relative clause which he wants

to pick up — the objects are moved (for example, the blackboard in the shot already mentioned in the example can't be seen enough? Well, it will be hung lower, etc.). Still, profilmic qualification tends to belong more to the prosody and to the stylistics of film than to its grammar.

2) Filmic qualification. This qualification of the noun–relative clause of which the film moneme is composed is obtained through the use of the camera and has well-noted characteristics.

Filmic qualification includes the distance of the lens from that set of real units that must be shot; that is, the definitions of extreme close-up, close-up, two shot and long shot, master shot, are technical definitions of qualification.

Let us continue with the example of the teacher: With the modes of creating substantives we have made a choice of objects, forms, and actions taken from reality which, framed together — that is, having become a moneme — form the noun-relative clause "a teacher who teaches." With the qualification described above, we can thus have "a teacher who teaches while laughing" or "an angry teacher who teaches" (profilmic qualification), and "a teacher who teaches seen close up," "a teacher who teaches seen in long shot," "a teacher who teaches an unexpected thing," etc. (filmic qualification).

It remains to be said that filmic qualification can be active or passive. It is active when it is the camera that moves or that, in any case, prevails (for example: a zoom shot of "the teacher who teaches," or a tracking shot of "the teacher who teaches"). It is passive when the camera is motionless or is not felt, while the real object moves (for example: the camera remains on the teacher, who moves toward and away from it as he teaches). Naturally, one also has a "deponent" qualification when the movement of the camera and of the object in reality annul each other or in any case have an equal value.

At this point I would like to clarify one fact. *Active and passive qualifications refer to the reproduced reality.* That is, if in the close-up of the moving teacher the camera is still, the qualification is active, because it is the teacher *who acts;* if, instead, in the close-up of the teacher the camera moves — drawing near, moving away, panning, etc. — the filmic qualification is passive, because this time the teacher is *affected* by the camera.

If the active qualification predominates, the film tends to be realistic, because reality acts in and on it, which implies the author's faith in the objectivity of reality (cf. John Ford).

If the passive qualification predominates, the film is lyrical-subjective, because it is the author with his style who acts, which implies a subjective vision of reality on his part (cf. Godard).

4. Modes of Verbalization (or Syntax). The technical definition of these modes is "editing."

But this time, too, we must distinguish two types or two phases of editing.

1) Denotative editing. It consists of a series of connections, elliptical by definition, between various shots or monemes, giving them first of all a "length" and subsequently a linking whose function is the communication of an articulated discourse. It is, in sum, the syntactical phase: coordination and subordination.

The first effect of this "denotative" or purely syntactical "editing" *is that the monemes lose their characteristic as first phase, that is, of being noun–relative clauses, and become quite simply the monemes typical of the film, with the respective qualification.* Since the one and only characteristic of editing is to establish an oppositional relationship, it is precisely through this oppositional relationship that it fulfills its syntactical function.

Denotative editing in fact puts the two shots in oppositional relationship, juxtaposing them by ellipsis: "the teacher *who* teaches" and "the students *who* listen," etc. But it is precisely in this oppositional relationship that syntax is born; that is, finally, the sentence "the teacher who teaches the students."

This series of extremely simple "oppositions" thus requires a type of syntax which we can call *additive* in opposition to the *accumulative* syntax which we have said occurs when the "relative clauses" accumulate within one shot, understood as a however-minimal sequence shot.

These additions are what the experts of editing call "links": That is, they link one shot to the next, establishing their duration. What follows is a series of clauses or a "set of clauses" which could better be defined as "syntactical complements," in that they are placed exactly between the clause and the complement.

I will give one example: I have two shots or monemes: the relative clauses "the teacher *who* looks" and "the students *who* look." If I add the second to the first, the clause "the students who look"‑becomes the direct object complement and thus I have the sentence, "the teacher *who* looks at the students."

It is sufficiently clear from this example that the syntax of cinema is inevitably progressive. It forms "series" of clauses, or better, of syntactical complements. This series, ongoing as the result of a series of additions, is progressive precisely because if, for example, I place the direct object clause first, the meaning of the whole changes ("the students who look at the teacher"). The special syntax of cinema is thus a rough linear progressive series: Everything which in language is parenthesis, change of tone, melodic line, curses, etc., is realized in cinema as expressive language, as we shall see, by the rhythms — that is, by the reciprocal relationships of the duration of the clauses.

2) Rhythmic (or connotative) editing. It is difficult to establish the real relationship between denotative editing and rhythmic or connotative editing; up to a certain point they coincide. Beyond a certain point the rhythmic editing would appear to be typical of a form of expressiveness which should be opposed to denotation as such.[9]

The rhythmic montage defines the duration of the shots, in and of themselves and relative to the other shots of the context.

The "duration" established by the rhythmic editing *is therefore before all else an additional qualification.* If fact, if I pause on the shot of "the teacher *who* teaches" only for the time necessary to perceive it, the qualification is profilmic; if I stop more or less than necessary, the qualification becomes, however, expressive; and if I stop *much* more or *much* less than necessary, the qualification becomes actively filmic, that is, it causes us to be aware of that camera which, even while shooting, could also have been motionless. Its presence is felt precisely in the irregularity of the length of the shot itself.

When instead the "duration" is not considered as such but relative to the other shots of the film, we enter into the real field of rhythmic editing.

Even in the most aridly communicative and inexpressive film — that is, in the most potentially exploitative film language — there is the presence of a rhythm which is born of the relations of length between the various shots, and of the length of the entire film. As simple relationship of duration between the various shots, the rhythm is necessary to the most prosaic and practical actual communication of the film.

The "rhythmeme" therefore assumes particular value in the language of cinema, both in communicative editing and rhythmic editing carried to the limits of expression. In the latter case it becomes the principal rhetorical figure in cinema, whereas in literature it appears to be secondary or at least in second place.

[. . .]

(1966)

The Nonverbal As Another Verbality[10]

It has always been said that not all thought is verbal. But perhaps because of the scarcity of my information, the incompleteness of my hurried readings, I have NEVER encountered a definition of the "nonverbal."

May I take the liberty of searching for something which resembles such a needed definition?

For some time now I have been speaking of a code of cinematographic decoding analogous to that of the decoding of reality. This implies the definition of reality *as Language*.

The book of the world, the book of nature; the prose of pragmatism, the poetry of life; these are commonplaces which come first in the wild prehistory of a "General Semiology of Reality as Language."

I have before me, in my garden in Eur,[11] a small oak tree: It is part of the reality which speaks; it encodes. The relationship is direct. I can speak of this oak to another and thus employ the written-spoken medium. This written-spoken medium is part of reality; in a General Semiology, on the latter [reality], languages would occupy the place of one of its many elements, etc., neither more nor less, etc.

But it is strange; man has always dissociated written-spoken language from reality. In the long history of cults, every object of reality has been considered sacred; this has never happened with language. Language has never appeared as hierophant.

Only in the heart of bourgeois culture was an actual, constant, important metalinguistic awareness born, and in fact language was made sacred, even if we remain in the literary context and do not spread out into that of religion — disregarding a generic mystical coalition. I am speaking of symbolism, of hermeticism, and in general of all the avant-garde movements of the second half of the nineteenth century and the first half of the twentieth.

The metalinguistic awareness which has in some way, for the first time, made language sacred has been a classist phenomenon of entropy: it has been a phenomenon lived entirely within the bourgeoisie.

The working class and Marxism have remained extraneous to this sacralizing process of the bourgeoisie: they acquired rationality, not the mystifying irrationality of the "confrontational" avant-garde movements.

Therefore, for the working class and for Marxist ideology language has remained a simple function, and the awareness of it was what it always was: the idea of a means of communication (perhaps also of the sacred). However, during all the long centuries in which there did not exist a "thing" or "phenomenon" of reality which did not know the glory of the tabernacle, language has always been considered the principal instrument in this relationship with reality. Magic formula, prayer, and miraculous identification with the thing indicated. Language has never lost its characteristic as "evocation," which was perceived in a purely instrumental fashion.

So far as I know, in defining the relationship between sign and signified, all of "scientific" linguistics, including structuralism, with the great Saussure, etc., has always ignored the original magic moment. Naturally linguistics is a science, and a science of the nineteenth and twentieth centuries. When pure, innocent Racism, etc., was still in force — the idea of the greatness of Europe, of the greatness of the white bourgeoisie, etc. — magic was all colored.

What does the "sign" make of the "signified": does it "signify" it? It's a tautology. Does it point to it? It isn't scientific. Does it identify with it? It's an old quarrel between "nomen" and "res," etc., etc.

In reality there is no "signified": *because the signified is also a sign.*

Allow me the poet's freedom to state free things freely.

Yes, this oak tree that I have in front of me is not the "signified" of the written-spoken sign "oak tree": *no, this physical oak tree here in front of my sense is itself a sign* — certainly not a written-spoken sign, but iconic-living, or however else one might wish to define it.

Therefore, in substance the "signs" of the verbal languages do nothing more than translate the "signs" of the nonverbal languages, or in the case in point, the signs in the written-spoken languages merely *translate* the signs of the Language of Reality.

The location in which this translation takes place is the interior.

Through the translation of the written-spoken sign, the nonverbal sign, that is, the Object of Reality, presents itself once again, evoked in its physicality, in the imagination.

The nonverbal, therefore, is nothing other than another verbality, that of the Language of Reality.

Whether I use writing or I use cinema, I merely evoke the Language of Reality in its physicality by translating it.

In any case, I always give it Primacy. This is the *Fas-Nefas* of every author.[12]

Reading my "monologizing" verses through the statement a reader thus finds himself in the presence of the nonverbal (including the statement which I adopt to communicate, that is, *to evoke*).

In every written text and in every spoken proposition (and not only in the screenplay) *one thus has a structure which wants to become another structure;* in other words, one has the process from the structure of the written-spoken language to the structure of the language of "reevoked" language, with all the regression that this implies.

In fact, when I say "oak tree" I regress to that original structure of language which is the Language of Reality, in order to then advance to the field of an imagination other than mine where the oak tree "sign of the language of Reality" is reconstituted as evoked (or remembered) physicality.

The process is the following: oak tree as sign of the Language of Reality — "oak tree" as written-spoken sign which *translates* it — oak tree as sign of the Language of imagined Reality.

Written-spoken languages are *translations by evocation:* audiovisual languages (cinema) are *translations by reproduction.*

The translated Language, therefore, is always the nonverbal language of Reality.

The Code of Codes

A blond young man, my dear Eco, advances toward you. You do not smell him. Perhaps because he has no smell, or because he is far away, or because other odors form a barrier between him and you, or perhaps because you have a cold. Strange, because he should have a certain odor on him. He is blond, I tell you, but his blondness is slightly sooty, as if streaked with ancestral patinas, neglected and excluded from the barbaric and bourgeois blond of the great rich countries of the North. One would not say that he is racially blond. A joke, perhaps, of destiny. Or perhaps some unfaithfulness of some good struggling mother whose genealogical tree is unknown (Degli Esposti, Degli Innocenti, Degli Angeli, Dei Morti di Fame),[13] perpetrated by some soldier of a cold, foreign mercenary army.

This blond hair is excessive; it forms what amounts to a fur hat, but the wind has disheveled that fur hat, and only a tall plume has remained, which (now that the wind has died down) forms a small monument out of proportion to the minute face. The minute face has lost eyes. They must be brown, but torment makes them opaque and seems to fill them with the yellow of old proletarian ills. With that yellow variegated gaze he looks around himself with a, so to speak, immobile mobility. He is overcome by fear. Worry about being there keeps him in suspense, hung up as if on a coat hanger. This impression is also increased by his get-up. It's a blue coat with gold buttons, from which a long handkerchief or a brazen multicolored scarf dangles, after having been twisted around his neck. The legs under the sailor's greatcoat are scrawny. On his feet he wears small boots. A crumpled book sticks out of a pocket of his coat. The pallor of his face, the lower-class features, the contrast between the dirty, sooty blond of his hair, the gaudy poverty of his clothing, the smallness of his legs — everything makes one think of a Neapolitan; perhaps a youth who comes from the province of Naples: let us suppose from the land of the Mazzoni. Yes, a peasant race (in a hinterland not far from the sea) more than a sailor. But that book which sticks out of his coat (a cheap edition of Dante)? And that lost look, isn't its insecurity masked by timidity and hatred, as in the poor immigrants? In fact he draws close to you and, as if you were transparent, he whispers toward you, "I love Benedetta."

In describing this youth in long shot who comes toward you and speaks a sentence, I, as you see, have used the system of signs of our written language. If I had met you at some conference at Frascati or Palermo, I would have used the system of signs of our spoken language.

What you have not understood is whether I have thus described for you with words Jerry Malanga in reality or Jerry Malanga in a film.[14]

You would say that I have cheated. No. I made an analytical and not a technical description. I have in fact used — with metaphorical ambiguity, out of honesty — the "screenplay" term, long shot.

By now I have repeated many times that the Code of Reality and the Code of Cinema (of the cinematographic *langue,* which does not exist because only films/*paroles* exist) are the same Code.

It is in the name of this code that I almost experimentally draw near to the identification of Jerry Malanga, or at least of "a Neapolitan immigrant in America and returned to Italy with an attitude in which Neapolitan folklore and beat folklore have strange points in common." All this second definition is — from a lively and artistic point of view — the product of a cognitive code which serves me to recognize both the real Malanga and the cinematographic one.

Well, no. I played a joke on you. The Malanga in the long shot that I have described to you in a "lively" style is neither the Malanga of reality (street or drawing room) nor the Malanga of the screen.

What Malanga is he, then?

I won't tell you, because I want to continue the joke.

I will tell you later, forcing you, for now, to follow the line of my argument.

In your book *Notes for a Semiology of Visual Communications,*[15] splendid in its clarity (and I hope useful not only to the fortunate Florentine students to whom it is addressed), there are some preliminary observations to be made.

A) You analyze a potentially infinite series of cognitive codes whose first and most simple units are at times the last and the most complex of what might be described as an underlying code. On various occasions you seem to arrive at the analysis of the most UNDERLYING of all the codes. And there you stop. One therefore has the impression that your book was written on the brink of an abyss. You do not lean out beyond that edge. You nearly touch it and then you back off, after having glanced at it absentmindedly. This code, the most UNDERLYING of all, is the one which concerns sensory perception, which you submit to the judgment of psychology, I believe, or to I don't know what other specific science, presenting it thus in your book as a given, to be examined thoroughly elsewhere.

Leafing through your book I could list for you all or almost all of the places in which you stop, announcing the existence of a relationship of sensory perception with physical reality, on which then falls precisely the deep silence of an abyss.

B) On page 142, devoting yourself to my amateurish comments with a patience for which I am very grateful (cf. the rudeness of certain university professors), you write: "These comments would also eliminate Pasolini's idea of a cinema as semiology of reality, and his belief that the elementary signs of the cinematographic language are the real objects reproduced on the screen (a belief, we now know, of a *singular semiological naiveté* [the italics are mine — PPP] and which is in contrast with the most elementary aims of semiology, which is to eventually reduce the facts of nature to cultural phenomena, and not to bring the facts of culture back to natural phenomena)."[16]

Dear Eco, things are exactly the opposite of how you interpret them. That I am naive, there is no doubt, and in fact, because I am not a petit bourgeois — with all the violence of a maniac also in not wanting to be such — I am not afraid of naiveté; I am happy to be naive and also perhaps sometimes to be ridiculous.

But certainly this is not what you wanted to say; you said "naiveté" as a euphemism for "artlessness." I would also be willing to accept artlessness (which does exist), but not in this instance. Because all my chaotic pages on this topic (the code of the cinema equal to the code of reality in the context of a General Semiology) *tend to bring Semiology to the definitive transformation of nature into culture.* (I have repeated seven or eight times that a General Semiology of reality would be a philosophy which interprets reality as language.) In other words, I would like to plumb the depths. I would not want to stop on the brink of the abyss on which you stop. I would not want, that is, for any dogma to have any value; while in you, unconsciously, at least two dogmas remain consecrated: the dogma of semiology as it is and the dogma of secularism.

I am completely secular; as a child I escaped the lessons of doctrine: I was not confirmed, my father was not a believer, my mother — believing in a world full of archaic sweetness — never even compelled me to go to mass. And so, not even anticlericalism in my family (whence eventually mystical revivals).[17] I am also fairly rational, so that even if I should rebel against the omnipotence and omnipresence of reason as the myth of the bourgeoisie (cf. Goldmann), I would do it reasoning sweetly.

Let us therefore suppose, "per absurdum" — I stress "per absurdum" — that God exists. Let us transform nature into culture in the only way that is possible in advance. And let us dedicate no more than half a page to this fatuous matter.

If the God of Confessions existed, what would the semiologists say of the "sema"? And could Jakobson still say that "objects" (those famous natural objects or things, such as stones, trees, noses, bottles, etc., etc.) are "signs of themselves" and, in such a manner, "reveal themselves"? Or, by chance, nature would not cease to be "nature" or self-revealing tautology, at the bottom of that abyss in which you leave our sensory relations immersed along with it? Sensory relations that constitute our psychophysical knowledge of natural reality, which is fulfilled according to the most UNDERLYING (but this nonetheless the most INTERACTING) of codes?

Now, because it is irritating to speak of God among secular people, let us limit ourselves to calling God Brahma, and let us shorten this to B.

The existence of B. (whose character is Vedic-Spinozan) causes the statement "reality is a language" to no longer be apodictic and unmotivated, but [to be] in some way sensible and functional: "reality is the language of B."

With whom does B. speak? Let us assume with Umberto Eco. (Who, having been extremely Catholic, I am told, now, concerning B., is a bit defensive.) Let us assume that in this moment B. speaks with Eco, using as sign, as ultimate sign, the hair of Jerry Malanga. But what difference is there between the hair of Jerry Malanga and the eyes of Umberto Eco? They are but two organisms of reality, which is a *continuum* without any break in continuity; a single body, as far as I know. The hair of Jerry Malanga and the eyes of Umberto Eco therefore belong to the same Body, the physical manifestation of the Real, of the Existing, of Being; and if the hair of Jerry Malanga is an object that "reveals itself" as "sign of itself" to the receptive eyes of Umberto Eco, it cannot be said that this is a dialogue; [it is] a monologue which the infinite Body of Reality has with itself.

At this point we can also free ourselves from the embarrassing notion of B. (which I do without trauma, as one who is secular without the religion, that is, the dogma, of secularism) and simply say that "Reality speaks with itself," that the "sema" speak to other "sema" in a single context in which revelation and comprehension, question and answer, are the same thing (transmitter and receiver are identical).

You object that it is not possible that the "objects of reality" can be the second level of articulation of cinema. But you yourself teach me that codes can be interactive. I therefore do not see why the minimal unit of an Ur-code — that is, the cognitive code of reality, that is, the self-revealing objects — cannot become a minimal level of another, higher code which is more cultural in a technical sense.

And after all, don't you yourself say it? "And from simplification to simplification, the dream of the structuralist is, in the end, that of identifying the Code of Codes, the *Ur-code,* so as to permit the discovery of rhythms and cadences (the same operations and elementary relations) within all human behavior, analogous to the cultural and biological ones" (p. 48).

Why have you allowed yourself to be awakened from this dream? Are you afraid of dreams? And why, if the structuralist can permit himself dreams, cannot the semiologist do so? And in the case that the semiologist, too, should want to dream, what is the best way of identifying the Ur-code, if not by considering "reality as language" (and not as a series of languages)?

"This Ur-code" — you add — "would consist of the very mechanism of the human mind rendered homologous to the mechanism which presides over the organic functions." Why do you thus stop every time (barely hinting at its existence) with a code of perception which man-in-nature has of nature?

Further on you say again: "... But the first warning to keep in mind in a semiological research is that *not all the signifying phenomena can be explained with the categories of linguistics*" (p. 107).

Therefore the attempt to interpret visual communications semiotically is of interest in this sense: It allows semiology to demonstrate the possibility of independence from linguistics.

Because there are in fact sign phenomena which are considerably less precise than the phenomena of visual communication strictly speaking (painting, sculpture, drawing, signal codes, cinema or photography), a semiology of visual communications will be able to constitute a bridge toward the semiological definition of other cultural systems (those which, for example, put into play usable objects, as happens with architecture or industrial design).

Magnificent! But why not take yet another step forward toward the total transformation of physical and human reality into cultural phenomena, and examine sign phenomena that are *considerably less precise,* as are, in point of fact, those of physical and human reality in its totality, that is, the "im-signs" (according to the terminology of Peirce)?[18]

For every definition of the sign, you say, there is a corresponding phenomenon of visual communication. For the "im-sign," for example, there is the corresponding example of the portrait of Mona Lisa or the live shot footage of a televised event. . . .[19]

Magnificent! But, still on the level of the direct psychophysical cognitive relationship, does the phenomenon of visual communication not also correspond to the "natural im-sign" consisting of Mona Lisa herself in flesh and blood (even though now dead), or to the Inter-Bologna soccer match itself, played one afternoon of one Sunday of this November and unfortunately lost by Bologna because of a questionable penalty kick?[20] Or do you want to relegate these "real im-signs" to the limbo of that nature which cannot be transformed into cultural phenomena?

What were the eyes of Leonardo or the eighty thousand pairs of eyes of the fans that Sunday if not the protagonists of a cognitive relationship with those "natural im-signs"?

And, after all, you yourself say it — overwhelmed by an unforeseen elegiac impulse: "When from the rosy light which spreads in the sky I deduce the imminent rising of the sun, am I already responding to the presence of a sign which is recognizable through learning?" (p. 109).

It is B., it is B., dear Eco, who says to himself, through the pink im-sign of the light and through your looking eyes, that a new day is breaking.

And at this level the Ur-code must be identified by the semiologists.

And so, through the very words of Morris, which instance a wonderful intuition, which is not, however, carried to its extreme consequences (a General Semiology), we have arrived at the center of the question: "The portrait of a person is to a considerable extent iconic, but is not completely so since the painted canvas does not have the texture of the skin, or the capacities for speech and motion, which the person portrayed has. The motion picture is more iconic, but again not completely so."[21] So says Morris, and you comment: "Such an approach, when pushed to its limit, would persuade both Morris and common sense to destroy the notion of iconism; 'a completely iconic sign would always denote since it would be itself a denotatum,' which is the same as saying that the true and complete iconic sign of Queen Elizabeth is not Annigoni's portrait but the Queen herself (or a possible science fiction *doppelgänger*)" (p. 110).[22]

The truth is subtle, damned, and impudent, nor does it acknowledge restraints or one-way signs! You said it jokingly. In fact, every one of us and every object and event in reality "is the iconic object of itself." Not only that but you yourself have established a possible Saussurean catalogue of things, making a joking reference to science fiction: the "double" of which you speak is nothing more than the abstraction of the "living *langue*" which has been deduced from the presence of the "living *parole*" constituted by Queen Elizabeth in person!

Also, the language with which B. speaks with itself in a Spinozan fashion is therefore divided into *"langue"* and *"parole"*!

And at this point I am going to jot down in two lines a thing which, to be minimally validated, would require an entire essay — so be it.

If reality is a language, it can therefore only be predicated on a Saussurean model, because, notwithstanding the act of independence from linguistics performed in practical terms by semiology, there is no possible "system of signs" which does not articulate itself in a code-abstraction (*langue*) and in a living-concreteness (*parole*). So: let us consider the Queen of England. The Queen of England exists only as an iconic symbol of herself in the context of the *"parole,"* that is, in her psychological, physical, moral, personal, sexual, carnal concreteness; but from this one "deduces" an abstract Queen of England on the codified and codifying level of *"langue";* here the Queen of England, although remaining always an abstract "iconic symbol of herself," loses every intimate and unrepeatable concreteness and becomes a public, social, and personal datum. The concrete person is therefore not the iconic symbol of herself as *"parole";* instead, the abstract person — that is, in social classifications — is the iconic symbol of herself as *"langue."* This happens for living and conscious persons as we two and the Queen of England are; it also happens for animals, things, events; the living im-signs, the semes. They, too, are concrete, figural symbols of themselves in their physical, noninterchangeable but violently singular presence; and they are figural symbols of themselves in the *"langue"* constituted by generalizations, classifications, genera, species — in short, by all that which is general, public, etc.

(1967)

Note

This letter has remained in a fragmentary state. But I want to at least finish the joke played on Eco.

Well, then, that "blond boy" presented at the beginning through the signs of the written-spoken system of Italian, and subsequently decoded according to the code of the latter, is not a "blond boy" in reality nor a "blond boy" on the screen. *He is a "blond boy" on the stage.*

In the stratification of systems, the underlying system lends itself as material for the "double articulation" of the higher system. The "blond boy" (or the Queen of England) could also be photographed, painted, or sculpted. In short, he could be an iconic sign of himself in the context of many systems of signs, each one with its specific code. But he would never be encodable in any of these systems of signs if he were not *first of all* decodable in the system of the signs of Reality as Self-revelation or as First Language, through its code, which is the Code of Codes.

This does not transform the cultural codes (literature, cinema, linguistics) into natural phenomena, but, on the contrary, transforms nature into cultural phenomena: It transforms all life into speech.

(January 15, 1971)

Notes

Those notes provided by the editors and translators of the English version of Pasolini's essays, Louise Barnett and Ben Lawton, are indicated by "LB/BL."

1. "Lin-sign," short for language sign, is Pasolini's term for the written or spoken word. It corresponds more or less to what structural linguists would call the "signifier"; and its counterpart in cinema is the "im-sign," or plastic image. — ED.

2. By the phrase "prevarication of its phoneme," Pasolini appears to suggest that in Mallarmé's and Ungaretti's poetry the meaning of a particular word is expanded by using the word in such a way that it "breaches the trust" ordinarily established between sound and meaning. He uses "prevarication" in unusual contexts elsewhere as well. — ED.

3. "Im-sign," or image sign, is discussed further by Pasolini in his "Cinema of Poetry" [in *Heretical Empiricism* (Bloomington: Indiana University Press, 1988)], pp. 167–86. — LB/BL

4. "By imagining the work of art as three-dimensional space, we would be able to say that the various critical methodologies have preferred to cover — from time to time — a single dimension, plucking surfaces or lines out of the work. . . . Structuralism, thanks to the greater organic quality of its presentations, can aim at a three-dimensional analysis. . . . The theory of relativity, however, has integrated a fourth dimension — time — with the three of Euclidean geometry. Now one could very well demand . . . a critical description of the work that integrates the new dimension with the three traditional ones. This means taking (historical) time into consideration, but in its aspect of dimension of a work, understanding a work of art, in short, as a *chronotope*." Cesare Segre, *I Segni e la critica* [Signs and criticism, Turin, 1969], p. 28; quoted by Pasolini in "From the Laboratory," *Heretical Empiricism*, pp. 75–76. Cf. M. M. Bakhtin's use of "chronotope": "The intrinsic connectedness of temporal and spatial relationships that are artistically expressed in literature." *The Dialogic Imagination*, edited by M. Holquist and translated by C. Emerson and M. Holquist (Austin: University of Texas Press, 1981), p. 84 — ED.

5. "Le cinéma: langue ou langage?" *Communications* 4 (1964):52–90, was reprinted in Metz's book *Essais sur la signification au cinéma* (Paris: Klincksieck, 1969), pp. 39–93, and is included in his *Film Language* (New York: Oxford University Press, 1974), pp. 31–91. — LB/BL

6. Eric Buyssens, *Les langages et le discours, essai de linguistique fonctionelle dans le cadre de la sémiologie* (Brussels, 1943). Buyssens writes: "Only discourse is at the same time an act and an abstraction: It is an ideal act" (p. 31).

7. Both *lingua* and *linguaggio* may be translated as "language." *Lingua,* however, the more standard and specific term, means language system; *linguaggio,* meaning any communicative activity, often refers to jargons or restricted vocabularies such as scientific language, legal language, or to the activity of speaking or expressing, as in "the language of flowers." — LB/BL

8. See André Martinet, *Eléments de linguistique générale* (Paris: A. Colin, 1963); translated by E. Palmer, *Elements of General Linguistics* (Chicago: University of Chicago Press, 1964), pp. 22–29. — LB/BL

   The "double articulation" that characterizes phonological language (the language that we speak and that I am writing now) may be defined as "a limited number of abstract signs, discrete units (phonemes) that are meaningless in themselves, which, in combination, go to make up a vast number of words or meaningful units (morphemes)." [Keith Cohen, *Film and Fiction* (New Haven: Yale University Press, 1979), p. 89.] The lack of double articulation, imputed to cinema by the French linguists and film semioticians, is here being challenged by Pasolini. — ED.

9. This confusion probably depends on the fact that while monemes consist of a reproduction of reality, their rhythms, that is, their relations, do not; everything in cinema is reproduced from reality, but not the rhythms which only accidentally coincide with those of reality. It is in the rhythms, therefore, that is, in the editing, that one can speak most of all of arbitrariness and conventionality in the language of cinema.

10. From an epistolary interview with S. Arecco (*Filmcritica,* March 1971). — LB/BL

11. Eur is a modernistic residential quarter of Rome envisioned by Mussolini as a planned new city. Pasolini moved there in 1963. — LB/BL

12. *Fas:* permitted by the gods; *Nefas:* offensive to the gods (literally, "unspeakable"). — LB/BL

13. Degli Esposti, "of the exposed"; Degli Innocenti, "of the innocent"; Degli Angeli, "of the angels"; are all last names traditionally given to foundlings. Dei Morti di Fame, "of the dying of hunger," with connotations of sexual frustration, is a Pasolini joke. — LB/BL

14. Jerry Malanga, an actor with the Living Theater of Julian Beck and Judith Malina. — LB/BL

15. *Appunti per una semiologia delle communicazione visive* (Notes for a semiology of visual communications) (Milan: Bompiani, 1967). Now incorporated in *La Struttura assente* (The absent structure) (Milan: Bompiani, 1968) as parts A, B, and C. Rather than translating *La Struttura assente,* which incorporates *Appunti* . . . , Eco wrote the book in English as *A Theory of Semiotics* (Bloomington: Indiana University Press, 1976). — LB/BL

16. *La Struttura assente,* p. 152. Hereafter page references will be to the first Italian edition of Eco's book and will appear in parentheses. — ED.

17. "Revivals" appears in English in the original. — LB/BL

18. Peirce writes: "A *Sinsign* (where the syllable *sin* is taken as meaning 'being only once,' as in *single, simple,* Latin *semel,* etc.) is an actual existent thing or event which is a sign." *Collected Papers of Charles Sanders Peirce,* edited by C.

Hartshorne and P. Weiss (Cambridge, MA: Belknap Press of Harvard University Press, 1960), vol. 2, p. 250.

19. Pasolini is referring to a chart in Eco's *Struttura*, p. 108. — LB/BL

20. Inter is a Milanese soccer team. — LB/BL

21. Charles Morris, *Signs, Language and Behavior* (New York: Prentice-Hall, 1946), p. 23.

22. Eco's own English version has been used here: *A Theory of Semiotics*, p. 192. — LB/BL

Part 3

Cinema: The Other
Apprenticeship

Jonathan Baumbach, 1933–   8

 leading experimenter in narrative form, Jonathan Baumbach teaches English at Brooklyn College of the City University of New York. His novels include *A Man to Conjure With* (1965), *What Comes Next* (1968), *Reruns* (1974), *Babble* (1976), *Chez Charlotte and Emily* (1979), and *My Father More or Less* (1982). His stories have appeared in *Partisan Review, Fiction, TriQuarterly,* and *Esquire,* among other journals and a collection of his stories, *The Return of Service,* was published in 1979. His most recent novel, *Separate Hours,* came out in 1990.

Baumbach wrote a critical study in 1965, *The Landscape of Nightmare: Studies in the Contemporary American Novel,* in which he surveys the works of major American novelists of the post–World War II era in terms of innocence, guilt, and redemption. Through detailed analyses of texts by Saul Bellow, Ralph Ellison, Bernard Malamud, Wright Morris, Flannery O'Connor, J. D. Salinger, William Styron, Edward Wallant, and Robert Penn Warren, he attempts to account for the nightmarish atmosphere pervading the lives of these authors' characters and the ways that atmosphere impinges on their individual consciousnesses.

With Ronald Sukenick, Baumbach founded the Fiction Collective, a free-wheeling group of writers intent on publishing fiction that cannot easily find an outlet in today's commercial book industry. He now codirects the collective, which has brought out novels of a wide variety of tastes and styles as well as two anthologies of its writers' works, *Statements: New Fiction From the Fiction Collective* (1975, 1977).

His dedication to risk-taking and to bringing experimental writing to the attention of the reading public is reflected in his own writing. Like Pier Paolo Pasolini, he maintains a loyalty to his ethnic and class roots. His early years in a Jewish neighborhood of Brooklyn, which he alludes to briefly in the essay that follows, frame a good number of the key scenes of his novels. *Reruns,* for example, a novel built around the experience and metaphor of seeing movies again and again, opens with a breakfast scene officiated by a mother "wearing a nurse's mask to keep her germs off the food,"[1] whose culinary loyalties are unevenly divided between husband and son (the narrator). Enforced eating, which we already associate with the loving tyranny of certain American Jewish households from the works of Philip Roth and Bernard Malamud, plays a counterpoint throughout the novel to the distracted consumption of movies, that all-pervasive product of popular culture that forms, as in Puig's works, the stuff of both reality and fantasy.

A hilarious yet unsettling scene accents the confusion between reality and fantasy one constantly feels in *Reruns.* The narrator, who is sitting in a movie theater in which *Marty Meets the King of Kings* ("a revival under new title of something we had already seen"[2]) is playing, alternately acts aggressively toward and is confronted by various members of the audience. As he and his "friends" are being ejected from the theater by a matron and three ushers, the screen actors (Ernest Borgnine, among others) merge with the characters groping around the dark auditorium for the exit. The matron escorting the narrator becomes indistinguishable from an ax-wielding matron in the coming attraction, and the narrator has an "odd sensation": "I glanced up at the screen, saw myself say what I had said, followed by Anna [one of his friends] saying what she had said."[3]

Fantasy plays an integral, if not predominant, part in all of Baumbach's works. Characters named Francis (not Frank) Sinatra and Judith (not Judy) Garland play major parts in *Chez Charlotte and Emily,* a multitiered narrative that must eventually take into account the screen personalities of the characters' namesakes. As Baumbach points out, Francis's story, which has several variants within the contours of the novel, is clearly marked within the realm of fantasy, or "the world of the imagination." This imaginary realm, though, is far from being the playful contrivance of a supernarrator; it derives from common movie plots and has all the trappings of a Hollywood melodrama. As in Godard's work, nearly every element is tinged with literary associations: Sinatra is a book editor, Charlotte and Emily evoke the Brontë sisters (recalling a scene from *Weekend* in which the protagonists meet up with authors and well-known fictional characters), and everyone is on the point of becoming an author — if they are not authors already.

Baumbach is attracted to the movies because, he says, of their "relative newness." It is not just the formal traits of cinema that interest him but also the melodramatic content of so many movie plots. He claims that at least five scenarios, borrowed from or inspired by film melodramas, are compressed into *Chez Charlotte and Emily*. Although these scenarios are not identifiable as one reads the novel, the melodramatic character of the action comes through loud and clear, as when Charlotte dies and "Francis falls to his knees on the sand, a bare speck in the universe."[4]

An important aspect of *Chez Charlotte and Emily* that seems to owe nothing to the cinematic influence is Baumbach's creation of characters who, through their uncanny disappearances and reappearances, seem to be extensions of one another. Baumbach has suggested that Francis functions as an extension of Joshua, another character and a novelist. Joshua is the one telling the story of Francis and the others, and so, like Marcel's retelling of Swann's love in Proust's great novel, he projects onto Francis his own character traits. Charlotte and Emily, who have a habit of dressing in each other's clothes, seem to resemble and often call to Francis's mind the other woman in his life, his wife, Nora. When Emily disappears at one point, Charlotte puts on Emily's clothes in order to discover what kind of relation Francis has with Emily. Baumbach uses doubling and disguising as a disquieting manner of testing interpersonal relations. It is as though Francis's sojourn on the island, like that of the Italian noblemen in *The Tempest*, were a lengthy initiation rite through which he is supposed to discover his own true nature.

One might further suggest, following the lead of psychoanalytic critics, that all of the characters are merely emanations of a basic male and female type that Baumbach wishes to examine. The male type is the novelist-adventurer. Joshua's repressed desires to be a hero are displaced onto his friend (or character?) Francis. Baumbach's male is at once sexually aggressive and inhibited. His artistic sense makes him interested in going behind the scenes, questioning the logic of what is happening to him, and standing back to appraise the scheme of his life. The female type remains out of focus until Judith, the prostitute, appears. A variation on the literary cliché of the degraded woman who is really worldly wise, she embodies the nurturing sexuality to which the other women, Nora and Genevieve, Joshua's wife, aspire. At the same time, like Charlotte and Emily, she has certain vulnerabilities that can be protected only by a strong man. After nursing Francis back to health and becoming his mistress, Judith writes her memoirs of life with Francis. Feeling that Judith has outdistanced him as a writer, Francis leaves her. However, when Judith tells him she has been receiving threatening phone calls, Francis appears on the scene and saves her at the last minute from being murdered.

Chez Charlotte and Emily, which is more chronological and sequential than *Reruns,* reveals formal cinematic inspiration in its crosscutting techniques. At the beginning of the novel, when Francis disappears (he swims too far into the ocean and is washed up on Charlotte and Emily's island), Nora begins to hypothesize about what might have happened. Rather than speaking of the two strands of narrative as occurring simultaneously, by means of a word like "meanwhile," the narrator jumps back and forth between them. Thus, as we witness Nora reasoning that Francis has probably pulled some stunt so that he could "disappear without messy recriminations," the scene suddenly switches: "Francis was almost positive that he had at least once or twice seen the two sisters together in the same room."[5] The effect of this abrupt shift is to emphasize the distance that now separates husband and wife. But when we inspect the two passages carefully, we realize that both deal with a character's thought process. Both have something to do with the whereabouts of someone else. Nora's reflections thus become a mirror image of her husband's, as though the two were communicating telepathically.

It will come as no surprise that the "ultimate" author, Baumbach, who tells us that the scenarios of this novel "are all like pieces of film," writes film criticism for the *Partisan Review.* His essay is sprinkled with references to well-known films, *Rashomon* (1951), *Lost Weekend* (1945), and *A Star Is Born* (1954), among others. Like Puig and other writers (such as Horacio Quiroga, Carlos Fuentes, Guillermo Cabrera Infante, and Faulkner), he apparently learned his novelistic craft, to some degree, from critically watching movies. He is an excellent example of the contemporary novelist who, in order to renovate a traditional form, does not seek to purify his medium or "refine it out of existence" but rather raids an adjacent art, the movies, to plunder its seemingly inexhaustible means of expression.

A final word should be added on Baumbach's style. Although he describes the narrative style of *Chez Charlotte and Emily* as "flat," it is certainly far more flamboyant than that of many other novelists. Compared to the style of *Reruns,* which is dominated by the tone of nightmare, that of *Chez Charlotte and Emily* is, indeed, peaceful. But the similarities in the narrative styles of these two novels are more telling than the differences. As with all good novelists, Baumbach's style is indicative of his message. The claustrophobic feel of the narrator's adventures in *Reruns* and the melodramatic style of *Chez Charlotte and Emily* both point toward the grim hopelessness of the modern human condition. Whether his characters are trapped by their private fantasies or by the conventions of popular culture, they lack a future. Not that the picture we get is full of gloom and doom: On the contrary, Baumbach depicts his characters' dilemmas with humor and deep sympathy. Like Donald Barthelme, Baumbach has a talent for condemning his characters to a hopeless universe of arbitrary rules and then freeing them from this hopelessness by bringing to light the hilarious absurdity of their everyday lives.

Notes

1. Jonathan Baumbach, *Reruns* (New York: Fiction Collective, 1974), p. 2.
2. Ibid., p. 70.
3. Ibid., p. 80.
4. Jonathan Baumbach, *Chez Charlotte and Emily* (New York: Fiction Collective, 1979), p. 34.
5. Ibid., p. 35.

Jonathan Baumbach

Seeing Myself in Movies

> The cinema is an involuntary imitation of dreams. It might have been invented to express the life of the unconscious whose roots go so deep into poetry.
>
> — Luis Buñuel

I spent a large part of my childhood watching movies, engaged in them in special, private ways as if they were pieces of my own unremembered dreams. Although I read a great deal and grew up in a bookish household, movies occupied me in more profound ways than books. More profound because I came to movies without obligation. They were unworthy, most of them (or so I grew up to believe), of the kind of respect we brought to books or paintings or theater. The pleasure movies supplied was outside the cultural avenues of establishment concern. We came to movies — I speak at once subjectively and for my generation — without the resistances we brought to those agencies of culture that were foisted on us for the good of our souls. Movies were our own discovery, an outlaw pleasure. We had no obligation to value them as art, to find ourselves changed by them. Our relationship to movies was nobody's business but our own. It was an illicit affair and so all the more charged with mystery. In some ways, the more banal the film, the deeper the fantasies it generated. The flickering image made indelible contact.

I went as a child mostly to Saturday matinees with one or two close friends, though sometimes by myself. Watching the movie, I was in a sense always by myself (or in the movie, a part of it), the audience like shadows in a dream landscape. The weekly visits were ritual. It was what we did for the most part with our Saturday afternoons. Television was still on the horizon. The dreamlike quality of movies occupied our fantasies.

I saw double features, set off by cartoons and a newsreel and sometimes a chapter of a serial, the entire show running well over three hours. I took pleasure from almost all of the movies I went to; their aesthetic qualities were irrelevant to my experience of them. That isn't wholly true. I was always somewhat judgmental, coming from a home where the making of distinctions was held in esteem. The less my brothers and I found to like in a movie, the more we evidenced intelligence. So I made certain distinctions between movies, but those distinctions, I suspect, were mostly outside the real experience I had those afternoons in the dark.

My imaginary life, my fantasies as a child, were in large part an outgrowth of my illicit experience with movies. I partook of the heroes' formidable qualities, and left the theater a hero in adolescent's disguise, my secret identity carried like a hidden sword. My prowess was not available to ordinary perception. On any given Saturday afternoon, I might have been the mysterious gunfighter in *Shane,* the forsaken sheriff in *High Noon,* the incorruptible detective in *The Maltese Falcon,* the son who had to defy his father to become worthy of him in *Red River,* the mythic revolutionary in *Viva Zapata,* the detective who fell in love with a woman in a painting in *Laura.* The list is arbitrary, or merely representative. The heroes in the movies were conceptually larger than life and were made even larger by their magnified images on the giant screen. It was not the frustration inherent in dreams that I took away from these films as a child, but a sense of the possibilities of magical triumph. Film embodied myth, overran the laws of probability. No doubt it filled me, filled my fantasies, with all kinds of unrealistic expectations. That's another story.

For years, until I somehow let go of them, I remembered the plots (and iconographic scenes and actors' names) from obscure movies of my childhood. I was an encyclopedia of such information, an authority on the dregs of private obsession. I would (at times) rehearse the plots of movies to myself before going to sleep — my dreams activated by the dreamlike shadows of films. The plots comforted me with their familiarity, with their familiar strangeness. My fantasy world was fully within my control; though the movie plots held surprises for me the first time I saw them, they became domesticated by incorporation into my fantasies.

I sense myself circling around my subject, trying to locate it like an image in a viewfinder. Do I write novels that are related to films because I am unable (for financial reasons, for reasons of personality) to make a film? It's possible — indeed, not unlikely. In any event, the issue here is how film has influenced my fiction, not why. (It is not an unreasonable belief that an art form is diluted when it feeds off other art forms. Yet I resist believing that what I do is less fictionlike because of its relation to film.) The coded mysteriousness of dreams has interested me as a writer from the outset, and perhaps film interests me because of its relation to dreams. And then, it may be the other way around, that dreams intrigue me because of their cinemalike ambience. I suspect that film and dream, which I use interchangeably in my work, interest me for similar reasons. External reality, let me confess, for all its dazzle, has never seemed as charged to me as the inner world.

A dream is like a murder mystery in which the detective, the victim, and the suspect are all versions of the same character. I use the shadowy logic (really illogic) of movie plots to simulate dreams. That is, I want to create fiction that has the logic and mystery of a dream while not seeming necessarily dreamlike. In my first two novels, *A Man to Conjure With* and *What Comes Next,* there are a number of dreams reported and identified as dreams. In my later novels, starting with *Reruns,* the dreams are the reality. Or, put another way, the novels are cinematic in a dreamlike way. In *Reruns,* which I'll deal with at greater length later on, all of the characters are extensions of the narrator, all have been willed into being by his perception of them. What I wanted to get at was the experience of going into a dark theater — which is very dreamlike, of course — and discovering that one is watching the movie of one's life. The discovery is not especially surprising, because all the movies one has watched have become pieces of one's life.

What interested me as a child about movies was everything, the medium itself. As an adult, as a writer, I am attracted to movies that are mystifying and mysterious, which is to say that things haven't changed all that much. The films I like today are more sophisticated versions of what attracted me to movies as a child. Let's get down to specific cases. The films that come to mind as having influenced me in one way or another are *Breathless* (Jean-Luc Godard), *L'Aventura* (Michelangelo Antonioni), *Diary of a Country Priest* and *Pickpocket* (Robert Bresson), *Vertigo* (Alfred Hitchcock), *Les Yeux sans visage* (*Eyes Without a Face*) (Georges Franju), *The Big Sleep* (Howard

Hawks), *Belle de jour* (Luis Buñuel), *Le Boucher* (Claude Chabrol), *Persona* (Ingmar Bergman), *Kiss Me Deadly* (Robert Aldrich), *Shoot the Piano Player* (François Truffaut), *The World of Apu* (Satyajit Ray), *Ride the High Country* (Sam Peckinpah), and *High and Low* (Akira Kurosawa). This list is partial and somewhat arbitrary. The filmmaker whose work has been most important to me is Jean-Luc Godard.

Godard's impact is probably most apparent in my third novel, *Reruns*. What influenced me about *Breathless* was not its subject but its rhythm, its fragmentation, its hyped-up speed, its refusal to acknowledge conventional limitations. *Breathless* offered the example of its riskiness and the example of its imaginative success. Godard's first full-length film violates almost all the rules — the received notions of how to tell a story in film — and is all the richer for having gone its own way.

Reruns is made up of a series of dreamlike scenarios in the life of a character who is continually reinventing himself. Only a little of what I intended for *Reruns* probably came to be realized. My ambition for that book was quixotic. I wanted to create a novel that was made of flashes of light and sound. I wanted to create an open-ended movie in text — dreams transformed into cinema. I wanted to put everything in that book and at the same time leave everything out. That is, I wanted to create a fiction that tells almost every story and then to erase the events of narrative, leaving only traces and images, clues of evocation.

Early in *Reruns,* the narrator (as a lost child) finds himself at the door of Dracula's castle. The family of vampires — a mirror image of his own family — take him in and for dinner serve him the head of a child with a snake coming out of its mouth. In a sense, the child-narrator is the dinner; it is the self on the other side of the mirror that he is offered for sustenance. That vampires are conventionally undead — that is, dead and still with us — seems to me a metaphor for unexpressed feelings. I had not consciously thought of this metaphor when writing the section; intuition led me to this idea about vampires. The Dracula films had a certain fascination for me as a child that I'll try to account for. They are about a creature that transcends mortality, though without any seeming pleasure in extended survival — a figure of extraordinary power and terrible vulnerability, a figure of almost absolute evil who enlists some sympathy from us. The creature must sleep in a coffin during the day, as if actually dead. The light of day has the power to reduce him to dust. Being undead is, on balance, perhaps worse than death. The fantasy permits us a sense of transcendence, while at the same time it makes us glad we're mortal. There is also an erotic component to the fantasy — something I was not consciously aware of as a child. Dracula has extraordinary power over women; he enslaves them by sucking their blood. It is not wholly distortion for a child to perceive his parents as vampires.

It is the dream quality of movies that has influenced my work the most — the haunting illogicality of film noir, the mythology of westerns and *policiers,* the dark night of the horror film. Images in movies are at once fleeting, here and gone, and impressed like an engraving on the memory. Movies talk to us — unconscious to unconscious. Watching a movie is like viewing a dream in a mirror. This may be a private response, though I suspect not. I think movies have had a profound, and not always salutary, influence on the way we view our experience. The main characters in my later novels tend to view the world as if it were a movie of their own invention.

Chez Charlotte and Emily is my most cinematic novel. Yet that was not the intent of that work, insofar as I was conscious of the intent. Let me briefly convey the novel's central narrative. A book editor, summering with his family at Cape Cod, swims out into the ocean beyond his depth and appears to drown. He is carried by the tide to a private cove, where he is washed ashore, unconscious and barely alive. He is rescued and nursed back to life by two enchanting sisters, twins named Charlotte and Emily. In living with Charlotte and Emily, the book editor leaves the real world to live, in a sense, in the world of the imagination. This world of the imagination (also the house of fiction), turns out, in fact, to be mostly a series of movie plots. The book editor, whose name, Francis Sinatra, has its own false associations, becomes the lover of both Charlotte and Emily, though it is also possible that there is only one sister. Francis (in one part of the story) is not sure he's ever seen the two sisters in the same room together. It is possible that Charlotte and Emily are different aspects of the same person (a reference to Brian De Palma's *Sisters,* which itself is derived from several of Hitchcock's films), that one of the twins has died and the other has assumed her personality. When he is with Emily (or the Emily side of the character), Francis narrates pieces of his life, some real, some invented. Emily records those narratives in her diary, changing them slightly to suit her sense of Francis, whom she knows as Tom. With Charlotte, Francis acts out various melodramatic scenarios — that is, Francis and Charlotte improvise the scenarios together — as a means of intensifying passion. The novel at various levels continually redefines itself; it is always in the process of renewed definition. Francis's story is essentially being told by Joshua — the novelist within the novel, the surrogate author reimagining his own life through the character of Francis.

Francis's life with Charlotte and Emily is a form of wish-fulfill-ment — a fantasy of nurturance and eros and the concomitant punish-ment for presumption, for taking without sufficient commitment in return. Escaping the stultifying domesticity of his "real" life, Francis seeks to become fully alive again (like the characters in books and films), unfettered by the restrictions of habit and obligation. No longer stuck in his domestic bargain with his dissatisfied wife, Nora, Francis moves into the world of Charlotte and Emily as a means of reinventing himself. He returns home at the end, barely changed by his adventures, momentarily refreshed.

I've been criticized for using distancing devices in my work, for not dealing with emotions directly. It has become fashionable to derogate literature that appears to deny or repress emotion. However, the issue is considerably more complicated than current discourse admits. The manipulation of feeling (and all art is to some extent manipulative) is not an end in itself. I have a sense that many readers want literature to move them powerfully because they feel emotionally inert — an aspect of what has been called postcivilization — frozen inside like some great winter lake. We all want to feel; it's one of the ways we know we're alive. I've tended to be wary of sentiment too easily arrived at (movies are sometimes the worst offender here); I don't like to have my feelings jerked around. What is one really feeling when one is moved to tears or grief or pain by a work that is patently dishonest? The emotion generated is a displacement, an evasion of some real occasion for feeling. To be moved falsely is to be cheated, is to lose some part of oneself. I find sentimentality vicious. My intent with these statements is not to justify my own practice — I, like others, admire certain direct emotional appeals — but to give some sense of what urges me in the direction I have chosen to move.

I use film plots and dreams in my fiction because of their powerful emotional content — because so much deep feeling is contained in them in tantalizing code — but also as distancing devices, as a way of keeping the reader from getting too close to the experience until he's found his way there through the maze. I want the reader to feel that he is going the wrong way all along, forced away from the work's emotional center, and then to arrive at some surprising and troubling place at the last moment. This is not to say that I accomplish what I intend — I mean my work to be affecting in a mysterious way — I am merely stating my objective.

Let's come back to *Chez Charlotte and Emily.* Francis's idyll, with all its bizarre and comic aspects, moves abruptly into nightmare. When Emily, feeling abandoned, throws herself into the ocean, Francis experiences a sense of overwhelming loss. If the sisters are, in fact, one, with Emily's death Francis loses them both. The section ends with a series of melodramatic revelations.

> Is it possible that he's never actually seen the two sisters at the same time?
> It is Charlotte's grinning corpse, dressed in Emily's clothes, that washes up like jetsam on the shore.
> Francis falls to his knees on the sand, a bare speck in the universe.

If the scene works as I meant it to, the reader should experience a sense of grief at the end of this chapter. The grief, the sense of loss, is at once parodic and real.

Joshua Quartz, the novelist within the novel, is telling the story to his wife, Genevieve, as a means of making contact with her. Francis is Joshua's surrogate (as Nora is Genevieve's), perhaps even an extension of himself. Francis's life with Charlotte and Emily (as well as his adventures after he leaves them) are daydreams made manifest. The experience is something like going to a movie and discovering yourself as one of the characters — the hero, perhaps, or the heroine. *Chez Charlotte and Emily* is about how one escapes the banality of everyday life — how one renews life for oneself — through the generative power of the imagination. Francis is a tourist in the house of fiction, which might also be perceived as the palace of cinema or the landscape of the imagination. He has a number of fantastic adventures before returning, like Ulysses, to his family.

Not all of the scenarios in this novel have analogues in actual films, but they are all like pieces of film. They have the configuration, or rhythm, of film narrative. They parody certain conventional scenes in films while at the same time they offer films the homage betokened by imitation.

In one scenario, Francis, believing his wife has remarried, becomes an alcoholic (like Ray Milland in *Lost Weekend*) and falls to what seems the lowest state imaginable. He is taken in by a prostitute with intellectual pretensions. The prostitute, Judith Garland, is a variation of the cliché of the secret nobility of the apparently degraded. Judith, like Charlotte and Emily, nurses Francis back to health and becomes involved with him in a symbiotic way. That is, she sees Francis as a mentor, becomes an author herself, and ultimately publishes her memoirs. When she outdistances her mentor, and becomes a celebrity (as in *A Star Is Born*), Francis leaves her.

After Francis's departure, the scenario takes a new twist. Judith is besieged by obscene phone calls and hires a bodyguard to look after her — in effect, to take Francis's place. The bodyguard makes himself invaluable to Judith, insinuates himself (as in *The Servant*) into her life. The phone calls continue, however, and become more menacing. One day Judith discovers that her bodyguard has been stealing her jewels, and she fires him.

When Judith meets Francis on the street — he is working for the holiday season as a street Santa Claus — she asks him if he is the one making the threatening calls. Francis denies doing so, though he feels touched by the charge and follows Judith home. He arrives in time to save her from a murderous attack by her former bodyguard, who has been the caller all along (as in *Midnight Lace*). By saving Judith's life, Francis redeems his obligation to her, and becomes a kind of hero.

The narrative is described almost as flatly in the novel as it is here. Aspects of at least five movies are compressed into this parodic scenario, which, in its cinematic ambience, is like a dream.

Francis lives through various archetypal experiences; he becomes the center of a succession of pop culture fantasies taken from actual or imagined films. Paralleling Francis's adventures, even perhaps as a reflection of them, Joshua, Genevieve, and Nora (Francis's wife) have their own literary/cinematic adventures. The world of *Chez Charlotte and Emily* becomes the world of image and text, imagined possibility made into simulated reality. Each episode has its own self-conflicted variation. (Kurosawa's *Rashomon* was the inspiration for the last shape-shifting scenario.) The strategy in the novel was to transform the seemingly unreal (certain pop mythologies) into dreamlike scenarios that are as affecting, in their own way, as renderings of deeply felt experience.

My recent novel, *My Father More or Less,* juxtaposes fragments of a film with a somewhat realistic narrative. The film is in the process of revision; its changing form reflects indirectly the emotional life of the filmmaker, who is one of the novel's two main characters.

In using film scenarios in my fiction, I don't see myself moving away from the nature of fiction. Fiction, being an older form, has more restrictive parameters. One of the attractions of film is its relative newness, the sense (at times) that it is still discovering its potentials. I strive to come to fiction with the kind of openness to possibility that the filmmaker brings to his medium. Received opinion claims that everything has already been done in fiction. I think it's a misperception that the novel has exhausted its formal possibilities, but it's a misperception that comes to us with the weight of authority. Taking after film, my fiction pursues the illusion that it is working a new medium and that things can be done with language that have not even been dreamt of before or have been dreamt of in the deepest of sleeps and have been long forgotten.

Ben Stoltzfus, 1927–   9

 en Stoltzfus is one of the rare U.S. writers whose works must be placed in a European rather than an American lineage. It was Henry James who first saw the need to juxtapose the North American experience and sensibility with the traditions of European psychological realism. Rather than looking back to Nathaniel Hawthorne, Herman Melville, or Poe, James took as his models such French novelists as Flaubert and Maupassant. Faulkner followed suit by rendering the unique experience of moral degradation and social turmoil in the deep South by means of techniques recently perfected by the major European modernists such as Joyce and Proust. Since the era of triumphant modernism, however, few Americans have been attracted by specifically European models of novelistic form.

Stoltzfus, born of American parents in Bulgaria, moved to the United States in 1943 after having lived his first sixteen years in Sofia, Istanbul, and Beirut. Thus, by the time he began to write fiction he had already had the kind of life experience that encourages comparisons between the Anglo-American tradition and that of other national literatures. He has studied French literature most extensively, and it is the French tradition that seems to predominate in his writing.

With the critical acclaim and controversy surrounding the *nouveau roman* (new novel) in France, a new source of inspiration became available to those American writers attracted to the preciseness of description, the emphasis on writing as an activity in itself, and the play of language that typified the works of such "new novelists" as Robbe-Grillet, Claude Simon, Michel Butor, and Nathalie Sarraute. Stoltzfus's novels can be clearly inscribed in this new tradition. His characters, though fairly well developed in terms of dominant psychological conventions, lack the full presence of mind we associate with nineteenth-century characters. Like the protagonists in Robbe-Grillet's novels, they begin bewildered and only very gradually reach a point of limited enlightenment. Stoltzfus arranges scenes in such a way that events do not evolve along a linear axis but rather appear as fixed, atemporal tableaux that, through whole or partial repetition, imply an eventual chronology.

His first novel, *The Eye of the Needle* (1967), is an intense study of childhood and first love amidst the concentration camps and anti-Semitism of the Nazi period in Eastern Europe. A young boy records fragmented perceptions of a closed-in world as the novel opens. One central focus is a needle as it is used to sew a patch: "The needle moves through the weave, stitches the design of white checks on the background of the cloth, continuously appears, disappears, and reappears on the white surface of the handkerchief."[1] At a certain point, the reader realizes that this needle, inscribed in the title of the novel, is one element in an image network of sewing and seeing whose significance is tentatively suggested by the biblical parable that serves as an epigraph to the novel: "It is easier for a camel to go through the eye of a needle than for a sinner to enter the kingdom of God." Later, the eye of the needle will double for a keyhole through which the boy peers at a woman with whom he has already, without realizing it, fallen in love. And finally, this opening becomes metaphorically associated with the woman's body as she introduces the boy to the mysteries of sex.

But the weaving of the needle does not remain an innocent, purely intratextual metaphor. As in the new novel, it becomes identified with writing and with the structure of Stoltzfus's novel itself. Needle and penpoint melt together as the boy, Marc, writes impassioned letters to Nadja. Through these letters, interspersed with repeated, obsessive scenes of torture and agony, we learn of the relationship between Nadja and a younger girl, Mara, whom Marc has now begun to love. Nadja delivers Mara, a Jew, into the hands of the Nazis, who deal with her in the same brutal manner with which they dealt with Marc's father. The novel ends with a swirling of intercalated descriptions of the woman sewing, an incessant snowstorm, and the boy watching the patterns.

The Eye of the Needle is a novel of initiation in which the relations between son and father and between an adolescent and his first love are painstakingly examined through the juxtaposition of traumatic scenes and key metaphors. Stoltzfus uses this same technique in his second novel, *Black Lazarus* (1972), which takes place in Berkeley, California, during the student movement and the black riots of the late 1960s. Here we find the shifting perspectives and intense repetitions applied more globally to a large-scale social conflict. The result is an unusually sharp, cubist view of the political turmoil in America that has ambiguously shaped the succeeding decades.

Stoltzfus, a literary critic of some note and professor of French, comparative literature, and creative writing at the University of California–Riverside, has also published studies of Robbe-Grillet, André Gide, and Hemingway. As his essay makes clear, he feels the writing activity is bound to reflect and even to adopt certain techniques first used in the cinema. For Stoltzfus, as for the French critic Alexandre Astruc, the camera can be likened to a pen, just as the pen can adapt for its own use the visual propensities associated with the camera. According to this analogy, modern films and novels not only resemble one another but are perfectly situated to influence one another as well. Stoltzfus's remarks are thus of great value for the way they begin to take account of the massive impact that movies have had on our contemporary literature and for the sensibility they reveal of one of our writers who has remained lucidly open to this impact.

Note

1. Ben Stoltzfus, *The Eye of the Needle* (New York: Viking, 1967), p. 19.

Ben Stoltzfus

Shooting With the Pen

Is it a film or a novel? Is it a camera or a pen? Ever since the films of the New Wave of the late 1950s and early 1960s, the audience has had the impression that film directors write with their cameras and that innovative novelists shoot scenes with their pens. The product, be it a film or a book, may be different materially, but the creative process for both is so similar — *"bricolage,"*[1] assemblage, montage, and mise-en-scène — that in the last thirty or forty years, the two genres have developed conventions that parallel each other and overlap.

It is no accident that in the cinema the two creative modes — realism and fantasy — have evolved simultaneously, that a Louis Lumière documentary, such as *Les Pompiers de Lyon* (*The Firemen of Lyons*), coexists with a Georges Méliès fantasy, such as *The Voyage to the Moon* (1902), or that the aesthetic canon requiring art to imitate nature coexists with its opposite — an art that refuses to imitate nature.

Whereas Méliès's *Voyage to the Moon* was pure fantasy, fancifully rendered, the 1969 *Eagle* that landed on the moon ("one giant leap for mankind") gave us documentary television footage to record this historical event. These two voyages, the real one and the false one, the historical and the imaginary, reflect, even symbolize, a profound artistic dichotomy, that is, the tension between a historical event as fact and its assimilation into the fictive process. This ambiguity and tension is also present in two of my novels, *The Eye of the Needle* (written in 1963 and published in 1967) and *Black Lazarus* (written in 1969 and published in 1972).

The Eye of the Needle describes the beginning of the Holocaust, placing it within the long history of the Judeo-Christian tradition; *Black Lazarus* situates the 1969 landing on the moon within a two-hundred-year span of black American history that culminates with the 1965 Watts riots in Los Angeles. Although sixty-five years had elapsed since Lumière's and Méliès's pioneering films, the objective chance, as the surrealists call it, between events in my fiction and events in *The Firemen of Lyons* and *Voyage to the Moon* is uncanny. *Black Lazarus* is similar to *The Firemen* in that it describes the efforts of firefighters, now in Los Angeles, to contain the fires of Watts. I am pleased to note in retrospect (the novel was not consciously planned this way) that *Black Lazarus* contains not only the aesthetic tension between documentary and fantasy that marked the beginnings of cinema but, in the references to firefighting in Watts and to the 1969 moonlanding, direct allusions to two of its earliest titles. This coincidence suggests that the acts of firefighting and moon worship have mythical dimensions that correspond to ongoing human fears and aspirations.

The immediate problem for me as a novelist was how to meld the realism of historical events into a fictive mode. How could I use the conventions of reflexive writing that were rapidly becoming the conventions of the New Wave — namely achronology, montage, simultaneity, discontinuity, the present tense, the jump cut, the seeing eye (or camera), the absence of inner monologue or stream of consciousness, contradictions, disruptions, and a general indifference to the physical description of characters (as opposed to a fairly detailed description of things), conventions that deny mimesis by foregrounding the artistic process — and still assert the validity of historical events. Jean Ricardou, in *La Prise de Constantinople* (1965, *The Fall of Constantinople*), and Claude Simon, in *La Bataille de Pharsale* (1969, *The Battle of Pharsala*), melded the historical with the fictive, but in doing so seem to have devalued the former in favor of the "writerly" process. For Ricardou, *la prise* becomes *la prose* (*La Prose de Constantinople* is the alternate title on the back of the jacket cover); for Simon, too, it is prose that gives the writing a reflexive and nonreferential autonomy. The title of Simon's work is really an anagram for "the battle of the phrase." For Ricardou and Simon, language foregrounds itself as history recedes, whereas for me the tragedies of the Holocaust and the black experience had to be given a weighting whose historical urgency would not be overshadowed by the formal patterns in which they were embedded.

The novels of Honoré de Balzac and Emile Zola are frequently cited as examples of realism or naturalism in which the conventions of writing dictate an imperious fidelity to the recording of the names, places, heredity, and mores of people from a variety of social strata during a particular historical period. It is surely no accident that history teachers flesh out their courses by assigning a Balzac novel or Gustave Flaubert's *Sentimental Education,* which chronicles the events of 1848. Nonetheless, Flaubert's fiction, for all its historical verisimilitude, displays a tension between realism and fantasy that disrupts the mirroring processes of art in order to foreground language, and, with it, the creative process. However, even before *Madame Bovary,* Laurence Sterne's *Tristram Shandy* and Denis Diderot's *Jacques le fataliste* had foregrounded the creative process by calling attention to the structures of their novels, by exposing the internal machinery of fiction, by revealing the very scaffolding of artistic construction that Flaubert, in *Madame Bovary,* was still striving so laboriously to conceal.

There are other examples one might cite, but those I listed I mention only in passing in order to suggest that, from cinema's beginning at the turn of the twentieth century, these two facets were displaying an aesthetic tension that Miguel de Cervantes's *Don Quixote* (the first novel) had manifested with such verve and imagination in the sixteenth. In the twentieth century, examples of nonmimetic art have proliferated with such abundance that I am astonished whenever I still hear people pontificating about art's inevitable mimetic role. Be that as it may, these days most people accept the idea that art can be an artifact that not only refuses to imitate nature but that also declares its independence from it. For instance, abstract art asserts that a painting is an object — an object that makes a statement about itself. In order to do this, art has become highly self-conscious, and, in foregrounding its own language, it invites the audience to participate in a reflective process that devalues artistic conventions and stresses the language of art as a perceptual system.

Such art teaches us that, in large measure, the apprehending system determines the relationship between the subject and the object, between the perceiver and the perceived. René Magritte, for instance, whose paintings appear to be realistic because the subjects are recognizable objects, nevertheless abolishes space, time, and gravity by painting landscapes that overlap (*The Beautiful Captive*), daytime scenes that are simultaneously nighttime scenes (*The Empire of Lights*), and boulders that float in the air like clouds (*Battle of the Argonne*). Magritte has one foot in realism and one foot in fantasy. The objects that he paints have a realistic appearance, but the visible contradictions that subvert the laws of time, space, and gravity assert a non-Euclidean relativity that is fantastic: It posits a 180-degree reversal of our expectations and of our experience. His paintings enable us to apprehend an entirely different world from the one we know.

If art is a perceptual system and not necessarily a mirror of reality, then the narrative interest shifts from the story that is being told to how it is told. Paintings are no longer portraits or landscapes but are instead surfaces of line and color arranged in a particular way. James Joyce's *Finnegans Wake* also foregrounds words and language (instead of plot), thereby inviting the reader's collaboration — a collaboration that will be inventive, re-creative, and imaginative. In this context, the French new novel has become the story of telling and not the telling of a story. Umberto Eco calls these works "open" — works whose indeterminacy and aleatory quality generate the audience's re-creative endeavors. Ideally, this collaboration between the audience and the artist provides insights into the nature of the creative process — language as an encoded system, the determinism of ideology, the liberating role of play, and the possibility of individual freedom.

Whenever artists play with the canon of convention, parody ideology, or exaggerated taboos, they demonstrate an independence vis-à-vis established tastes and restrictions. Alain Robbe-Grillet's film *Le Jeu avec le feu* (Playing with fire, 1975) is one parodic example that uses incest as one of its motifs. Jean-Luc Godard's *Weekend*, by exaggerating the realism of automobile slaughter on the highways, counters Siegfried Kracauer's belief that cinema should be realistic. François Truffaut's *Day for Night*, a film about the making of a film, foregrounds the language of cinematography. Like *Tristram Shandy*, or André Gide's *The Counterfeiters*, or Vladimir Nabokov's *Pale Fire*, these films expose the machinery of the creative process. They do so, in large measure, by violating social and artistic norms.

Every ideology maintains that it is natural or God-given, and all societies expect men and women to obey these natural and divine laws. Mimesis is the inevitable by-product of an ideology that postulates natural correspondences and divine harmonies. By imitating nature, and in describing man and society as imbedded in nature, art was expected to reflect universal values. Normative art, then, is usually the innocent — that is, unthinking — reflection of an encoded ideology. In fiction, the encoded ideology posits the need for plot, chronology (always linear), flesh-and-blood characters, and suspense. The litmus test for any best-seller is the degree to which the book does not violate these conventions. Whenever a film, such as Jean Renoir's *Rules of the Game* (1939), or a novel, such as Gide's *The Counterfeiters* (1926), subverts the audience's expectations (in both these works the violations, when compared to those in the films of Godard or the novels of Claude Simon, were minimal), it suffers the consequences of incomprehension or neglect. In both cases, Renoir and Gide subvert tragedy and character as normative codes by introducing randomness and chance. They both play with unpredictability. It was twenty years before the New Wave would rehabilitate the "failure" of *The Rules of the Game*. Even today, the antirealism of *The Counterfeiters* — its implausible proliferation of events, chance, frequent shifts in point of view, its scenes of wrestling an angel — continues to disconcert its readers. One would have thought that by now reflexive films such as Alain Resnais's *Last Year at Marienbad* (1961) or reflexive novels such as Robert Coover's *Spanking the Maid* (1982) should have established themselves as acceptable fare, if one considers the now distant efforts toward reflexivity of Renoir and Gide, not to mention Sterne, Joyce, and Roussel. But so strong is ideology's hold that the canon of realism seems to persist with an ineradicable tenacity. Although the general public seems more receptive to fantasy and reflexivity in film than in fiction (and I don't mean science fiction), there are indications of change. The relative successes of John Fowles's *The French Lieutenant's Woman* (1969), with its four different endings, John Barth's *Giles Goat-Boy,* redeemed perhaps by its humor, and Italo Calvino's works, which appear regularly in this country in paperback editions, suggest a gradual, although still minor, shift in public sensibilities and acceptance. The mass audience no doubt continues to prefer conventional action-packed blockbusters such as *Gone With the Wind* (the novel as well as the film), *2001, Raiders of the Lost Ark,* and *E.T.*

In her book *L'Age du roman américain* (1948; trans. *The Age of the American Novel,* 1972), Claude-Edmonde Magny chronicles the influence of film on American fiction between the two world wars, the influence of the American novel of action on French writers, and the narrative shift from introspective writing to objective description. Magny's term *"le style américain"* connotes all three aspects of this narrative discourse, which is characterized by the primacy of the visual. Insofar as all of us writing today have experienced the impact on our writing of film and television — fiction, documentaries, commercials — Magny is not wrong to stress this influence.

Today we see films on television that are intercut with commercials and the news. Switching channels provides montage, simultaneity, and disruption. Insofar as the news and commercials have become entertainment and situation melodramas have become educational (alcoholic husbands, incestuous fathers, and child molesters), the lines between distinct genres have been blurred. As technology bombards our visual and auditory senses with the accelerating images of an evolving ideology, fiction and reality begin to overlap. Realities that were once considered separate entities now converge. This blurring process suggests that the system (be it the language of documentary or the language of fiction) that organizes these realities is one and the same; that the language — any descriptive system — that describes reality determines our perception of it. Within this ambiguous state of affairs, the artist's role may not reside in spinning yarns or in telling stories but in calling attention to how this organizing process defines itself as well as the reality we perceive through it.

The extraordinary impact and immediacy on the audience of the filmic image, which, on the screen, is bigger than life and sometimes more intense, organizes reality in ways that emphasize, on the one hand, the hieroglyphic incoherence of dreams (as seen particularly in the surrealist and avant-garde cinema of the 1920s) and, on the other, the realism of our waking lives. In my novels I try to blend the two processes. The fabric of my fiction is woven with the woof of realistic threads on a warp of imaginary ones. It is a network of truth and a tissue of lies. This interweaving of images, places, seasons, people, and events, always in the present tense, as in a film, forces the audience to focus on the simultaneity of all experience.

The past determines the present, which, in turn, determines the future. In *Hiroshima mon amour* (1959), this meshing of time and space fuses love and death, past and present, France and Japan, war and peace, victims and victimizers, into a moving discourse that is more than a documentary and less than fiction. The term docudrama seems imprecise, yet insofar as the film defines the parameters of a collective human tragedy, personified in the fictional encounter of the two main actors, the word may not be far off the mark.

In *Hiroshima mon amour,* the close focus shot of the man's hand, emphasizing tactile movement and sensory experience, triggers the flashback to Nevers, the town where the emotional tragedy of the French girl's love for a German soldier took place. It parallels the physical tragedy of the dropping of the atom bomb on Hiroshima. The images of past and present move back and forth (always in the present tense), bridging geographical distance and abolishing chronological time. It is useful to note in passing that Marcel Proust's discoveries concerning the resuscitating powers of involuntary memory have indeed been assimilated by New Wave directors.

Although *Last Year at Marienbad* (1961) uses similar flashbacks, montage, and jump cuts, the events Robbe-Grillet alludes to in the film have no historical significance and are, in fact, false. "Last year at Marienbad" is no more than "this year at Marienbad," since no meeting took place, everything is invented, and the imagined projections of a possible future are fictitious. *Last Year at Marienbad,* although emphasizing once again the present tense of filmic (and fictional) discourse, embodies a fictional lie — the imaginary discourse that Robbe-Grillet would exploit more fully in a subsequent film, *The Man Who Lies* (1968). Considering that Robbe-Grillet wrote the scenario for *Last Year at Marienbad,* his script defines the distance between his sensibilities as a writer-director and those of Resnais. Robbe-Grillet is more interested in the form of narrative discourse, with all its interlocking textures that tend to deny mimesis, whereas Resnais seldom loses sight of the historical reality that undergirds his efforts. The intensity of a documentary such as *Night and Fog* (1955), whose images resurrect the haunting presence of the German concentration camps of World War II, reminds us that Resnais is never far from the world that his camera is tracking. Although *La Guerre est Finie* (1966) manages to suggest the overlapping of memory and imagination, its formal qualities are belied by the theme of political commitment.

One of the reasons I like Magritte's art and Resnais's films is that they use reality or historical fact in a formal context that seems to deny the manifest realism of their works. Although both men create false documentaries, they have given us true fictions. In a sense, and following their example, I write my works with a seeing eye — a camera that enables light to pass through the lens. "The eye of the needle" is a metaphor of fear and of sight that determines the focus of the novel, the angle of vision, the mise-en-scène, and the montage. Everything, as in the cinema, is seen in the present tense. And *Black Lazarus,* likewise, gives us two hundred years of black American history that are experienced in an instant — the instant that ignited the fires of Watts.

Even though the cinema has given us a reality that rivals the intensity of our daily lives, New Wave cinematographers, like the writers of reflexive fiction, have destroyed the idea that a film or fiction should be no more than a mirror of the world. Whenever montage systematically juxtaposes past, present, and future images, it abolishes time as well as the conventions of linear discourse. The real and the imaginary, as in *Last Year at Marienbad,* are forced to coexist, thereby abolishing verisimilitude. The overriding importance of the narrative system devalues the significance formerly attributed to the psychology of the characters, the depth of their motivations, and the tragedy of their individual destinies. By emphasizing the subjectivity of every point of view, the hand-held camera (its movements now visible on the screen) devalues the alleged objectivity of perception that the smooth tracking camera once tended to support. The once cohesive and monolithic quality of narrative point of view has been disrupted and fragmented, but the pieces, when reassembled, as in a cubistic painting, have a coherence that transcends the parts. A cubist painting, unlike the so-called holes in the wall — the landscapes of the past — is a manmade construction (not a mirror of reality) that refuses to imitate nature.

A film such as *Hiroshima mon amour* mirrors history insofar as it uses events relating to World War II. But in structuring this reality with Proustian and cubist sensibilities, it reorders our perceptions of love, death, and time. *Hiroshima mon amour* combines fact and fantasy. A skeptical audience will no doubt say that all art does that, which is true. The essential difference, however, is that reflexive art highlights the fictive process that incorporates whatever reality may or may not be there. To that end, we now have generative words and generative images in addition to flashback, montage, simultaneity, and narrative disruption. Generative themes introduce a playful, aleatory dimension, stressing the reproductive possibilities of chance and free association.

Joyce, Roussel, the surrealists, and Proust, among others, have tapped the generative capacities of words, names, sounds, colors, and places in order to foreground the slippage of meaning, the play of signifiers, and the pleasure of the text as a self-regulating system. *Finnegans Wake* (1939) dramatizes language and its productive capacities by stressing the internal reflexive activity of narration. The inventiveness and complexity of Joyce's neologisms make meaning not something already accomplished and waiting to be expressed but rather a horizon of expectations, a perspective of semiotic production. Roussel's texts also function as generative devices. *Locus Solus* (1914) is a "game" of machines invented to create a world that is itself the product of linguistic machinery. Roussel creates puns on one phrase to produce another, then writes a story to unify the two: "*Une demoiselle à prétendants*" (a girl with suiters) becomes "*une demoiselle à reître en dents*" (a paving beetle for [making] a knight out of teeth). The text, by displaying a closed system of differences, encourages the production of meanings and thus devalues the notion of determinate signs.[2] Roussel's work demythifies reality as well as those literary forms that claim to mirror it. He plays on double and different identities, on time that repeats and abolishes itself, on words whose slippery meanings convey the reverse of what they seem to say — paronomastic (or wordplay) structures that undermine the stability and predictability of a "sacrosanct" world.

Playing with language was, of course, a favorite game of the surrealists in the 1920s, who used words and colors as generative themes for images and meaning. A word such as "*rubis*" (ruby) leads to the word "*rose*," which leads to the sound for dew (*rosée*). Any of these sounds may lead to a fish called a "*rouget*" (in "Au beau demi-jour"), as easily as the color rose leads visually to the color red (*rouge*), or the sound "rose" to a rose window ("Rosace" in André Breton's "Hôtel des éntincelles" and *Le Revolver aux cheveux blancs*). Breton's verbal playfulness and inventiveness produce "*aux mollets de moelle*" (calves of marrow) and "*au cou d' orge . . . à la gorge . . . d' or*" (neck of barley . . . to the throat . . . of gold) (in "L'Union libre"); and puns such as "*la mourre*" (a game of fingers and numbers) and "*l' amour,*" or "*le coeur m' en dit*" (the heart tells me so) and "*le coeur mendie*" (the heart begs) (in *Les états-généraux*).

Du côté de chez Swann (1913), like surrealist writings, provides its own examples of paronomasia. The "*madeleine*" is both a "*patisserie*" and the Madeleine, a Parisian monument; "*une de mes églises*" (one of my churches) is a pun on the word "churches" and thereby signifies both the village, Méséglise, and the narrative. Claude Simon's *Triptyque* (1973) multiplies the internal reflexive allusions of the text, moving us back and forth on a discontinuous horizontal axis. Signifiers, instead of signifying, refer to other signifiers whose mimetic role is undermined by mirrors, pictures, posters, postcards, and film clips to which they refer or from which they emerge. The simultaneous narration of three sexual encounters (at a beach city, in a valley, and in a northern suburb), using words, images, and connotations that overlap from one setting to another, sets up resonances that come into focus whenever the spotlight, the projector, the lens, or the eye (that is, any of these circles) illuminates the events of the novel's triadic structure. Paronomasia and polysemy have allowed a game of construction designed to facilitate the semantic slippage through which a work derives its meaning: It proliferates (pro-life-rates). Language, by displaying a system of differences, allows the responsive imagination to play with ambiguity, thereby generating new meaning. Each word, color, or image, in addition to connecting with reality outside the text, links itself with other words, colors, or images inside the text in order to form a closed, reflexive system. This closed network invites the reader to play with the textual weave in order to produce meaning. Readers no longer consume the text, they produce it.

In Robbe-Grillet's *Le Voyeur* (1955), the figure eight is a generative theme that brings dissimilar objects together: bits of string rolled into a figure eight, eyeglasses, two contiguous cigarette burns on a newspaper clipping, knotholes on a wooden door, the wheels of a bicycle, the island's double-circuit pathway. In Robert Pinget's *Passacaille* (1969), the opening words, "So calm. So gray. Not a ripple in view" (*Le calme. Le gris. De remous aucun*), generate the novel's rhythms and cyclical patterns. In Robbe-Grillet's *Projet pour une révolution à New York* (1970), the generative theme is the color red, a color that arson, murder, and rape share because red is the color of fire, blood, and the revolutionary flag. In Robbe-Grillet's film *Trans-Europ-Express* (1966), the words in the title connote fear, sex, and death. The word *Trans* slips into *transes* (meaning "fears"). *Europ,* the Paris to Antwerp train, becomes *Europe,* a girlie magazine concealed within the covers of *L'Express* (France's equivalent of *Time* magazine). *Express* is simultaneously the train and the name of the newsmagazine, featuring "l'homme qui est mort quatre fois" (The man who died four times). The slippage between images of fear, eroticism, and violence generated by the words and themes of the film's title — a slippage that is transported and accelerated by the very movement of the train — links the continuously shifting associations, such as the high-speed shots of the rails converging and separating as though they, too, were commenting on the narrative (as they are). Another Robbe-Grillet film, *L'Eden et après* (The Eden and after, 1970) is based on a series of twelve generative themes that are, in some ways, comparable to Arnold Shoenberg's twelve-tone musical system. The comparison, though, is a loose one and must not be pushed too far. The problem with all such auto-generative texts is the public's general inability to understand the organizing principle. The system is perceived as disruptive by an audience looking for the conventional patterns of plot, suspense, character, and chronology. By and large, the conventions of the traditional novel and film are defined as order, whereas variations from the established norm, such as the use of generative themes based on assemblage, are perceived as disorder. Whatever criticisms are leveled at the alleged disorder of Schoenberg's atonal system apply also to comparable generative systems in fiction and cinema.

To illustrate this point, Umberto Eco, in *L'oeuvre ouverte* (1965), traces the development of the tonal system in music from J. S. Bach to Schoenberg. Bach formalized tonal music according to a scale of twelve tones organized in a hierarchy. Later, Ludwig van Beethoven introduced dissonances and intervals that did not exist in Bach's hierarchies, so that a listener could no longer say with confidence which note was dominant or tonic or subdominant. Richard Wagner moved even further from Bach's tonal system by refusing to resolve dissonances. Wagner's "vague harmonies" were generalized even more by Schoenberg, who reasoned that in order to abolish the hierarchy of notes, each note should be repeated as often as every other. Thus were born Schoenberg's "serial arrangements" in which a work was fragmented into a certain number of pieces: The twelve notes of the scale could be repeated in different orders, but no note was repeated until the other eleven had been used.

Alexandre Astruc, in his landmark essay of 1948, called on filmmakers to assert their artistry by means of a discourse that was as flexible and subtle as written language.[3] His *caméra-stylo* (camera-pen) was to set the tone for the New Wave. However, before the New Wave, Vsevolod Pudovkin, in *Film Technique,* and Dziga Vertov, in *The Man With a Movie Camera* (1929, in which he advocates a radical devaluation of realism by means of a back-and-forth play between fact and fiction), used the lens of the camera to provide an optical (and narrative) point of view whose selectivity would guide the audience's emotions and response. This camera-pen is at work in *The Eye of the Needle:*

> A sudden turbulence swirls the dust particles, swirls them in and out of the visible ray of light, always bringing new particles to replace those which have apparently disappeared beyond the barrier of the upper diagonal. The lower diagonal is absolutely parallel to the upper one and it is only within this narrow band of light, not wider perhaps than six inches, that the disturbance is noticeable. It is impossible to blow the dust particles out of the light beam and, in spite of the effort, new grains appear, swirl, disappear, and evolve within the now decreasing violence of the movement. (p. 20)

This narrow band of light may be sunlight passing through a window, or it may correspond to the selective vision of an observer, or it may be the light of a projector transferring its images onto a screen. The effect in all three cases is the same: It restricts the field of vision, thereby limiting the audience's response to images that will be generated by fear or desire. Light will also pass through the "prism" of artistic discourse, thereby foregrounding the creative process — the movements of the needle weaving the colors of the four seasons into flowers on each corner of the white handkerchief (white page, white screen). "The Eye of the Needle" is the title of the novel, but it is also the eye of the perceiver (point of view, camera lens) and the eye that holds the thread. In addition, it is the biblical "eye" through which the camel cannot pass. By using a selected pattern of images and thread, the "eye," in time, connotes and denotes a variety of holes and openings. The eye is thus a generative word and image that will, in due course, connote optics, art, fear, guilt, and eroticism. A detailed description of a camel on a pack of cigarettes has meaning only because it corresponds to a "collision" or "conflict" between a religious attitude and a sexual one. However, insofar as the novel's chronology is circular, the montage of images, events, and scenes derives from Sergei Eisenstein's use of the shot as a montage cell. Eisenstein's juxtaposition of a dog and a mouth in order to elicit the concept "to bark," or of a knife and a heart in order to elicit the concept "sorrow," is analogous to the juxtaposition of a needle and a camel. Within the novel's biblical-erotic interface, this juxtaposition signifies guilt and hopelessness. Thus, the point of view (camera position) materializes the conflict between the organizing logic of guilt and hopelessness and the inner logic of the two entities. Fear of damnation is translated into a preoccupation with religious symbols, such as the cross — symbols that metamorphose into swastikas — or the Star of David. When the swastika and the Star of David collide, they elicit the concept of a Nazi superman in conflict with a Judeo-Christian humility. The narrative discontinuity that relies on montage for a linking of ideas functions on two simultaneous levels — the historical and the mimetic — levels that cannot be brought together unless the audience produces meaning by reacting to the juxtapositions. In effect, the montage of objects, images, people, and events — the artistic discourse — generates the meaning. Within this foregrounding of language, the role of the audience is to assemble the montage elements in order to re-create the generative interplay of all the parts. To understand the dialogue is to become aware that form is also content.

An identical process is at work in *Black Lazarus*. Martial, the black teenager who works under the sign of the red star at a Texaco car wash, draws red stars on the pages of a history book. The juxtaposition of the red star and history, whatever Marxian connotations it may have, communicates the rage and rebellion Martial feels as a black person trying to advance within a capitalistic system run by the white establishment. A montage (paragraph descriptions) of the moonlike signs of the major oil companies (Union 76, Gulf, and Shell) rising above the freeways of the night, along with the full moon on which the astronauts have just landed and a giant billboard showing a white "bitch goddess" (Diana — the moon) selling desire, if not whiskey ("feel the black velvet"), elicits the imagery of power, success, and eroticism. Martial's point of view (the camera angle) that "sees" this montage generates the collision of privilege — his and theirs — black and white — and the inevitable frustrations of a young black whose name derives from the red planet, Mars (mythical connotations of bellicosity), and whose anger manifests itself in fantasies of rape (the astronauts "landing" on the moon — a white Diana).

A juxtaposition of historical events (images of the slave trade and of slaves working in the South) with contemporary images of white opulence structures a sociopolitical narrative whose cinematic qualities invite the audience to re-create the conditions that led to the Watts riots. As the black historian Lerone Bennet, Jr., phrases it: "Everything, including time, changes in a revolutionary time, and the clocks inherited from the old regime are usually too slow or too fast." Rebellion accelerates time, and it is this acceleration that *Black Lazarus* tries to convey. The novel projects images of the past and of the present onto a screen whose signifying caption is "burn, baby, burn!" — an explosive message of arson, aggression, and violence that contrasts with the message of nonviolence of Martin Luther King, Jr. Eventually, fantasies of another holocaust — nuclear war — emerge from allusions to "sowing the wind" and "reaping the whirlwind," from images of black slaves working in the fields in the South and descriptions of black rebels setting fire to Watts. Finally, biblical prophecy from the book of Revelation is juxtaposed with descriptions of contemporary pollution, obsolescence, exploitation, and indifference.

It is important to note that if a montage is well constructed, the ideas will follow. My fiction — in which I use the same techniques as cinema montage, whose frames and images, if properly read, convey meaning — invites audience collaboration. The "linking" of scenes and the "collision" of images guide the audience in a particular direction. However, without the necessary participation and re-creation of the generative source (fear for *The Eye of the Needle,* anger for *Black Lazarus*) — the biological cell from which all the images emerge — there can be no understanding of the whole. The emphasis here is not on passive consumption of meaning (as we consume and discard food or cars) but on producing meaning. In order to produce meaning, the audience must participate in the montage, assemble the images, play with them, and experience the re-creative freedom that produced the work in the first place. Activating the formal interplay of the parts — a continuous slippage backward and forward of all the separate cells (geographical, affective, visual, auditory, time-framed, and so forth) — generates content and eventually the message: fear of eternal damnation in *The Eye of the Needle* and the revolt of righteous indignation in *Black Lazarus*. Nonetheless, the tension between the formal interplay and the historical content is constant and serves to underscore the artistic process. Such art is an ordering system that belies mimesis even though it uses realistic images as building blocks (cells). Such a narrative discourse calls attention to the fact that art is not a mirror of nature — that it is, instead, an artifact that structures our perception of reality and is itself a reality in conflict with all forms of documentary realism.

For instance, in *The Eye of the Needle* there is a description of a small, worn key on which the letters "me" are still legible. This key fits into the keyhole of the door of the bathroom in which Nadja, the boy's tutor, bathes. The boy spies on the woman through the keyhole. Although it restricts his field of vision, it does allow him to see her sexual parts. The erotic connotations of the key and the keyhole are obvious. The letters "me," through synecdoche, elicit the word "camel" (ca[me]l). Although the camel cannot pass through the eye of the needle, the key does fit into the keyhole. Thus, the key is to the keyhole as the camel is to the eye of the needle. Furthermore, the "me" (boy) is to the key as fear of damnation (boy) is to the camel. Thus, the eroticism of the keyhole (the boy has been seduced by the woman) conflicts with his religious beliefs (sin will lead to hell). The boy's affective imagery can be diagrammed as follows:

```
            key                     key  = eroticism    =    desire
          /     \                 /           ↑                    \
  "me" =<         >= boy =<                 (conflict)              >= insanity
          \     /                 \           ↓                    /
            camel                   camel = damnation   =     fear
```

In conclusion, if the montage is skillfully executed and the audience is reading it correctly, that is, collaborating in the re-creative endeavor, then the juxtaposition of described people, objects, places, events, and imaginings gives the audience a picture of desire in conflict with fear. The two worlds of the boy's affective life collide as a result of the montage dialectic.

In both novels, the montage of images that leads to a linking of ideas, as in the cinema, constitutes the grammar and syntax of the narrative discourse. However, in addition to Eisenstein's montage and Pudovkin's linkage, there is an associative process at work that generates logical transitions from disruptions in narrative continuity that otherwise may seem chaotic, abrupt, and illogical. Thus, fear of death generates a fear of holes, of black objects, of crows, of black robes, of hair, of shadows, and so forth. The opposite of black is white, and in *The Eye of the Needle* white surfaces contrast with black ones: snow, the snowing of peach blossoms, the white feathers of a magpie, the black cross outlined in white on the fuselage of a World War II German airplane, the white and black squares of a chessboard, and so forth. Or a burning cigarette may generate smoke that generates fire that generates a concentration camp furnace that generates the fires of hell — a suffering that is both physical and spiritual. This suffering alludes to the deportation of the Jews as well as to the deportation of souls.

In *Black Lazarus*, the black and white squares of a linoleum floor on which Rena, Martial's sister, bounces her red ball, adumbrate the novel's structural image of black and white: Martial is a black protagonist living in a white world. The black velvet dress worn by the reclining model pictured on the whiskey billboard contrasts with her white skin. The cargo of black slaves crammed into a ship's hold contrasts with the white sails. Night opposes day. A black Cougar (Martial's car) violates Mrs. Rhea's white suburban space. A black panther (denoting the animal but also alluding to the Black Panthers of the 1960s) attacks a white lamb. The lamb denotes the animal but connotes Martial's fantasy of Mrs. Rhea (Désirée). Heroin is white but the ghetto is black. Cotton is white but the fingers picking it are black. The black and white triangles of an imaginary Vassarely print summarize the novel's formal patterns:

> The black and white triangles decrease in size as the eye moves from the periphery to the center of the circle where, once again, the pattern spirals the eye out, then in again in a continuous, pulsating, whirling movement that wobbles, spins, expands and contracts this picture of

the sun so normally constructed in its prolonged, continuous, and, it would seem, never-ending revolutions. Triangles which were symmetrical become asymmetrical, overlap, metamorphose into rectangles, squares, and parallelograms whose linear movement rotates them in and out in a multiple succession of augmenting or diminishing geometric shapes.

One would think that this exercise in pure form would leave no chinks or cracks for the imagination to slip into, so perfect is the abstraction of design, so apparently inhuman the construction of the line, so mathematical the treatment of the composition. Yet this exercise in optics thrills the eye, throws it back upon the self where the inner sun revolves in time, invents a place, and peoples it with fear and terror, love and hate, and the myths of the collective mind. (pp. 95–96)

I should say in conclusion that in addition to the influence on my fiction of *Hiroshima mon amour, Last Year at Marienbad,* and New Wave films in general, other films, particularly French ones of the 1940s and 1950s, have had an impact on my work. René Clément's *Forbidden Games* (1952), with its striking opening sequence showing the machine-gunning of a column of refugees, is a good example. The obsession with death of Paulette, the Parisian girl, and Michel, the peasant boy, leads them to a preoccupation with dead animals and the "forbidden" burial games. I was interested in their selective morbidity and the portrayal of the adult world through children's eyes.

Another film, Claude Autant-Lara's *Le Diable au corps* (*Devil in the Flesh,* 1947), which was set during World War I and features Gérard Philipe as a schoolboy (François) in love with a married woman, Marthe, also gave me insights into how to handle the adult world as portrayed through the eyes of adolescence. The war, which is shown as a transgression of civilized codes, is analogous to the young couple's adultery, which is a transgression of civil codes. Their liaison is a passion that destroys, and Marthe dies giving birth to François's child. As he follows the funeral and the church service from a distance, François, through a series of flashbacks, relives his now vanished happiness. The boy in *The Eye of the Needle* relives his past anguish from his bed in a mental hospital.

Another Autant-Lara film, *Le Blé en herbe* (*Reckoning Seed,* 1954), provided me with poignant images of adolescent love and the seduction of a boy by an older woman, events that duplicate, almost, the boy–girl–older woman triangle in *The Eye of the Needle*.

Georges Rouquier's *Farrebique* (1946) contains dramatic images of nature, things, and time. Time is accelerated as clouds stream across the sky, as flowers open in seconds, as vine tendrils cling to the wheel spokes of a passing cart. I'm sure that I incorporated this pageant of the four seasons, the lyrical shots of nature, the coming of spring, and life on a French farm in the Massif Central into scenes in *The Eye of the Needle*.

Last, though not least, there was a special quality in Jean Delannoy's *La Symphonie pastorale* (1946) that influenced the texture of *The Eye of the Needle*, particularly the snowbound landscapes of the Swiss Alps, the whiteness of the snow contrasting with the dark outlines of the village houses and the shadows of the trees. The white and black in Delannoy's film were, as I recall, very impressive, visually, and helped me to impose a similar visual contrast in *The Eye of the Needle* and *Black Lazarus*. Also, the peaceful mantle of snow belied the passions and desire that were hidden from view. That effect, I thought, worked very well. Finally, it was Michèle Morgan's face as Gertrude that I kept seeing whenever I described Mara, the young girl who is deported by the Germans and with whom the boy is in love.

Notes

1. *Bricolage,* a French word introduced into the vocabulary of critical theory by Claude Lévi-Strauss, refers to the gathering together of whatever disparate objects are at hand (originally, gadgets or parts for repairing) in order to form a larger structure. *Bricoleur* is often translated as "handyman." — ED.

2. According to linguists, the production of meaning in language is predicated upon the *differentiation* of sound units, or phonemes, arranged in a series. In most communication processes these differences are agreed upon by speaker and listener. But in the works by Roussel discussed here the underlying difference, which may go unnoticed by the casual reader, is based on two phrases whose sounds are identical but whose meanings are wildly divergent. Thus, the differentiating factor results not from a structure inherent in language but rather from what Stoltzfus calls a "closed system" established within the text. — ED.

3. The essay is entitled "La Naissance d'une nouvelle avant-garde: la caméro-stylo" and appeared in *L'Ecran Français* 144 (1948). It was translated by Peter Graham as "The Birth of a New Avant-Garde: La caméra-stylo" in his *The New Wave* (Garden City, NY: Doubleday, 1968), pp. 17–23. — ED.

Manuel Puig, 1932–1990

o writer since Gustave Flaubert more consistently, more relentlessly attacked the mores of the middle class than Manuel Puig. Like Flaubert, he did so by using writing techniques that have revolutionized the language of the novel. Puig is not alone in his language manipulation; in fact, the field of the contemporary Latin American novel is well populated with linguistic innovators: Cabrera Infante, Alejo Carpentier, Severo Sarduy, to name the most obvious. But though his novels share many of the themes of these and earlier fiction writers, such as Cervantes and Anton Chekhov, it is ultimately to Flaubert that one must turn to discover Puig's most important forebear.

Just as Flaubert critiqued life under the first repressive bourgeois regime in France — that of Louis Napoleon during the Second Empire, which ushered in an era of unrivaled pretentiousness and bad taste — so Puig subjected to close, merciless scrutiny the everyday life of Argentines under the hollowly chauvinistic regime of Juan Perón. His first novel, *La Traición de Rita Hayworth* (1968), comprises events from 1933 to 1948, a period that overlaps Perón's rise to power and election as president in 1943. Translated in 1971 as *Betrayed by Rita Hayworth*, the novel charts, among other things, what Emir Rodríguez Monegal has called "the mediocrity, the resentment, the frustration of the whole political body" of Argentina.[1] Though Puig's search for a Spanish publishing house for *Rita Hayworth* was beset with difficulties and controversies, the novel was almost immediately translated into French and was chosen by *Le Monde* as one of the best novels of 1968–1969.

Rita Hayworth is a novel of initiation with no conventional narrative mode; it formed an auspicious beginning to a writing career that became one of the most celebrated in Latin America. In this novel, we see some of the major themes that would preoccupy Puig's later works: the suffocating alienation of the suburban Argentine bourgeoisie; the inadequacy of the people's language to express the depth of their emotions; the lurid attraction the Argentine bourgeoisie felt toward Hollywood movies, which became a surrogate design for living; and the painful process of sexual role development in an exceedingly macho society. Although this *Bildungsroman* lacks a clear, central protagonist in traditional terms, it revolves around the character of Toto, a little boy growing up in the La Plata region north of Buenos Aires, who, doting on a father who ignores him, develops a rich imaginative life by going every afternoon to the movies with his mother and by sharing with her an omnivorous appetite for the images and myths promulgated by women's magazines, radio soap operas, and advertising.

It has been said that Puig constructed no distance between the alienated subjects in *Rita Hayworth* and the reader, but this contention is only partly true. The novel is composed of various discursive modes, the early chapters being predominantly spoken, such as Choli's telephone conversation with Mita that includes only Choli's words, and the later chapters predominantly written, such as Esther's diary and Berto's letter. Strictly speaking, there is no narration. The characters are always before us, and consequently there is no summary, no recapitulation or back illumination of the sort ordinarily supplied by a narrator. In the grand tradition of modernism, Puig chose to understate, to present this tawdry scenario in what appears to be its raw state and thereby to encourage the reader to infer the various "betrayals" taking place.

However, this novel presents more than a slice of life; it is more than an extended journalistic human interest story. Distance comes in precisely through Puig's use of a triply alienated language. The main point is that the language of the characters is not their own. As all the major Latin American novelists of the last thirty years have made clear, the Spanish spoken by Latin Americans is not really their language but rather a bastardized form of the Castillian Spanish imposed on South America at the time of the Conquest. More important for Puig was that this already hybrid tongue lacks authenticity because of its incapacity to express deep feelings and subtle ideas. Rodríguez Monegal calls it a "triple language" because its sources of inspiration are filmscripts (or, rather, the poorly translated Spanish subtitles of Hollywood movies), the language of popular novels and biographies, and the dialogue of radio and television soap operas.[2] At a loss for how to communicate emotion sincerely, Puig's characters revert to various forms of popular culture for an appropriate cliché and thus reveal to us, through this indirect distancing, the degree of their cultural and linguistic imprisonment.

What makes *Rita Hayworth* so moving is precisely the indirectness with which Toto's story is revealed to us. Rather than describing in detail Toto's sexual initiations and humiliations as they happen, Puig has them recounted by a third party, after the fact. Toto's terrorization at the hands of some older boys, for example, is described by Hector. Similarly, the way that Toto's gentle, slightly effeminate nature annoys the other boys is not narrated by means of a direct encounter. Instead, we read an anonymous note sent by one of them to the dean of the high school complaining about the "goody goody Cassals." The horror of an effeminate nature in a macho society is amplified by this indirect manner of disclosure. Nothing can be more deviant in the highly conformist Argentine society of the time than homosexuality; and several of the characters, even Mita, Toto's mother, attest to this tendency in Toto.

The narrative stance in *Rita Hayworth* bears a distinctly cinematic quality: No narrator intervenes at any moment to guide the reader toward significant details or to tell the reader which events will have important reverberations. It is a technique that Puig would become attached to; with a few exceptions, none of his novels employs a narrator who stands outside or above or alongside the characters. In Puig's works, as in Faulkner's great monologue novels, the characters describe, laud, or condemn themselves *by* themselves. Their words are our only handle on the fictional world. In cinema, the camera acts as this same sort of arranger, though mute, of things, people, and events.

Puig's subsequent novels carry on both the stylistic innovation and the subject matter of *Rita Hayworth*. *Boquitas pintadas* (1969), translated as *Heartbreak Tango* (1973), adopts the conventions of the serial and the epistolary novel to tell a story of Nené's lackluster infatuation with the late Juan Carlos. *The Buenos Aires Affair* (1973) uses journalistic devices reminiscent of Nathaniel West's *Miss Lonelyhearts* to tell another story of impossible love. *El Beso de la mujer araña* (1976), translated as *Kiss of the Spider Woman* (1978), describes the gradually developing affection between a flamboyant homosexual interior decorator and a student revolutionary in a Buenos Aires prison cell by presenting only their conversations and private reveries. This novel, which many would consider Puig's chef d'oeuvre, has been permanently banned in Argentina because of the incisiveness of its political exposé and became the basis for an excellent film starring William Hurt as the homosexual, Molina. Puig's recent novels include *Pubis angelical* (1979), *Maledición eterna a quien lea estas páginas* (1980), translated as *Eternal Curse on the Reader of These Pages* (1982); and *Sangre de amor correspondido* (1982), translated as *Blood of Requited Love* (1984).

Besides providing the screenplay for Hector Babenco's adaptation of *Kiss of the Spider Woman,* Puig wrote the filmscript for *Boquitas pintadas* (1974) and the screen adaptation for José Donoso's *El Lugar sin límites* (*Infinity,* 1978). As he relates in his essay, his experience in Rome at the Centro Sperimentale di Cinematografia was a decisive factor in his development. Working under the aegis of such directors as Roberto Rossellini, Puig discovered in cinema not only the remnants of his earliest artistic sensibility but also a means of narrating that could revolutionize conventional novelistic prose. If movies are in his work the symptom of a cultural alienation whose roots go very deep into Argentine society and history, the cinema as a separate signifying medium is the mine from which Puig digs his most innovative devices. As Marta Morello Frosch has shown, cinema thus constitutes a "borrowed language," one that, through its double perspective of cultural alienation and technological innovation, becomes the ironic vehicle of communication for a linguistically impoverished populace.[3] It is not so much the filmic ideas, she insists, as the filmic style that influences Puig's characters. Toto, for example, in a magnificent scene of sexual misunderstanding, retells a movie sequence about a carnivorous underwater plant that devours fish. He acts out the scene with paper dolls and declares his certainty that this act is exactly the same as human copulation.

Films are the medium, moreover, of a new kind of narration that, before Puig, had not been seen in the novel: the recounted movie. Most evident in *Kiss of the Spider Woman,* this new narration, as practiced by Molina, consists of taking a film plot and retelling it by paying attention to those details that indirectly reveal the character of the person narrating. The very tense, locution, and phenomenological stability of this interpolated rendition create a sense of the recounted experience — except it is not a life experience at all, but the experience of an artistic object, an instance of a play within a play, or rather, a movie within a novel. Consider Molina's account of a scene from the panther woman film (*Cat People*, 1942):

> But come to think of it maybe I'm wrong, I think she had more of a braid around her head, that's more like that part of the world. And a long dress down to the floor, and a fox stole over her shoulders. And she comes to the table and looks at Irena as if with hatred, or not quite, more the way a hypnotist looks, but an evil look in every way. And she speaks to Irena in an incredibly strange language, pausing there by the table.[4]

Notice that the narrative stance is at once that of a person examining an object in the process of development and also that of a quasi-participant in the drama, one who mistakes at first the style of the woman's hair and possibly misinterprets the meaning of the look in her eyes. The action continues implacably in the present, and we are left to imagine, along with Molina's cellmate, Valentin, the emotional tenor of the scene. Such narration functions not only to remove us temporarily from the squalid conditions of the jail but also to construct an object of erotic fascination for Valentin, who becomes more and more eager to learn of the fate of the attractive heroine.

Puig had been developing this unique cinematic narration since his first novel. In *Rita Hayworth,* Delia tells about her maddening affair with López, who after several nights of passionate lovemaking, suddenly drops her. She constructs a hypothetical reliving of her last night with him in the mode of a long, dramatic film shot:

> I never thought that Sunday would be the last time, if he'd told me so I would've concentrated on every minute of it so I'd never forget it, I would have held him so tight my fingers would've hurt, and I would have told him all the things I'd do for him, not eat, not sleep ... that I'd convince him to come back. ... But that was already too much to ask, I would have been content with simply knowing it was

the last time, I could have worn my best dress for him, and silk stockings, and no holding back on the perfume, the vestibule floor shining like a mirror lined with flower pots — ferns — I'd borrow from Mita. . . . I would have played all I had. And I wouldn't have waited for him in the vestibule, I'd have waited for him on the street corner, that way I'd see him coming from a block away and he'd get bigger and bigger until he'd be so close I'd start backing up, counting one, two, three, four . . . the time it would take him to reach me in the dark vestibule and take me in his arms . . . eleven, twelve, thirteen, fourteen . . . and as little as he was, far away from the corner, he's so big now, in front of me, that he covers all the space in front of me, he covers all of me with his head and neck and shoulders.[5]

The most interesting aspect of this development is its suggestion of a close link between fantasy life and cinematic narration. Delia's fantasy reads almost exactly like Molina's recounted film. Particular attention is paid to the details of dress. Quick revisions are accommodated as Delia changes the hypothetical meeting place from the vestibule to the street corner. And finally, as though she were the film screen itself, Delia describes López's approach toward her as though her eyes were a camera: López grows "bigger and bigger" until he "covers all the space in front of me." Just as in Molina's interpolations, in which we become aware of a person recalling an art object at the very moment he is recounting its narrative contents, in Delia's fantasy we are aware not simply of the strongly wished-for revision of her last night with López, but also of the process by which she sets up the fiction — her flair for the dramatic, her careful planning of her wardrobe, and her essential passivity as she counts the moments before he takes her into his arms.

In all these ways, then, films act to construct what Morello Frosch calls the characters' "mental horizons."[6] Even more than the magazine articles, the soap operas, and the popular song lyrics sprinkled through the novels, cinema becomes the intersubjective medium *and* message of Puig's world. Critics have identified in Puig's work an attack on the conventions of the Latin American novel and the consequential "demolition of a literary myth." If that attack is significant, it is ironically launched by means of a cultural artefact imported from North America. And if Puig critiqued the empty values and hollow lives of his contemporaries, it was through another, thoroughly ideological medium, whose values are themselves just as limited and unenlightening as the other cultural forms pervading the society. In these terms, Puig is once again unique. He took further than any other Latin American writer one of the basic paradoxes of Latin American life, the love-hate relationship with North America. Developing societies like Mexico, Colombia, and Argentina depend crucially on U.S. aid to exploit fully their own natural resources. Yet U.S. aid comes cloaked with a heavy superstructural layer of tinsel-laden dreams and images. It is to his credit that Puig subjected this layer, summed up in the style and content of Hollywood movies, to exhaustive scrutiny.

Notes

1. Emir Rodríguez Monegal, "A Literary Myth Exploded," *Review* 72 (Winter–Spring 1971–72):62.

2. Ibid., p. 63.

3. Marta Morello Frosch, "The New Art of Narrating Films," *Review* 72 (Winter–Spring 1971–72):52.

4. Manuel Puig, *Kiss of the Spider Woman*, trans. T. Colchie (New York: Knopf, 1978), p. 10.

5. Manuel Puig, *Betrayed by Rita Hayworth*, trans. S. J. Levine (New York: E. P. Dutton, 1971), p. 111.

6. Frosch, "The New Art," p. 55.

Manuel Puig

How the Provincial Argentine Left Literature for the Movies, Thereby Discovering the Immense Potentials of the Novel

Living in a town in La Pampa[1] was not the ideal condition for one who felt uncomfortable with the reality of the place in which luck or misfortune had landed him. Other points of reference were far away: fourteen hours by train to Buenos Aires, an entire day's trip to the sea, almost two days' travel to the mountains of Córdoba or Mendoza. But there was another and closer reference point: On the town's movie screen a parallel reality was projected. Reality? For many years I believed so. A reality I was certain existed outside of the town and in three dimensions. I received the first proof to the contrary in Buenos Aires, when I went to school there in 1946 for my *bachillerato*.[2]

The reality of the pleasure, that tantalizing reality, did not exist in Buenos Aires. Would it exist outside of Buenos Aires? I had to leave my country to find out: Only at age twenty-three was I able to save the money to pay for the twenty-one-day trip which then separated Buenos Aires from Europe. I wasted no time in discovering that not even in Rome, where I chose to settle, did that yearned-for parallel reality exist. Least of all did it exist in the official film school, the Centro Sperimentale di Cinematografia, which lay in the very heart of the Cinecittà. I had arrived there with a cargo of idolatry — von Sternberg, Frank Borzage, the well-known faces of Greta, Marlene, Michèle Morgan, the poets Prévert and Cocteau — which was hardly suitable, because it was 1956 and the prevailing ideology was neorealism. At

---

Translated by Margaret Peden.

the school one had to move to the beat of two repressions, each with its own tempo, though fundamentally akin. First, it was a state school that in this period was under Christian Democratic rule. Second, the director and administration were of the super-Catholic sort that still existed in the '50s — puritans to a point that today would be laughable. For example, the low necklines of the female acting students were objectionable; decorum was required; and any kind of sexual activity was considered offensive. I am referring to heterosexual activities among students; homosexuality was out of the question. As far as drugs were concerned, the mere mention of the word evoked in them some sinister opium den in Macao. In other words, it was the asceticism of a convent.

Running apparently counter to that repressive discipline was the ideology of the faculty, imbued with neorealism. Everything had started in the immediate postwar period with *auteur* films such as *Open City* by Rossellini, *Shoeshine* by De Sica, and *La Terra trema* by Visconti. From those filmmakers' works the film critics and theoreticians had attempted to extract a dogma, a series of principles they wielded like bludgeons against any film different from the type approved by Zavattini and his followers. That's right: Not only was knowing how to narrate reactionary; *auteur* cinema was also reactionary. The term *auteur* still did not exist; adopted by *Cahiers du Cinéma* around that same period, it had not yet been popularized in 1956.[3] I remember an example of pure cinema that Zavattini proposed: A working woman leaves her house and goes shopping, she looks at glassware, compares prices, gets shoes for the children — all within the actual time of the action, which could easily fill the usual hour and one-half projection time. And the director's view, of course, could never intervene; the director's view could not be subjective — that was a mortal sin. That cold, impersonal, yet revelatory camera resolved everything. But a camera revelatory of what? A superficial photographic realism.

I should add that 1956 was a major crisis year for the theoreticians of neorealism; the public was pulling away from them, and, instead of causing them to rethink their positions, this made them even more rigid. That year saw the premiere of De Sica's *Il Tetto* (*The Roof*). Filmed under the Zavattinian reign of terror, it was a popular and critical flop at the international film festivals. Only the neorealist theoreticians defended it because it was shot according to the house rules, which had succeeded in choking the creative breath out of De Sica. How did it all end up? Filmmakers stopped any serious experimentation, and thus a brilliant crusade begun in the postwar period by authors, not critics, came to a halt. But why did production stop? Because the public had turned away: The political, muck-raking film had become so purist and so dry that only the elite audience could follow it. The general public, the lower classes, the working classes, which in Italy had a passion for cinema and could afford a ticket, did not understand that sort of film that was apparently directed at them. An elitist cinema — of the happy few, "for the people."

It didn't work. Well, there I was, feeling torn. On the one hand, I liked the idea of a popular cinema of contestation; but I also liked the well-told film that seemed to belong exclusively to the reactionaries. I debated all of this in my first scripts, which ended up being nothing more than copies of old Hollywood films. I was enthusiastic while I wrote them, but once I was finished I didn't like them. I was taken at first by the possibility of recreating moments for the childlike spectator, protected in the shadows of the movie house; but while the dream was pleasant, the awakening was not.

Finally, I realized that it might be more interesting to explore the narrative possibilities of my own reality, and I began to write a script that inevitably became a novel. Why inevitably? I didn't consciously decide to move from the cinema to the novel. I was planning a scene in the script in which one of my aunts, in voice-over, introduced the action in the washroom of a house in town. That voice had to be at most three lines long, yet it continued without stopping for thirty pages. There was no way to make her keep quiet. She had only banalities to tell about; but it seemed to me that the accumulation of these banalities gave a special significance to the exposition.

That incident with the thirty pages of banalities took place one day in March 1962, and I myself haven't been able to keep quiet since then. I've continued with my banalities; I wasn't going to be outdone by my aunt.

Now let's theorize, as Zavattini did. I believe that what led me to that change in medium of expression was the need for more narrative space. Once I was able to confront the reality, after so many years of fleeing toward film, I was interested in exploring it, analyzing it, in order to try to understand it. And the classic space of an hour and one-half of screen time did not suffice. Cinema requires synthesis, and my themes required a different approach; they required analysis and accumulation of details.

From that novel I moved on to two others, always with the conviction of never returning to cinema. But in 1973 the Argentine director Leopoldo Torre Nilsson asked me for the rights to *Boquitas pintadas* (*Heartbreak Tango*), and, after much hemming and hawing, I accepted the offer and also agreed to handle the adaptation. Torre Nilsson, as producer and director, gave me complete freedom, but I didn't feel comfortable with the task because I had to follow a procedure contrary to that which had helped to liberate me. I had to summarize the novel, trim it down, find formulas that could synthesize what originally had been exposed analytically.

Four years later there was another call from the cinema. In Mexico the director Arturo Ripstein asked me to adapt Donoso's short novel, *El Lugar sin límites* (*Infinity*). Initially, I said no, but Ripstein insisted, and I reread the text. It was a long short story rather than a novel, and what had to be done in this case was add material to fill out the script. I felt much better about that job, and from the good working relationship with Ripstein arose another project: the adaptation of a story by the Argentine writer Silvina Ocampo, "El Impostor" (The imposter), for producer Barbachano Ponce's return to cinema. What did those two stories (I'm referring to *El Lugar sin límites* and "El Impostor") have in common? At first glance, nothing. But after completing both adaptations, I saw a clear kinship. Both narratives were allegories, poetic histories, without realist pretensions, though in the final analysis they referred to very well-defined human problems.

My novels, unlike these adaptations, always try to be direct reconstructions of reality; hence, their analytic character. Synthesis, by contrast, suits allegory and dream. What better example of synthesis than our dreams each night? Cinema requires synthesis and, as such, is the ideal vehicle for allegory, for dreams. Which brings me to another supposition. Is it for that reason that films of the 1930s and 1940s have aged so well? They were, without a doubt, dreams in images.

Let's take two examples: In Hollywood, "B" pictures such as *Seven Sinners* (Tay Garnett, 1940) and *The Best Years of Our Lives* (William

Wyler, 1946), seen as "superproductions" and loaded down with Oscars, were prized for their cinematography.

What has happened to these two films over the last forty years? *Seven Sinners* never tried to resemble any real-life situation. It was an unbiased reflection on power and established values — one more allegory on this theme. *The Best Years of Our Lives,* in contrast, set out to give a realistic image of the return of American soldiers after World War II. And it succeeded. But after all these years, even though a lot can be said for that film as a valid period piece, it is *Seven Sinners* that people would call a work of art. Yes, examining what's left of the history of cinema, I encounter more and more proof of how little remains of those attempts at realism in which the camera seems to skim the surface without managing to pass into any dimension other than that of photographic realism — that is, remaining within two dimensions.

Now, having briefly pointed out those differences that I see between cinema and literature, I shall go on to answer a question that I have been formulating for a long time. Can cinema and television do away with literature — with narrative, to be more specific? My impression is that no, it is impossible for this to happen, because there are two different readers involved. In cinema, attention is drawn to so many different points of attraction that concentration on a complicated conceptual discourse becomes difficult, if not downright impossible. With a film, one has to divide one's attention among the demands of the image, those of the spoken words, and those of the background music. One must pay special attention, moreover, to the impact of the image in movement. There are the same requirements for a painting, where one counts on the static quality of the image. The concentration allowed, in contrast, by the printed page gives the narrator room for another type of discourse, more complicated conceptually. Besides, the book can wait, the reader can stop to reflect; but not so with the cinematic image.

In conclusion, there are stories that only literature can take up, because the reader's attention determines them thus. In the final analysis, what decides everything is the nature of human attention. It does have limits; it can focus on certain material and not on other. It gets tired; it can penetrate depths on the written page that when shown on the screen would be impossible to grasp.

I had a curious experience in this regard. Three years ago I saw an Italian film, *The Suspect,* by Francesco Maselli. It is a very complicated political story, done with painstaking detail. During the projection I became alarmed because I couldn't follow the narrative. The characters were asking questions that seemed to have no connection to one another. I supposed that, written down, these same bits of dialogue would be more intelligible — or would they? What was happening? Was it all gibberish, or was the spectator's attention simply unable to grasp everything presented to it? This question interested me, and through my editor in Rome I obtained the original screenplay. I read it and understood everything perfectly. There were, of course, two or three obscure passages that became clear when I went back to reread them. But this procedure was not possible in the movie house. There the projection cannot be stopped.

From all this, I think I can affirm that reading a film is different from reading a novel, that this film "reading," even if it contains something of the literary reading, also has a good deal of the reading of a painting. This would be a third type of reading, which, though sharing characteristics of both literary and plastic reading, is nevertheless different. And what am I getting at with all this? It's a way of showing my ever-renewed admiration for the advantages of printed narrative, with its wide margin for an author's experimentation and, at the same time, the broad territory it proffers to that author for an encounter with the reader.

Notes

1. Puig was born and raised in the small Argentine town of General Villegas, near the border between the provinces of Buenos Aires and La Pampa. — ED.

2. The *bachillerato* would correspond to the North American high school diploma. — ED.

3. *Auteur* cinema, a term put into currency by André Bazin and other critics writing for *Cahiers du Cinéma* during the 1950s, referred to a corpus of films that bore the stylistic imprint of the director who had made those films. *Auteur* directors were those who developed recognizable motifs and stylistic traits independent of the subject matter of each film. — ED.

Bibliography

All titles refer to novels or short story collections unless otherwise indicated.

Jonathan Baumbach

The Landscape of Nightmare: Studies in the Contemporary American Novel. New York: New York University Press, 1965. (*criticism*)

A Man to Conjure With. New York: Random House, 1965.

Moderns and Contemporaries: Nine Masters of the Short Story (edited with Arthur Edelstein). New York: Random House, 1968. (*anthology*)

What Comes Next. New York: Harper & Row, 1968.

Writers as Teachers/Teachers as Writers (edited by Baumbach). New York: Holt, Rinehart & Winston, 1970. (*essay*)

Reruns. New York: Fiction Collective, 1974.

Babble. New York: Fiction Collective, 1976.

Chez Charlotte and Emily. New York: Fiction Collective, 1979.

The Return of Service. Urbana: University of Illinois Press, 1979.

My Father More or Less. New York: Fiction Collective, 1982.

The Life and Times of Major Fiction. New York: Fiction Collective, 1986.

Separate Hours: A Novel. Boulder: Fiction Collective Two, 1990.

Jorge Luis Borges

Fervor de Buenos Aires (Passion for Buenos Aires). Buenos Aires: Serantes, 1923. (*poetry*)

Inquisiciones. Buenos Aires: Proa, 1925. (*essays*)

El tamaño de mi esperanza (How great my hope is). Buenos Aires: Proa, 1926. (*essays*)

El idioma de los argentinos (Speech of the Argentines). Buenos Aires: M. Gleizer, 1928. (*essays*)

Evaristo Carriego. Buenos Aires: M. Gleizer, 1930. Trans. N. T. di Giovanni, *Evaristo Carriego: A Book About Old Time Buenos Aires.* New York: Dutton, 1984. (*biography*)

Historia universal de la infamia. Buenos Aires: Megáfono, 1935. Trans. N. T. di Giovanni, *A Universal History of Infamy.* New York: Dutton, 1972.

Historia de la eternidad (History of eternity). Buenos Aires: Viau y Zona, 1936. (*essays*)

El Jardín de senderos que se bifurcan (The garden of forking paths). Buenos Aires: Sur, 1941. Trans. in *Ficciones.* Buenos Aires: Sur, 1942.

Seis problemas para don Isidro Parodi (with A. Bioy Casares, under pseudonym H. Bustos Domecq). Buenos Aires: Sur, 1942. Trans. N. T. di Giovanni, *Six Problems for Don Isidro Parodi.* New York: Dutton, 1983.

Ficciones. Buenos Aires: Sur, 1944. Trans. A. Kerrigan et al., *Ficciones.* New York: Grove, 1962.

Dos fantasías memorables (Two memorable fantasies) (with A. Bioy Casares, under pseudonym H. Bustos Domecq). Buenos Aires: Oportet y Haereses, 1946.

Un modelo para la muerte (A model for death) (with A. Bioy Casares, under pseudonym B. Suárez Lynch). Buenos Aires: Oportet y Haereses, 1946.

Nueva refutación del tiempo (*New Refutation of Time*). Buenos Aires: Oportet y Haereses, 1947. (*essays*)

El Aleph. Buenos Aires: Losada, 1949. Trans. N. T. di Giovanni, *The Aleph and Other Stories, 1933–1969.* New York: Dutton, 1970.

La Muerte y la brújula (Death and the compass). Buenos Aires: Sur, 1951.

Otras inquisiciones. Buenos Aires: Sur, 1952. Trans. R.L.C. Simms, *Other Inquisitions.* Austin: University of Texas Press, 1964. (*essays*)

La Hermana de Eloísa (Heloise's sister) (with L. M. Levinson). Buenos Aires: Ene, 1955.

El hacedor. Buenos Aires: Emecé, 1960. Trans. M. Boyer and H. Morland, *Dreamtigers.* Austin: University of Texas Press, 1964.

Antología personal. Buenos Aires: Sur, 1961. Trans. A. Kerrigan et al., *A Personal Anthology.* New York: Grove, 1967.

Labyrinths: Selected Stories and Other Writings (edited by D. A. Yates and J. E. Irby). New York: New Directions, 1964.

Obra poética, 1923–1964. Buenos Aires: Emecé, 1964. Trans. N. T. di Giovanni, *Selected Poems, 1923–1967.* New York: Delacorte, 1972.

Introducción a la literatura inglesa (with M. E. Vázquez). Buenos Aires: Columba, 1965. Trans. L. C. Keating and R. O. Evans, *An Introduction to English Literature.* Lexington: University of Kentucky Press, 1971. (*essays*)

Crónicas de Bustos Domecq. Buenos Aires: Losada, 1967. Trans. N. T. di Giovanni, *Chronicles of Bustos Domecq.* New York: Dutton, 1976.

Introducción a la literatura norteamericana (with E. Zemborain de Torres). Buenos Aires: Columba, 1967. Trans. L. C. Keating and R. O. Evans, *An Introduction to American Literature*. Lexington: University of Kentucky Press, 1971. (*essays*)

El libro de los seres imaginarios. Buenos Aires: Kier, 1967 (rev. ed. of *Manual de zoología fantástica*. Mexico: Fondo de Cultura Económica, 1957.) Trans. N. T. di Giovanni, *The Book of Imaginary Beings*. New York: Dutton, 1969.

Nueva antología personal (New personal anthology). Buenos Aires: Emecé, 1968.

Elogio de la sombra. Buenos Aires: Emecé, 1969. Trans. N. T. di Giovanni, *In Praise of Darkness*. New York: Dutton, 1972.

El otro, el mismo. Buenos Aires: Emecé, 1969. (*poetry*)

El informe de Brodie. Buenos Aires, Emecé, 1970. Trans. N. T. di Giovanni, *Doctor Brodie's Report*. New York: Dutton, 1971.

El Matrero. Buenos Aires: Edicom, 1970.

El Congreso. Buenos Aires: El Archibrazo, 1971. Trans. N. T. di Giovanni with author, *The Congress*. London: Enitharmon, 1974.

El oro de los tigres. Buenos Aires: Emecé, 1972. Trans. A. Reid, *The Gold of Tigers: Selected Later Poems*. New York: Dutton, 1977. (*poetry*)

Borges on Writing. Edited by N. T. di Giovanni, D. Halpern, and F. MacShane. New York: Dutton, 1973. (*essays*)

Les Autres: Scenario original (The others: original scenario) (with A. Bioy Casares and H. Santiago). Paris: C. Bourgois, 1974. (*screenplay*)

El Libro de arena. Buenos Aires: Emecé, 1975. Trans. N. T. di Giovanni, *The Book of Sand*. New York: Dutton, 1977.

La Rosa profunda. Buenos Aires: Emecé, 1975. Trans. in *The Gold of Tigers*. New York: Dutton, 1977. (*poetry*)

Libro de sueños (Book of dreams). Buenos Aires: Torres Aguero, 1976. (*transcripts of dreams*)

La Moneda de hierro (The iron coin). Buenos Aires: Emecé, 1976. (*poetry*)

Adrogué. Adrogué: Eds. Adrogué, 1977. (*prose and poetry*)

Historia de la noche (History of night). Buenos Aires: Emecé, 1977. (*poetry*)

Nuevos cuentos de Bustos Domecq (New wtories of Bustos Domecq) (with A. Bioy Casares). Buenos Aires: Librería de la Ciudad, 1977.

Rosa y azul. Madrid: Sedmay, 1977.

Siete noches. Mexico: Fondo de Cultura Económica, 1980. Trans. E. Weinberger, *Seven Nights*. New York: New Directions, 1984. (*lectures*)

Borges en/y/sobre cine (edited by E. Cozarinsky). Madrid: Fundamentos, 1981. Trans. G. Waldman and R. Christ, *Borges in/and/on Film*. New York: Lumen, 1988. (*film reviews*)

La cifra (The cypher). Buenos Aires: Emecé, 1981. (*poetry*)

Veinticinco agosto 1983 y otros cuentos (August 25, 1983, and other stories). Madrid: Siruela, 1983.

Atlas (with M. Kodama). Buenos Aires: Sudamericana, 1984. Trans. A. Kerrigan, *Atlas*. New York: Dutton, 1985. (*prose and poetry*)

Prosa completa. 4 vols. Barcelona: Ediciones B, 1984.

Los conjurados. Madrid: Alianza, 1985. (*poetry*)

Textos cautivos: ensayos y reseñas en "El Hogar" (1936–1939) (Captive texts: Essays and reviews in *El Hogar* [1936–1939]). Barcelona: Tusquets, 1986. (*essays and reviews*)

El Aleph borgiano (edited by J. G. Cobo Borda and M. Kovasics de Cubides). Bogotá: Biblioteca Arango, 1987. (*reviews*)

A/Z. Madrid: Siruela, 1988.

Obras completas, 1975–1985. Buenos Aires: Emecé, 1989.

William Burroughs

Junkie: Confessions of an Unredeemed Drug Addict (under pseudonym William Lee). New York: A. A. Wyn, 1953; published under own name, New York: Ace Books, 1964; rev. ed., Baltimore: Penguin, 1977.

The Naked Lunch. Paris: Olympia, 1959.

The Exterminator (with Brion Gysin). San Francisco: Auerhaun, 1960.

Minutes to Go. Paris: Two Cities Editions, 1960. (*"cut-up" poems*)

The Soft Machine. Paris: Olympia, 1961; New York: Grove, 1966.

The Ticket That Exploded. Paris: Olympia, 1962; rev. ed. New York: Grove, 1967.

Dead Fingers Talk. London: Johnathan Calder, 1963.

Nova Express. New York: Grove, 1964.

The Wild Boys: A Book of the Dead. New York: Grove, 1969.

The Job: Interviews with William S. Burroughs. New York: Grove, 1970.

The Last Words of Dutch Schultz: A Fiction in the Form of a Filmscript. London: Cape Goliard, 1970.

The Third Mind (with Brion Gysin). New York: Viking, 1978.

Ah Pook Is Here. London: Jonathan Calder, 1979.

Blade Runner: A Movie. Berkeley: Blue Wind, 1979.

Book of Breething. Berkeley: Blue Wind, 1980.

Port of Saints. Berkeley: Blue Wind, 1980.

Cities of the Red Night. New York: Holt, Rinehart & Winston, 1981. (First vol. of trilogy that includes *The Place of Dead Roads* and *The Western Lands*)

Early Routines. Santa Barbara: Cadmus, 1982. (*pre-1960 sketches*)

Letters to Allen Ginsberg (1953–1957). New York: Full Court, 1982.

The Place of Dead Roads. New York: Holt, Rinehart & Winston, 1983.

The Burroughs File. San Francisco: City Lights, 1984.

Exterminator. Baltimore: Penguin, 1985.

The Adding Machine: Selected Essays. New York: Holt & Co., 1986.

Queer. Baltimore: Penguin, 1986.

The Western Lands. New York: Viking, 1987.

Interzone. New York: Viking, 1989.

Tornado Alley. Cherry Valley, N.Y.: Cherry Valley, 1989.

Marguerite Duras

Les Impudents (The impudent). Paris: Plon, 1943.

La Vie tranquille (The tranquil life). Paris: Plon, 1944.

Un Barrage contre le Pacifique. Paris: Gallimard, 1950. Trans. H. Briffault, *The Sea Wall*. New York: Farrar, Strauss, 1967.

Le Marin de Gibraltar. Paris: Gallimard, 1952. Trans. B. Bray, *The Sailor From Gibraltar*. New York: Grove, 1966.

Les Petits chevaux de Tarquinia. Paris: Gallimard, 1953. Trans. P. DuBerg, *The Little Horses of Tarquinia*. London: Jonathan Calder, 1960.

Des Journées entières dans les arbres. Paris: Gallimard, 1954. Trans. A. Barrows, *Whole Days in the Trees*. New York: Riverrun, 1984.

Le Square. Paris: Gallimard, 1955. Trans. S. Pitt-Rivers and I. Morduch, *The Square*. New York: Grove, 1959.

Moderato cantabile. Paris: Minuit, 1958. Trans. R. Seaver, *Moderato Cantabile*. New York: Grove, 1960.

Hiroshima mon amour. Paris: Gallimard, 1959. Trans. R. Seaver, *Hiroshima Mon Amour*. New York: Grove, 1961. (*screenplay*)

Les Viaducs de la Seine-et-Oise (The viaducts of Seine-et-Oise). Paris: Gallimard, 1959. (*play*)

Dix Heures et demie du soir en été. Paris: Gallimard, 1960. Trans. A. Borchardt, *Ten-Thirty on a Summer Night*. New York: Grove, 1963.

Une aussi longue absence (A long absence). Paris: Gallimard, 1961. (*screenplay*)

L'Après-midi de Monsieur Andesmas. Paris: Gallimard, 1962. Trans. *The Afternoon of Monsieur Andesmas*, in S. Pitt-Rivers et al., *Four Novels*. New York: Grove, 1965.

Le Ravissement de Lol V. Stein. Paris: Gallimard, 1964. Trans. R. Seaver, *The Ravishing of Lol Stein*. New York: Grove, 1967.

Théâtre I (*Les Eaux et les forêts* [Water and forests], *Le Square, La Musica*). Paris: Gallimard, 1965. (*plays*)

Le Vice-consul. Paris: Gallimard, 1965. Trans. E. Ellenbogen, *The Vice-Consul*. London: Hamish Hamilton, 1968.

L'Amante anglaise. Paris: Gallimard, 1967. Trans. B. Bray, *L'Amante Anglaise*. New York: Grove, 1968.

Three Plays (*The Square, Days in the Trees, The Viaducts of Seine-et-Oise*). Trans. B. Bray and S. Orwell. London: Calder & Boyars, 1967.

L'Amante anglaise. Paris: Cahiers du Théâtre National Populaire, 1968. (*play*)

Théâtre II (*Suzanna Andler; Des Journées entières dans les arbres; Yes, peut-être* [Yes, perhaps]; *Le Shaga; Un Homme est venu me voir* [A man came to see me]). Paris: Gallimard, 1968. (*plays*)

Détruire, dit-elle. Paris: Minuit, 1969. Trans. B. Bray, *Destroy, She Said*. New York: Grove, 1970.

Abahn Sabana David. Paris: Gallimard, 1970.

L'Amour. Paris: Gallimard, 1971.

India Song: texte, théâtre, film. Paris: Gallimard, 1973. Trans. B. Bray, *India Song*. New York: Grove, 1976. (*play/screenplay*)

Nathalie Granger. Followed by *La Femme du Gange* (*Woman of the Ganges*). Paris: Gallimard, 1973. (*screenplays*)

Les Parleuses (with Xavière Gauthier). Paris: Minuit, 1973. Trans. K. A. Jensen, *Woman to Woman*. Lincoln: University of Nebraska Press, 1987.

Le Camion (The truck). Paris: Gallimard, 1977. (*screenplay*)

L'Eden cinéma. Paris: Mercure de France, 1977. (*play*)

L'Eté 80 (The summer of '80). Paris: Minuit, 1980. (*play*)

L'Homme assis dans le couloir (The man sitting in the hallway). Paris: Minuit, 1980.

Le Navire Night (Steamship *Night*). Followed by *Césarée, Les Mains négatives* (Negative hands), *Aurélia Steiner, Aurélia Steiner, Aurélia Steiner*. Paris: Mercure de France, 1980.

Véra Baxter ou les plages de l'Atlantique (Vera Baxter, or Atlantic beaches). Paris: Albatros, 1980.

Les Yeux verts (Green eyes). Paris: L'Etoile, 1980. (*essays*)

Agatha. Paris: Minuit, 1981. (*play*)

Outside: Papiers d'un jour. Paris: Albin Michel, 1981. Trans. A. Goldhammer, *Outside: Selected Writings*. Boston: Beacon, 1986. (*essays*)

L'Homme Atlantique (Atlantic man). Paris: Minuit, 1982.

La Maladie de la mort. Paris: Minuit, 1982. Trans. B. Bray, *The Malady of Death*. New York: Grove, 1986.

Savannah Bay. Paris: Minuit, 1982.

L'Amant. Paris: Minuit, 1984. Trans. B. Bray, *The Lover*. New York: Pantheon, 1985.

Théâtre III (*La Bête dans la jungle* [based on H. James's story "The Beast in the Jungle"], *Les Papiers d'Aspern* [based on H. James's novel *The Aspern Papers*], *La Danse de mort* [based on A. Strindberg's play *Dance of Death*]. Paris: Gallimard, 1984. (*plays*)

La Douleur. Paris: P.O.L., 1985. Trans. B. Bray, *The War: A Memoir*. New York: Pantheon, 1986. (*essay*)

La Mouette de Tchékov (Chekhov's seagull). Paris: Gallimard, 1985.

La Musica deuxième (The music, second time). Paris: Gallimard, 1985.

Les Yeux bleus cheveux noirs. Paris: Minuit, 1986. Trans. B. Bray, *Blue Eyes, Black Hair*. New York: Pantheon, 1987.

Emily L. Paris: Minuit, 1987. Trans. B. Bray, *Emily L*. New York: Pantheon: 1989.

La Vie matérielle (Material life). Paris: P.O.L., 1987. (*essay*)

La Pluie d'été (Summer rain). Paris: P.O.L., 1990. (*essay*)

Alexander Kluge

Lebensläufe. Stuttgart: Henry Goverts, 1962. Trans. L. Vennewitz, *Attendance List for a Funeral*. New York: McGraw-Hill, 1966. Rpt. as *Case Histories*. New York: Holmes and Meier, 1988.

Schlachtbeschreibung. Freiburg: Walter, 1964. Trans. L. Vennewitz, *The Battle*. New York: McGraw-Hill, 1967.

Abschied von gestern (*Yesterday Girl*) (edited by E. Patalas). Frankfurt: Filmkritik, n.d. (*screenplay*)

Die Artisten in der Zirkuskuppel; ratlos (*Artists Under the Big Top: Perplexed*). Munich: R. Piper Verlag, 1968. (*screenplay*)

Öffentlichkeit und Erfahrung (Public sphere and experience) (with Oskar Negt). Frankfurt: Suhrkamp, 1972. (*essay*)

Gelegenheitsarbeit einer Sklavin: zur realistischen Methode. Frankfurt: Suhrkamp, 1973. Screenplay trans. J. Dawson, *Alexander Kluge and The Occasional Work of a Female Slave*. New York: Zoetrope, 1977. Essay trans. J. T. Acuff, *Toward a Realistic Method: Commentaries on the Notion of Antagonistic Realism*. Austin: University of Texas Press, 1980.

Lernprozesse mit tödlichem Ausgang (Learning process with lethal conclusion). Frankfurt: Suhrkamp, 1973.

Neue Geschichte, Hefte 1–18, "Unheimlichkeit der Zeit" (New stories, notebooks 1–18, uncanniness of time). Frankfurt: Suhrkamp, 1977.

Die Patriotin (The patriot). Frankfurt: Zweitausendeins, 1979.

Ulmer Dramaturgien: Reibungsverluste (Ulm dramatic theory: Friction losses) (with Klaus Eder). Munich: Hanser, 1980. (*essay*)

Geschichte und Eigensinn (History and obstinacy) (with Oskar Negt). Frankfurt: Zweitausendeins, 1981.

Bestandsaufnahme: Utopie Film (Taking stock: cinema as utopia). Frankfurt: Zweitausendeins, 1983. (*essay*)

Die Macht der Gefühle (*The Power of Emotion*). Frankfurt: Zweitausendeins, 1984. (*screenplay*)

Der Angriff der Gegenwart auf die übrige Zeit (*The Blind Director*, literally, "the Assualt of the present on the rest of time"). Frankfurt: Suhrkamp, 1985.

Pier Paolo Pasolini

Poesie a Casarsa. Bologna: Libreria Antiquaria Mario Landi, 1942. (*poetry*)

Poesie. San Vito Al Tagliamento: Stamperia Primon, 1945. (*poetry*)

I Pianti (The mourned). Casarsa: Pubblicazioni dell'Academiuta, 1946. (*poetry*)

Dov'è la mia patria (Where is my homeland). Casarsa: Pubblicazioni dell'Academiuta, 1949. (*poetry*)

Roma 1950 "diario" (1950 Rome "diary"]. Milan: All'insegna del pesce d'Oro, 1950. (*poetry*)

Tal cour di un frut (In the heart of a boy). Tricesimo: Friuli, 1953. (*poetry*)

Il canto popolare (The popular song). Milan: La Meridiana, 1954. (*poetry*)

Dal diario (From the diary). Caltanisetta: Sciascia, 1954. (*poetry*)

La meglio gioventù (Superior youth). Florence: Sansoni, 1954. (*poetry*)

Ragazzi di vita. Milan: Garzanti, 1955. Trans. E. Capouya, *The Ragazzi.* New York: Grove, 1968.

Le ceneri di Gramsci. Milan: Garzanti, 1957. Trans. D. Wallace, *The Ashes of Gramsci.* Paterborough, Cambridgeshire: Spectacular Diseases, 1982. (*poetry*)

L'usignolo della Chiesa Cattolica (The nightingale of the Catholic church). Milan: Longanesi, 1958. (*poetry*)

Una Vita violenta. Milan: Garzanti, 1959. Trans. W. Weaver, *A Violent Life.* London: Jonathan Cape, 1968.

Donne di Roma (Women of Rome). Milan: Il Saggiatore, 1960. (*texts accompanying photographs*)

Passione e ideologia (1948–1958). Milan: Garzanti, 1960. (*essays*)

Sonetto primaverile (Spring sonnet). Milan: All'insegna del pesce d'oro, 1960. (*poetry*)

Accattone. Rome: F. M., 1961. (*screenplay*)

La religione de mio tempo (The religion of my time). Milan: Garzanti, 1961. (*poetry*)

Mamma Roma. Milan: Rizzoli, 1962. (*screenplay*)

L'odore dell'India. Milan: Longanesi, 1962. Trans. D. Price, *The Scent of India.* London: Olive, 1984. (*essays*)

Il sogno di una cosa. Milan: Garzanti, 1962. Trans. S. Hood, *A Dream of Something.* London: Quartet, 1988.

Il Vantone di Plauto (adaptation of Plautus's *Miles Gloriosus*). Milan: Garzanti, 1963. (*play*)

Poesie in forma di rosa (Poetry in the form of a rose). Milan: Garzanti, 1964. (*poetry*)

Il Vangelo secondo Matteo (*The Gospel According to St. Matthew*). Milan: Garzanti, 1964. (*screenplay*)

Alì dagli occhi azzurri (Blue-eyed Ali). Contains screenplays of *La Notte brava* and *La Ricotta.* Milan: Garzanti, 1965. Partial trans. J. Shepley, *Roman Nights and Other Stories.* Marlboro, Vt.: Marlboro, 1986.

Uccellaci e uccellini (The Hawks and the Sparrows). Milan: Garzanti, 1966. (*screen-play*)

Edipo Re. Milan: Garzanti, 1967. Trans. J. Mathews, *Oedipus Rex*. New York: Simon & Schuster, 1971. (*screenplay*)

Teorema. Milan: Garzanti, 1968.

Pasolini on Pasolini: Interviews With Oswald Stack. London: Thames & Hudson, 1969.

Medea. Milan: Garzanti, 1970. (*screenplay*)

Trasumanar e organizzar (To transhumanize and organize). Milan: Garzanti, 1971. (*poetry*)

Empirismo eretico. Milan: Garzanti, 1972. Trans. L. K. Barnett and B. Lawton, *Heretical Empiricism*. Bloomington: Indiana University Press, 1988. (*essays*)

Calderón. Milan: Garzanti, 1973. (*poetry*)

La Divina Mimesis. Turin: Einaudi, 1975.

La nuova gioventù (New youth). Turin: Einaudi, 1975.

Il Padre selvaggio (The savage father). Turin: Einaudi, 1975. (*cine-roman*)*

Scritti corsari ("pirate writings"). Milan: Garzanti, 1975. (*essays*)

Trilogia della vita (Il Decamerone, I racconti di Canterbury, Il Fiore delle Mille e una notte). Bologna: Cappelli, 1975. (*screenplays*)

Affabulazione, Pilade. Milan: Garzanti, 1977. (*plays*)

Lettere luterane. Turin: Einaudi, 1977. Trans. S. Hood, *Lutheran Letters*. Manchester: Carcanet New Press, 1983. (*essays*)

San Paolo (St. Paul). Turin: Einaudi, 1977. (*play*)

Porcile, Orgia, Bestia de stile (Pigsty, Orgy, Stylish Beasts). Milan: Garzanti, 1979. (*plays*)

Poesie e pagine retrovate (edited by A. Zanzotto and N. Naldini). Rome: Lato Side, 1980. (*poetry and miscellany*)

Amado mio (My beloved), preceded by *Atti impuri* (Impure acts). Milan: Garzanti, 1982.

Poems. Trans. N. MacAfee and L. Martinengo. New York: Random House, 1982.

Roman Poems. Trans. L. Ferlinghetti and F. Valente. San Francisco: City Lights, 1986.

Il Portico della morte (The portico of death) (edited by C. Segre). Rome: Associazione Fondo Pier Paolo Pasolini, 1988. (*essays*)

Manuel Puig

---

* *Cine-roman* is a term first used by the *nouveau roman* writers to refer to a literary text resembling the scenario of a film, including directions for camera movement and separate sound and image tracks but readable as a novel-like work independent of the film.

Manuel Puig

La Traición de Rita Hayworth. Buenos Aires: Jorge Alvarez, 1968. Trans. S. J. Levine, *Betrayed by Rita Hayworth.* New York: E. P. Dutton, 1971.

Boquitas pintadas: folletín. Buenos Aires: Sudamericana, 1969. Trans. S. J. Levine, *Heartbreak Tango: A Serial.* New York: E. P. Dutton, 1973.

The Buenos Aires Affair: Novela policial. Buenos Aires: Sudamericana, 1973. Trans. S. J. Levine, *The Buenos Aires Affair: A Detective Novel.* New York: E. P. Dutton, 1976.

El Beso de la mujer araña. Barcelona: Seix Barral, 1976. Trans. T. Colchie, *Kiss of the Spider Woman.* New York: Knopf, 1978.

Pubis angelical. Barcelona: Seix Barral, 1979. Trans. E. Brunet, *Pubis Angelical: A Novel.* New York: Random House, 1986.

Maldición eterna a quien lea estas páginas. Barcelona: Seix Barral, 1980. Trans. by Puig, *Eternal Curse on the Reader of These Pages.* New York: Random House, 1982.

Sangre de amor correspondido. Barcelona: Seix Barral, 1982. Trans. J. L. Grayson, *Blood of Requited Love.* New York: Vintage, 1984.

Bajos un manto de estrellas. Barcelona: Seix Barral, 1983. Trans. R. Christ, *Under a Mantle of Stars.* New York: Lumen, 1985. Includes theatrical version of *El Beso de la mujer araña.* (*play*).

Cara del villano; Recuerdo de Tijuana (Peasant face; Tijuana souvenir). Mexico: Seix Barral, 1985. (*plays*)

Cae la noche tropical (Tropical nightfall). Barcelona: Seix Barral, 1988.

Alain Robbe-Grillet

Les Gommes. Paris: Minuit, 1953. Trans. R. Howard, *The Erasers.* New York: Grove, 1964.

Le Voyeur. Paris: Minuit, 1955. Trans. R. Howard, *The Voyeur.* New York: Grove, 1958.

La Jalousie. Paris: Minuit, 1957. Trans. R. Howard, *Jealousy.* New York: Grove, 1959.

Dans le labyrinthe. Paris: Minuit, 1959. Trans. R. Howard, *In the Labyrinth.* New York: Grove, 1960.

L'Année dernière à Marienbad. Paris: Minuit, 1961. Trans. R. Howard, *Last Year at Marienbad.* New York: Grove, 1965. (*cine-roman*)

Instantanés. Paris: Minuit, 1962. Trans. B. Morrissette, *Snapshots.* New York: Grove, 1968.

L'Immortelle. Paris: Minuit, 1963. Trans. A. M. Sheridan Smith, *The Immortal One.* London: Calder & Boyars, 1971.

Pour un nouveau roman. Paris: Minuit, 1963. Trans. R. Howard, *For a New Novel: Essays on Fiction.* New York: Grove, 1965. (*essays*)

La Maison de rendez-vous. Paris: Minuit, 1965. Trans. R. Howard, *La Maison de Rendez-vous.* New York: Grove, 1966.

Projet pour une révolution à New York. Paris: Minuit, 1970. Trans. R. Howard, *Project for a Revolution in New York.* New York: Grove, 1972.

Rêves de jeunes filles (with D. Hamilton). Paris: Laffont, 1971. Trans. E. Walter, *Dreams of a Young Girl.* New York: Morrow, 1971. (*texts accompanying photographs*)

Les Demoiselles d'Hamilton (with D. Hamilton). Paris: Laffont, 1972. Trans. M. Egan, *Sisters.* New York: Morrow, 1973. (*texts accompanying photographs*)

Glissements progressifs du plaisir. Paris: Minuit, 1974. (*cine-roman*) (Progressive slippages of pleasure).

Construction d'un temple en ruines à la déesse Vanade (Construction of a temple in ruins to the goddess Vanade). Paris: Le Bateau-Lavoir, 1975.

La Belle captive (The beautiful captive). Paris: Bibliothèque des Arts, 1976.

Topologie d'une cité fantôme. Paris: Minuit, 1976. Trans. J. A. Underwood, *Topology of a Phantom City.* New York: Grove, 1976.

Temple aux miroirs (Temple with mirrors) (with I. Ionesco). Paris: Seghers, 1977.

Un régicide (A regicide). Paris: Minuit, 1978 (written in 1949).

Souvenirs du triangle d'or. Paris: Minuit, 1978. Trans. J. A. Underwood, *Recollections of the Golden Triangle.* New York: Grove, 1986.

Traces suspectes en surfaces (Suspect and surface traces) (with R. Rauschenberg). West Islip, N.Y.: Universal Limited Art Editions, 1978.

Djinn. Un trou rouge entre les pavés disjoints (Djinn: a red hole in a cracked sidewalk). Paris: Minuit, 1981. Trans. Y. Lenard and W. Wells, *Djinn.* New York: Grove, 1982.

Le Rendez-vous (The rendezvous) (with Y. Lenard). New York: Holt, Rinehart & Winston, 1981. (*grammar textbook*)

Le Miroir qui revient. Paris: Minuit, 1984. Trans. J.Levy, *Ghosts in the Mirror / Alain Robbe-Grillet.* London: J. Calder, 1988. (*autobiography*)

Angélique, ou l'Enchantement (Angélique, or the enchantment). Paris: Minuit, 1987.

Ben Stoltzfus

The Eye of the Needle. New York: Viking, 1967.

Gide's Eagles. Carbondale: Southern Illinois University Press, 1969. (*criticism*)

Black Lazarus. New York: Winter House, 1972.

Gide and Hemingway: Rebels Against God. New York: Kennikat, 1978. (*criticism*)

Alain Robbe-Grillet: The Body of the Text. Rutherford, N.J.: Farleigh Dickinson University Press, 1985. (*criticism*)

Alain Robbe-Grillet: Life, Work, and Criticism. Fredericton, N.B., Canada: York, 1987. (*criticism*)

Red White and Blue. Fredericton, N.B., Canada: York, 1989.

Ronald Sukenick

Wallace Stevens: Musing the Obscure. New York: New York University Press, 1967. (*criticism*)

Up. New York: Dial, 1968.

The Death of the Novel and Other Stories. New York: Dial, 1969.

Out. Chicago: Swallow, 1973.

98.6. New York: Fiction Collective Two, 1975.

Long Talking Bad Condition Blues. New York: Fiction Collective Two, 1979.

In Form: Digressions on the Act of Fiction. Carbondale: Southern Illinois University Press, 1985. (*criticism*)

The Endless Short Story. New York: Fiction Collective Two, 1986.

Down and In: Life in the Underground. New York: Collier, 1988. (*essay*)

Filmography

The following lists are intended to provide the reader with a broad outline of each writer's contact, direct and indirect, with the practice of filmmaking and the aesthetics of cinema. Some of the authors have written screenplays for films; some have written novels on which films have been based. In a few cases, the writers have directed films. Many of the authors provided the names of films that have influenced their writing.

Jonathan Baumbach

Films that have influenced Baumbach's writing:

The Big Sleep (Hawks, 1946).

Notorious (Hitchcock, 1946).

Lady From Shanghai (Welles, 1948).

Diary of a Country Priest (Bresson, 1950).

Rashomon (Kurosawa, 1951).

Limelight (Chaplin, 1952).

Naked Night (Bergman, 1953).

L'Avventura (Antonioni, 1959).

Breathless (Godard, 1959).

Eyes Without a Face (Franju, 1959).

8 1/2 (Fellini, 1963).

Band of Outsiders (Godard, 1964).

Fist in His Pocket (Bellochio, 1965).

Pierrot le fou (Godard, 1965).

L'Amour fou (Rivette, 1968).

Mississippi Mermaid (Truffaut, 1969).

Une Femme douce (Bresson, 1971).

Discreet Charm of the Bourgeoisie (Buñuel, 1972).
Obsession (De Palma, 1976).

Jorge Luis Borges

Films that have influenced Borges's writing:
Films by Josef von Sternberg and Ernst Lubitsch.

Films based on literary works by Borges:
Días de odio (Days of hatred) (Torre Nilsson, 1954). Based on "Emma Zunz."
Hombre de la esquina rosada (R. Mugica, 1961). Based on "Streetcorner Man."
Emma Zunz (A. Magrou, 1969). Based on story of same name.
The Spider's Strategem (Bertolucci, 1970). Based on "Theme of the Traitor and the Hero."
El Muerto/Cacique Bandeira (H. Olivera, 1975). Based on "The Dead Man."
Los Orilleros (Men of the border) (R. Luna, 1975). Based on original story by Borges and A. Bioy Casares.
Splits (L. Katz, 1978). Based on "Emma Zunz."
A Intrusa (C. H. Christensen, 1979). Based on "The Intruder."

Screenplays written by Borges:
Invasión (Santiago, 1969).
Les Autres (The others) (with A. Bioy Casares and H. Santiago) (Santiago, 1974).

William Burroughs

Films made by Burroughs in collaboration with Anthony Balch:
Towers Open Fire, 1964.
The Cut-Ups, 1965.
Ghosts at No. 9, 1978.

Films about Burroughs and films in which he acted:
Chappaqua (Conrad Rooks, 1965).
Prologue (Robin Spry, 1970).

Kerouac (Robert Frank's documentary made at the 1982 Kerouac Conference in Boulder, Colorado).

Burroughs (Howard Brookner, 1983).

Kerouac (J. Antonelli, 1984).

Home of the Brave (Laurie Anderson, 1986).

What Happened to Kerouac? (Richard Lerner and Lewis Macadams, 1986).

Films influenced by Burroughs's work:

Performance (N. Roeg, 1970).

Blade Runner (R. Scott, 1982).

"Wild Boys" (video) (Russell Mulcahy [with Duran Duran]).

Films based on literary works by Burroughs:

Taking Tiger Mountain (T. Huckabee and K. Smith, 1983). Based on *Bladerunner: A Movie.*

The Naked Lunch (D. Cronenberg, 1988).

Marguerite Duras

Screenplays written by Duras:

Hiroshima mon amour (Resnais, 1959).

Moderato Cantabile (P. Brooks, 1960).

The Sailor from Gibraltar (T. Richardson, 1967).

Duras also wrote the screenplays (or film treatments) for most of her own films: *Détruire, dit-elle, Nathalie Granger, La Femme du Gange, India Song, Son nom de Venise dans Calcutta désert, Véra Baxter, Le Camion, Le Navire Night, Aurelia Steiner, Cesarée,* and *Les Mains négatives.*

Films directed by Duras:

Détruire, dit-elle (Destroy, She Said), 1969.

La Musica (with P. Seban), 1970.

Jaune le soleil (Yellow the sun), 1971. Based on her novel *Abahn Sabana David.*

Nathalie Granger, 1972.

La Femme du Gange (Woman of the Ganges), 1973.

India Song, 1975.

Des journées entières dans les arbres (Whole days in the trees), 1976. Based on her play of same name).

Son nom de Venise dans Calcutta désert (Her name of Venice in Calcutta desert), 1976.

Véra Baxter ou les plages de l'Atlantique (Vera Baxter, or Atlantic beaches), 1976.

Le Camion (The truck), 1977.

Le Navire Night (Steamship *Night*), 1978.

Aurélia Steiner, also known as *Aurélia Steiner Melbourne,* 1979.

Aurélia Steiner, also known as *Aurélia Steiner Vancouver,* 1979.

Césarée, 1979.

Les Mains négatives (Negative hands), 1979.

Il Dialogo di Roma (Dialogue of Rome), 1983. (*documentary*)

Les Enfants (The children) (with J. Mascolo and J.-M. Turine), 1985.

Films based on literary works by Duras:

La Diga sul Pacifico (*The Angry Age,* also known as *The Sea Wall*) (R. Clement, 1958). Based on her novel *Un Barrage contre le Pacifique.*

Moderato Cantabile (P. Brook, 1960). Based on her novel of same name.

Une aussi longue absence (*The Long Absence*) (H. Colpi, 1961).

Dix Heures et demie du soir en été (J. Dassin, 1966). Based on her novel of the same name.

Le Marin de Gibraltar (*The Sailor from Gibraltar*) (T. Richardson, 1967). Based on her novel of same name.

Alexander Kluge

Brutalität in Stein (Brutality in stone) (with P. Schamoni), 1960.

Lehrer in Wandel (Teachers in transition) (with K. Kluge), 1963.

Porträt einer Bewährung (Proven competence portrayed), 1964.

Abschied von gestern (*Yesterday Girl*), 1966.

Frau Blackburn, geb. 5 Jan. 1872, wird gefilmt (Mrs. Blackburn, born Jan. 5, 1872, gets filmed), 1967.

Die Artisten in der Zirkuskuppel: ratlos (*Artists Under the Big Top: Perplexed*), 1968.

Ein Arzt aus Halberstadt (A doctor from Halberstadt), 1970.

Der grosse Verhau (The grand slam), 1970.

Die unbezähmbare Leni Peickert (The indomitable Leni Peickert), 1970.

Willi Tobler und der Untergang der sechsten Flotte (Willi Tobler and the sinking of the sixth fleet), 1971. Rereleased in 1977 as *Zu böser Schlacht schleich' ich heut nacht so bang* (In such trepidation I creep off tonight to evil battle).

Wir verbauen 3 x 27 milla. dollar in einer Angriffsschlachter (We'll blow 3 x 27 billion dollars on a destroyer), 1971.

Gelegenheitsarbeit einer Sklavin (*Part-Time Work of a Domestic Slave*), 1973.

(Episode in) *Die Reise nach Wien* (The trip to Vienna), 1973.

In Gefahr und grösster Not bringt der Mittelweg den Tod (The middle of the road is a very dead end) (with E. Reitz), 1974.

Der starke Ferdinand (*Strongman Ferdinand*), 1976.

Deutschland im Herbst (*Germany in Autumn*) (with Fassbinder, et al.), 1978.

Die Patriotin (*The Patriot*), 1979.

Der Kandidate (The candidate), 1980.

Krieg und Frieden (War and peace) (with V. Schlöndorff, S. Aust, and A. Engstfeld), 1982.

Die Macht der Gefühle (*The Power of Emotion*), 1983.

Der Angriff der Gegenwart auf die übrige Zeit (*The Blind Director*, literally, "The assault of the present on the rest of time"), 1986.

Vermischte Nachrichten (Miscellaneous news), 1986. (Composed of segments from the television program *Ten to Eleven*, which Kluge has been hosting in recent years.)

Pier Paolo Pasolini

Films that have influenced Pasolini's work:

Open City (Rossellini, 1946).

Bicycle Thief (De Sica, 1949).

The Burmese Harp (Ichikawa, 1956).

Shadows (Cassavetes, 1960).

It's a Mad, Mad, Mad, Mad World (Kramer, 1963).

Belle de jour (Buñuel, 1967).

Films by Charlie Chaplin, Carl Dreyer, Fritz Lang, Ernst Lubitsch, Kenji Mizoguchi.

Screenplays written or collaborated on by Pasolini:

La Donna del fiume (*Woman of the River*) (M. Soldati, 1954).

Il Prigioniero della montagna (The prisoner of the mountain) (L. Trenker, 1955).

Marisa La Civetta (Bolognini, 1957).

Le Notti di Cabiria (*Nights of Cabiria*) (Fellini, 1957).

Giovani Mariti (*Young Husbands*) (Bolognini, 1958).

Morte di un Amico (*Death of a Friend*) (F. Rossi, 1959).

La Notte brava (*Night Heat*) (Bolognini, 1959).

Il bell'Antonio (Bolognini, 1960).

Il Carro armato dell' 8 Settembre (The armored car of September 8) (G. Puccini, 1960).

La Giornata balorda (*From a Roman Balcony*) (Bolognini, 1960).

La Lunga notte del '43 (*The Long Night of '43*) (F. Vancini, 1960).

La Ragazza in vetrina (*Girl in the Window*) (L. Emmer, 1961).

Ostia (S. Citti, 1970).

La Commare secca (The grim reaper), 1962.

Storie scellerate (*Bawdy Tales*) (Citti, 1973).

Pasolini also wrote the screenplays for most of his own films:
> *Accattone, Mamma Roma, La Ricotta, La Rabbia, The Gospel According to St. Matthew, Comizi d'amore, The Hawks and the Sparrows, La Terra vista della luna, Che cosa sono le nuvole, Oedipus Rex, Teorema, Medea, Appunti per una Orestiade africana, Pigsty, The Decameron, The Canterbury Tales, The Arabian Nights,* and *Salò, or the One Hundred Twenty Days of Sodom.*

Films directed by Pasolini:

Accattone, 1961.

Mamma Roma, 1962.

La Ricotta, 1962. Episode in *RoGoPaG* or *Laviamoci il cervèllo.*

La Rabbia (The frenzy) (with G. Guareschi), 1963.

Comizi d'amore (Assembly of love), 1964.

Il Vangelo secondo Matteo (*The Gospel According to St. Matthew*), 1964.

Che cosa sono le nuvole? (What are clouds?), 1966. Episode in *Capriccio all'Italiana.*

La Terra vista dalla luna (The earth seen from the moon), 1966. Episode in *Le Streghe* (*The Witches*).

Uccellacci e uccellini (*The Hawks and the Sparrows*), 1966.

Edipo Re (*Oedipus Rex*), 1967.

La Fiore di campo (The flower in the piazza) also known as *La Sequenzia del fiore di carta* (*The sequence of the Paper Flower*), 1967. Episode in *Amore e Rabbia* (*Love and Anger*).

Teorema, 1968.

Medea, 1969.

Il Porcile (Pigsty), 1969.

Il Decamerone (*The Decameron*), 1971.

I racconti di Canterbury (*The Canterbury Tales*), 1972.

Il fiore delle mille e una notte (*The Arabian Nights*), 1974.

Salò o le 120 giornate di Sodoma (*Salò, or the One Hundred Twenty Days of Sodom*), 1975.

Films based on literary works by Pasolini:

La Canta delle marane (Mangini, 1960). Based on chapter from *Ragazzi di vita*.
La Commare secca (Bertolucci, 1962). Based on his story of same name.
Una Vita violenta (P. Heusch and B. Rondi, 1962). Based on his novel of same name.

Films in which Pasolini acted:

Il Gobbo (*The Hunchback of Rome*) (C. Lizzani, 1960).
Requiescant (C. Lizzani, 1967).

Manuel Puig

Films that have influenced Puig:

The Great Ziegfeld (R. Z. Leonard, 1936).
Gone With the Wind (V. Fleming, 1939).
Rebecca (Hitchcock, 1940).
Blossoms in the Dust (M. LeRoy, 1941).
Ziegfeld Girl (R. Z. Leonard, 1941).
Frenchmen's Creek (M. Leisen, 1944).
Mildred Pierce (Curtiz, 1945).
Saratoga Trunk (S. Wood, 1945).
Spellbound (Hitchcock, 1945).
The Best Years of Our Lives (Wyler, 1946).
Quai des Orfevres (Clouzot, 1947).
Sunset Boulevard (Wilder, 1950).
A Place in the Sun (Stevens, 1951).
Musicals starring Ginger Rogers and Eleanor Powell.
Films by Josef von Sternberg, Frank Borzage, Jean Cocteau, and films scripted by Jacques Prévert.
Films starring Louise Rainer, Marlene Dietrich, Greta Garbo, Greer Garson, Tyrone Power, Robert Taylor, Ingrid Bergman, Joan Crawford, Rita Hayworth, and Michèle Morgan.
Films by Italian neorealist artists, especially Rossellini's *Open City* (1946), De Sica's *Bicycle Thief* (1949), and Visconti's *La Terra trema* (1948).

Screenplays written by Puig:

Boquitas pintadas (Torre Nilsson, 1974). Based on his novel of same name.

El Lugar sin límites (Infinity) (A. Ripstein, 1978). Based on novela by J. Donoso.
El Impostor (A. Ripstein). Based on a story by Silvina Ocampo.
Pubis angelical (R. de la Torre, 1988). Based on his novel of same name.
Seven Tropical Sins (D. Weisman, 1990).

Screenplays for films that have not been produced:
Summer Indoors.
La Cara del villano (Peasant face).
Recuerdo de Tijuana (Tijuana souvenir)

Film based on novel by Puig:
Kiss of the Spider Woman (H. Babenco, 1985). Screenplay written by L. Schrader.

Alain Robbe-Grillet

Screenplays written by Robbe-Grillet:
L'Année dernière à Marienbad (Last Year at Marienbad) (Resnais, 1961).
Robbe-Grillet also wrote the screenplays for some of his own films:
   L'Immortelle and *Glissements progressifs du plaisir.*

Films directed by Robbe-Grillet:
L'Immortelle (The Immortal Woman), 1963.
Trans-Europ-Express, 1966.
L'Homme qui ment (The Man Who Lies), 1968.
L'Eden et après (The Eden and after), 1970.
Glissements progressifs du plaisir (Progressive slippages of pleasure), 1974.
Le Jeu avec le feu (Playing with fire), 1975.
N. a pris les dés (N. took the dice), 1975. Reworking of *L'Eden et après* for French television.
La Belle captive (The beautiful captive), 1983. Based on his novel of same name.

Films based on literary works by Robbe-Grillet:
In the Labyrinth (Robert Lrikala, 1962). Based on his novel of same name.
Les Gommes (The Erasers) (Lucien Deroisy, 1969). Based on his novel of same name.

Les deux chambres distantes et/ou les deux chambres discrètes (Two distant chambers and/or two separate rooms) (Nakagawa, 1975). Based on his story "La Chambre secrète" (The secret chamber).

La Plage à distance (The distant beach) (Nakagawa, 1977). Based on his story "La Plage."

La Chambre secrète (The secret room) (J. F. Urrusti, 1978). Based on his story of same name.

Ben Stoltzfus

Films that have influenced Stoltzfus's writing:

The Firemen of Lyons (Lumière, 1898).

Trip to the Moon (Méliès, 1902).

Le Diable au corps (*Devil in the Flesh*) (Autant-Lara, 1946).

Farrebique (Rouquier, 1946).

La Symphonie pastorale (Dellanoy, 1946).

Forbidden Games (Clément, 1952).

Le Blé en herbe (*Ripening Seed*) (Autant-Lara, 1953).

Hiroshima mon amour (Duras/Resnais, 1959).

Last Year at Marienbad (Resnais, 1961).

L'Immortelle (*The Immortal Woman*) (Robbe-Grillet, 1963).

Trans-Europ-Express (Robbe-Grillet, 1966).

Weekend (Godard, 1967).

L'Homme qui ment (*The Man Who Lies*) (Robbe-Grillet, 1968).

Ronald Sukenick

Films that have influenced Sukenick's writing:

Works of Fellini.

Film work:

Script (with Roger Corman), not produced.

Out (Eli Hollander, 1982). Based on his novel of same name.

Index